CANADIAN WHISKY

DAVIN DE KERGOMMEAUX

CANADIAN WHISKY

THE PORTABLE EXPERT

McCLELLAND & STEWART

Library and Archives Canada Cataloguing in Publication

De Kergommeaux, Davin
Canadian whisky : the portable expert / Davin de Kergommeaux.

ISBN 978-0-7710-2743-7

1. Whisky – Canada. 2. Whisky – Canada – History. I. Title.

TP605.D45 2012   641.2'520971   C2011-907956-9

We acknowledge the financial support of the Government of Canada
through the Canada Book Fund and that of the Government of
Ontario through the Ontario Media Development Corporation's
Ontario Book Initiative. We further acknowledge the support
of the Canada Council for the Arts and the Ontario Arts Council
for our publishing program.

Published simultaneously in the United States of America
by McClelland & Stewart Ltd., P.O. Box 1030, Plattsburgh,
New York 12901

Library of Congress Control Number: 2011945920

Typeset in Bookman

Printed and bound in Canada

ANCIENT FOREST
FRIENDLY

This book is printed on acid-free paper that is 100% recycled,
ancient-forest friendly (100% post-consumer waste).

McClelland & Stewart Ltd.
75 Sherbourne Street
Toronto, Ontario
M5A 2P9
www.mcclelland.com

1 2 3 4 5   16 15 14 13 12

For Janet with love and appreciation.

To Ronan with patience and anticipation.

Contents

Tasting notes for over one hundred Canadian whiskies are included throughout the book. These begin with the name of the whisky and percent alcohol, followed by nosing and tasting highlights and the initials of the physical distillery where the whisky was made, if this is known. The initials are as follows: AD – Alberta Distillers; BV – Black Velvet; CM – Canadian Mist; GB – Glenora; GI – Gimli; HA – Highwood; HW – Hiram Walker; KR – Kittling Ridge; SW – Still Waters; VF – Valleyfield; ND – not disclosed.

A Note on Measurements

Canada uses the metric system for most measurements and, except for historical quantities and measures, this book conforms with that practice. Where gallons are used, these are "wine gallons" and can be converted to litres at 1 gallon = 3.78 litres. Similarly, those readers more familiar with Imperial measurements can convert litres to gallons at 1 litre = 0.26 gallons.

Introduction

his is a story of Canada. It is a story of a colony becoming a nation, however regionally divided. It is a story of early Canadians finding creative ways to adapt largely European practices to a new and often hostile environment. It is a story of craftsmanship, ingenuity, family feuds, fortunes made, and legacies lost. The story begins with farmers protecting grain from pests, and millers turning waste into something they could sell and use to feed cattle. It begins with Canadian grain, with Canadian water, and with that other abundant ingredient: wood from Canada's extensive forests.

The story of Canadian whisky tells of Canadians processing raw materials to sell locally and for export. Yes, it is popular in Canada, but almost from the beginning Canadian whisky enjoyed global repute. Today it is sold in more than 160 countries around the world. Nonetheless, despite its international reach, little attention has been paid to Canadian whisky as a distinct whisky category. Like Canadians themselves, it tends to fly under the radar. And often the best whisky does not make it out of the country. Neither, unfortunately, does its story. Abroad and, discouragingly, at home too, much of the received wisdom about Canadian whisky is simply fantasy. Pity.

Many of today's dearly held whisky truths derive from myths that have been passed on most often innocently, but at other times co-opted and embellished to help promote particular brands or styles of whisky. Sometimes people filled in the blanks to complete a familiar rags-to-riches story. Other times they left out inconvenient facts in order to lead readers or listeners to a more desirable conclusion. Still other times they simply made things up. After all, distillers, their publicists, and jingoistic whisky lovers are hardly the first to subscribe to the principle of never letting the truth get in the way of a good story. Sometimes their conjectures have become truths by simple repetition.

Every now and then, when someone decides to publish something about Canadian whisky, they revive the same few (and limited) sources, essentially regurgitate them on discussion boards, in articles, and sometimes even in books and on company websites. Fresh historical sources, though, are very difficult to find because the industry is very secretive and rarely allows prying eyes within its walls. So, for example, an erroneous interpretation of J.P. Wiser's German nationality – misreading *Deutsch* for "Dutch" – has been broadly promulgated. Two hundred distilling licences sold in Upper and Lower Canada in 1840 have become an astounding 200 distilleries. A map of Canada's early distilleries interprets as a "whisky region" what turns out to be all parts of the country that were settled at the time but did not have ready access to the more easily distilled molasses. Attempts to discredit the nearly 200-year-old legacy of Canadian rye, based on foreign post-Prohibition definitions of so-called "real" rye, have led some people to think that Canada should adjust its own long-standing definition. This, despite the reality that Canadian-style rye represents overwhelmingly the majority of world rye whisky production.

Foreign journalists who have tried to understand Canadian whisky have found the story difficult to tease out. Not only is the country huge and travel within its borders expensive, but the Canadian production processes are unfamiliar and often interpreted in light of whisky knowledge from elsewhere. Misconceptions have been dutifully reported and reinforced. Yes, there is copper in the stills at Canadian Mist. No, American bourbon is not used to make Canadian whisky taste like rye. And no, there is no grain neutral spirit in Canadian whisky.

Canadian whisky is not Scotch and it is not bourbon. It is rye, and has been for nearly two centuries. Neither does Canadian whisky descend directly from Irish or Scotch whisky, nor did it evolve in parallel with whisky in America. Rather these two now different North American styles developed along distinct but intertwined paths as part of a single evolution. The historical record tells us that in North America making whisky did indeed begin first in the United States, but over time ideas, recipes, equipment, practices, and distillers moved freely back and forth across the border, as did whisky itself. However, two distinct periods of American history offered Canadian whisky makers opportunities to take the lead, as it were, and also led drinkers in the U.S. to associate whisky with their northern neighbour, Canada.

The first of these moments in time was the American Civil War (1861-65), which disrupted alcohol production throughout the Union and Confederate states. Canadian distillers were ready and able to fill the void south of their border. The second disruption came in the form of a piece of legislation called the *Volstead Act*. In 1920 *Volstead* ushered in nearly fourteen years of Prohibition in the United States.

In his definitive history of Prohibition, *Last Call*, Daniel Okrent rightly identified this period as "a sequence of curves and switchbacks that would force the rewriting of the fundamental contract between citizen and government." It was socially convulsive and created deep divides between groups who might otherwise have gotten along. Progressives, feminists, libertarians, secularists, and fundamentalists who maybe liked the occasional shot suddenly found no comfort in the legislation or the increasingly theatrical antics of those for or against it. When Prohibition ended, American distillers had to start over, and that they did, often using new processes, new recipes, and the latest equipment. It was a radical, industry-wide shift, not a gradual transition.

Despite its stated purpose, Prohibition did not remove alcohol from the United States. It simply encouraged the marketplace to find more and more creative ways to flout or bypass an essentially unenforceable law. Although Canadian whisky may have made up 10 percent of the alcoholic beverages consumed during Prohibition, the ensuing folklore, aided and

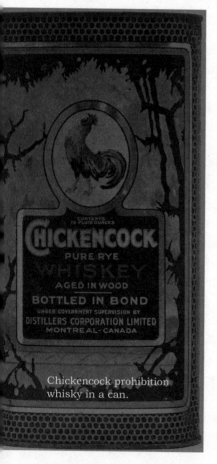

Chickencock prohibition whisky in a can.

abetted by screenwriters and novelists, has created the false but nearly universal belief that Canadian whisky was the drink of choice during Prohibition. For obvious reasons very little was documented – written records could incriminate the players on both sides of the border – and what little was written down was often deliberately destroyed.

This book tells the story of Canadian whisky by taking the reader inside the bottle, the distillery, the warehouse, and the marketplace. It tells the story as it is revealed in early documents and as it is recalled in the memories of people who have lived many decades of Canadian whisky history. It presents insights gleaned through discussions and visits with people who make Canadian whisky at each of Canada's nine established whisky distilleries. It is not intended to set the "official record" straight; however, it does challenge many dearly held beliefs.

One thing is certain, though: in the marketplace the most important ingredient in whisky is not the water, neither is it the grain. No – the most important ingredient is the story.

THE SUBSTANCE OF CANADIAN WHISKY

Chapter 1

The Grains

here's a lot of landscape in a bottle of Canadian whisky. Golden wheat fields that stretch to the horizon across barely undulating flatlands define the Canadian prairies. Meanwhile, more than 2,000 kilometres to the east in southern Ontario, on the other side of the Canadian Shield, roads from encroaching suburbia criss-cross similar expanses of maize, or Indian corn (most commonly simply called "corn"). Interspersed with patches of bush, soybeans and, more recently, electricity-generating windmills, corn remains a defining presence. If, as Canadian regulations decree, whisky is "a potable alcoholic distillate obtained from a mash of cereal grain," then Canada is indeed rich in the raw materials. In addition to corn and wheat, Canada grows more of the best rye grain than can possibly be used at home, and harvests equally plentiful crops of malting barley. Is it any wonder that from the earliest colonial days Canadians have made whisky?

Early whisky grains

Although Canadian settlers did not invent whisky, they did bring whisky-making skills and tools, and – just as important – whisky-making grains with them from their many homelands. It was Dutch and German immigrants who brought rye, the grain that would become the signature

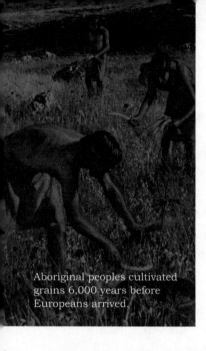

Aboriginal peoples cultivated grains 6,000 years before Europeans arrived.

of Canadian whisky, to North America. These European immigrants understood that rye was hardy enough to prosper in places where other crops might fail. Barley came to Canada primarily from England and the Netherlands, not Scotland as many still assume. Wheat also came from England, as well as from other European countries. The softest-flavoured, sweetest, and creamiest of whisky grains though, corn, originated right here in North America 6,000 years before Jacques Cartier set foot at Stadacona, or a little further south, the Pilgrims at Plymouth, for that matter.

In order to get the whisky-making process started, grain is mixed with water to make a "mash." When a mixture of different grains is used to make whisky, the closely guarded recipe giving the proportions of each type of grain is called a mash bill. Early in the nineteenth century, influenced by their neighbours from western Europe, Canada's pioneering distillers began to spice up their wheat mashes by adding a little bit of rye grain to them. Dutch and German immigrants already knew just how flavourful rye grain could be. However, Canada's first commercial distillers were mostly from England and they were quite unfamiliar with the spiciness of rye. Occasionally they used barley and corn to make the liquid slurry mash they would ferment into distiller's beer, but far and away the most common grain used commercially to make whisky in pioneer Canada was wheat.

Once the idea of adding rye grain to a mash took hold there was no looking back. Yet mash bills and grain inventories from the nineteenth century show that the proportion of rye used for a batch of whisky almost never reached one part in five. Indeed, some early mash bills show rye at 1 percent of the grain mashed, though most were closer to 5 or 10 percent. To distinguish this new distillation from "common whisky," that is, whisky made without using any rye grain, the rye-flavoured variety quickly became known simply as "rye." Although it commanded a slightly higher price, rye soon supplanted common whisky in all but the most impoverished households. At the same time, the word *rye* entered the Canadian lexicon to the point that whisky is now the first thing Canadians think of when they hear it and only later do they make the link to bread or grain.

Today's whisky grain

Although almost any cereal can be mashed and fermented to make whisky, the most commonly used today is corn. Rye, which still gives Canadian whisky its nickname, continues to be used almost solely for flavouring, with the notable exception of some all-rye whiskies produced by Alberta Distillers. Wheat, so plentiful, is

Pioneer farmers found tall rye grain easy to harvest by hand.

rarely used in Canada anymore, except at Highwood distillery, which was specifically engineered to create wheat-based whisky. In Canada, corn is still number one.

Some grain science

And now for some whisky-making science. The grains used to make whisky are actually seeds from corn, rye, barley, and wheat plants. Each seed contains a tiny embryonic plantlet and a large, starchy endosperm that stores food for the plant when it starts to sprout. This starchy endosperm must be converted to sugars before it can be fermented into alcohol. That's the case, whatever the grain. Usually this process begins by cooking the grain in hot water.

Each seed contains starch-degrading enzymes, which are activated only when the seed begins to sprout. In nature, these enzymes convert the starch to sugars, which nourish the sprouting seed. Distillers use similar natural enzymes to convert starch into sugars, which they then feed to yeast cells. Then the yeast metabolizes the sugars into ethanol and carbon dioxide. Some distilleries include what is called "malted" grain in their mash bills. Malting involves keeping the grain moist until it just starts to sprout, then drying it to prevent it from fully germinating. The malting process is handled by specialized companies called maltsters. Malted grain contains prodigious amounts of the enzymes that convert starch into fermentable sugars. Barley is the grain that most commonly is malted. Because heat would destroy its active enzymes, malted grain is not cooked before it is added to the mash. However, malt is not used for most Canadian whiskies. It has been replaced by natural microbial enzymes that produce the same effects as enzymes from sprouting grain.

A single seed of rye.

The non-starchy parts of the grain contribute oils, minerals, proteins, and micro-ingredients that nourish the yeast during fermentation and contribute flavour to the final product. Most of the non-starch grain components are later recovered and made into high-protein animal feed.

Corn

It is ironic that the Pilgrims came ashore at Plymouth Rock in 1620 hoping to replenish their dwindling beer supplies, as North America's original inhabitants neither brewed nor distilled alcoholic beverages. Doubly ironic is the fact that the seed of a plant the indigenous population had developed for food is exceptionally well suited to making the finest whiskies. Indeed, Native Americans living in what would become Canada and the United States had developed more than 300 different

Ontario corn ready to harvest.

varieties of corn (*Zea mays*) by the time the first European immigrants arrived early in the seventeenth century.

With a higher starch content than other grains, corn yields more alcohol. It is also much easier to process than other whisky grains because its mash is more fluid. However, unlike other grains, kernels of corn contain two types of starch, one of which requires higher cooking temperatures than are needed for other starches. Thus, it takes more energy to cook corn than it does for other grains. Corn produces a distillate that is sweet, soft, creamy, and fruity. Normally distillers use yellow dent corn, a cross between indigenous flint and flour types.

Rye

Rye (*Secale cereale*) is both cold-hardy and drought resistant, making it especially well suited to the harsh climate and poorly prepared soils of pioneer Canada. Rye's long stems also made it easy for early settlers to harvest. As anyone who has eaten rye bread knows, rye has a strong, somewhat spicy, and slightly bitter taste. When converted into whisky this translates into lovely strong flavours of clove, ginger, and cinnamon spices, hot pepper, fruit, and a complex floral sweetness, with a refreshing bitterness. The rye spirit that begins spicy and fruity develops scrumptious rich and complex flavours when aged in oak. Some whiskies made solely from rye grain can be a little overwhelming to the uninitiated palate. Consequently, from the earliest days of its use in Canadian whisky making, rye grain has been added judiciously. Some Canadian whiskies, such as the award-winning Alberta Premium, are made entirely from rye grain, though generally speaking a little goes a long way.

Rye has its challenges. It contains less starch than other grains, and thus has a higher proportion of nitrogen (protein) and also a lower alcohol yield. These high levels of nitrogen can lead to foaming problems during fermentation and distillation. This can be a pain in the neck for distillers, but rye's unique flavours are well worth the trouble.

Barley

For many people, barley (*Hordeum vulgare*) is the first grain that comes to mind when they think about whisky. In Canada, though, if it is used at all, barley is generally a minor component of the mash. All the same, Canada – most particularly the western provinces of Alberta and Saskatchewan – has ideal soil and weather conditions for

Alberta Premium
40% alc/vol

Crisp, flinty, clean rye spices greet searing white pepper, maple syrup and the softest tannins. Rich and fruity with a refreshing grapefruit pithiness. The brawn of youth and the clout of maturity. AD

Alberta Premium 25 Year Old
40% alc/vol

Powerful but elegant, creamy but dry. Cedar, gingery fruit, and earthy rye. A study in contrasts: earth and wood, ripe dark fruit and sourish pineapple, creamy toffee, cleansing zest, and an exotic lumberyard of aromatic wood. AD

Malting barley in the field.

growing barley. When Canadian distillers use malted grain, they almost always use barley malt because it is so readily available. Malting barley is big business in Canada, but make no mistake: the primary Canadian customer for malted barley is the brewing and not the distilling industry.

In Nova Scotia, plump-grained, starch-laden malt is favoured by Glenora Distillery, which makes its single malt whisky entirely from malted barley. However, for the corn-based, mixed-grain whisky that dominates Canadian whisky making in the rest of the country, it is shrivelled, enzyme-rich malt that is preferred. Distillers want barley with the greatest possible enzyme content because malt is much more expensive than unprocessed grain. Maltsters separate distillers malt (for whisky) from brewers malt (for beer) by passing it through vibrating screens after malting is completed.

While some Canadian whisky makers use malted barley, until recently, when the price of barley dropped significantly, unmalted barley was pretty much unknown. A little bit is now mashed at the Gimli, Hiram Walker, and Alberta Distillers plants. Seagram mythology tells us that Sam

Bronfman always kept a bit of unmalted barley whisky on hand to use for flavouring.

Wheat

With the exception of Molson's distillery in Montreal, which was an adjunct to a brewery and used both barley malt and mixed grains, Canada's earliest commercial distillers began as millers who distilled excess grain on the side. Primarily, that grain was wheat (*Triticum aestivum*). In the eighteenth and nineteenth centuries, before Europeans planted grain on the prairies, and long before Canadian Confederation, southern Ontario was known as "Canada's Breadbasket" because great stretches were so well suited to growing wheat. Millers ground this wheat into flour and held back a 10 percent tithe as payment for their services. They also found themselves with large quantities of milling waste, called "wheat middlings," which, on its way to becoming animal feed, found its way first into whisky mashes. No wonder someone suggested they add a bit of rye.

Over the centuries many varieties of wheat have been developed, including hard and soft wheats, and spring and winter wheats. Experience has shown that the starch in soft winter wheat is the most suitable for distilling. Mash produced from wheat grist is less fluid than corn mash, and this is why Highwood Distillers, the only Canadian distillery to specialize in distilling from wheat, cooks the grains whole. Traditionally, wheat has yielded much less alcohol than corn, but some recently developed varieties are beginning to catch up. Wheat spirit is usually sweetish, lighter bodied, and more delicately flavoured than corn, rye, or barley spirit.

Black Velvet 3 Year Old
40% alc/vol

Creamy caramel and sweet dark fruits with bursting ginger drops, zesty lime, and fresh-sawn lumber, then dry grain, rye spices, and spirity hot white pepper. BV

Black Velvet Deluxe
40% alc/vol

Ripe fruit, dusty rye, spices, caramel, and gently biting spirit. Creamy sweet butterscotch and fresh timber followed by glowing hot pepper and roasting hot ginger. Fresh, lively, and bright. BV

Each of the major whisky grains, along with another, called triticale (a wheat-rye hybrid used occasionally in Canada to make whisky), must be mixed with water to make the mash and dissolve the sugars, making them readily available to the yeast. Though this water may come from pristine lakes, glacier-fed streams, deep, deep wells, or city mains, it must always be the cleanest, freshest, and purest water the distillery can access. With all the care taken to select the most suitable grain to make whisky, it wouldn't make sense to process it with anything but the very best water.

Chapter 2

The Water

Grain is mashed and fermented in water. Partway through distillation more water may be added to help remove some insoluble by-products of fermentation. Once the spirit has been distilled, water is added again, this time to adjust the strength of the alcohol to an optimum level so it will derive the maximum flavour when it spends time maturing in barrels. Then, when the mature whisky is ready for bottling, water is added yet again, this time to bring it down to bottle strength. In all, as much as ten litres of water are added to the mash and the distillate for every litre of whisky produced. This water must be pure and clean and completely free of odours. Add to this another sixty litres of water used to heat the stills and to cool and clean the equipment, and you can quickly see why the first thing people look for when establishing a distillery is a reliable source of pure, clean water. Fortunately, Canada has plenty of it.

Some water science

There's more to water, however, than meets the eye. As it flows over the land, water picks up all kinds of minerals and chemicals, creating solutions that may be acidic or alkaline, soft or hard. While Scottish distillers extol the virtues of their soft water, American distillers wax lyrical

Canada has abundant supplies of pure, clean water.

about their hard limestone water. Can both be right? Of course they can. Yes, mineral content has an influence on fermentation; however, as Harold Ferguson, who for more than forty years used limestone-rich Lake Huron water to distill Canadian Mist, puts it, "I'd choose to make whisky out of the cleanest water I could get, you can adjust everything else."

It is true, though, that water that has passed through limestone favours the creation of certain congeners, the chemicals that give whisky its flavour. Soft Scottish water, however, provides a different advantage. It has a lower pH; that is, it is less alkaline (and therefore more acidic) than limestone water, and as a consequence it favours the action of yeast during fermentation. Some Canadian distillers use a sour mash process to overcome the alkalinity of limestone water. Distillation residues, called "thin stillage," are added to the mash to make it more acidic. A more acidic mash discourages the growth of bacteria that might otherwise spoil the resulting flavours. For this reason many distilleries have now replaced the sour mash process with changes in hygiene and sanitation.

Bush Pilot's Private Reserve
40% alc/vol

Oily yet dry, rich yet austere, with crisp oak. Sweet vanilla caramel becomes musty fresh-boiled corn with a hint of cardboard. Herbal tea murmurs mint then gushes sweet baking spices and hot white pepper. ND

Canada Gold
40% alc/vol

Very fruity with creamy corn liquor, vanilla, and undercurrents of sourness, earthiness, perfume, and Christmas spices. Seductive peppery heat. KR

Canada House
40% alc/vol

Simple Canadian rye with a caramel crisp start and kiwi fruit, then elements of bitter rye bread. Warming and clean with a longish, spicy, and mildly peppery finish. AD

Water is filtered, adjusted, and purified long before it ever reaches the first grain. The water added to bring the spirit down to barrel strength is also purified. Then, when the time comes for bottling, the water added to bring the blended barrel-strength whisky down to bottling strength is purified to ensure that its contribution to the flavour of the whisky is effectively nil.

Recycling energy

Rising energy costs and environmental concerns have led many Canadian distillers to install heat- and energy-recovery systems, enabling them to recycle the energy used to heat the water. Hiram Walker distillery, for example, has succeeded in reducing energy usage by almost a third over a five-year period, allowing it to hold energy costs steady despite the steeply rising rates charged by energy providers. As well, filtering and purification practices ensure that when water is returned to the environment it has been re-oxygenated and the impurities have been removed.

This industrial environmentalism is no mere fad. Fifty years ago the Corby distillery in Corbyville, Ontario, installed a massive heat-recovery plant along with

Canadian Club 20 Year Old
40% alc/vol

Rich, oaky synthesis of dark fruit, toffee, vanilla, hot pepper, dusty rye, and citrus zest. Cloves and nutmeg with fresh-cut lumber and dry roasted grain end in citrus pith. HW

Canadian Club 30 Year Old
40% alc/vol

Vibrant and deceptively complex with sweet dark fruit, zippy pepper, inklings of ginger, and filthy-rich tobacco. Fresh-cut lumber balances dusty old books as pink grapefruit does creamy dollops of butterscotch. HW sedimentation and filtration systems that ensured the water being returned to the Moira River was cleaner than it was when Corby's withdrew it to use for processing. The thriving trout population in the Moira River right beside the distillery became a point of pride for Corby's management and distillery staff.

Distilling remains an agricultural process, and just as it was fifty years ago in Corbyville, the harmony of nature is never far from the distiller's mind. As grain is turned into whisky its waste is fed to cattle. Water that is used to process the grain is cleaned and returned to nature. And wood, the final whisky ingredient, is harvested from mature trees in managed oak forests, leaving room for a new generation of saplings to grow in their place.

Chapter 3

The Wood

As clear as water, with a sweet, spicy, and some would say harsh, flavour. That's Canadian whisky spirit when it first comes off the still. It's drinkable and early settlers in Canada certainly drank lots of it. But it does not appeal to the modern palate. And by law, it's not really whisky. Before it can earn that name it must spend at least three years maturing in oak barrels. Comparing the mature product to the new distillate quickly demonstrates that ageing really does smooth out the rough edges while adding new flavours, dimensions, and complexities.

Ageing regulations

For centuries European wine and brandy makers knew the benefits of oak ageing. It was an easy knowledge transfer by their whisky-making colleagues. Along with knowledge, though, came government regulation. In Canada, a legal requirement for ageing was introduced in 1887, the first such law in any nation. Initially, the minimum ageing period was one year, in 1890 it became two. The stated purpose was to improve the quality of the product. However, most of the larger Canadian distillers at the time already aged their whisky before sending it to market. That first ageing law had another purpose altogether: increasing government tax revenue. Ageing requirements were hard on small producers

Empty barrels await filling at Alberta Distillers.

who were the most likely to evade taxes. Within a couple of years not a single "nuisance distiller" remained. In 1974 the requirement that Canadian whisky be aged for two years was increased to three and it was specified that ageing must take place in "small wood," oak barrels no larger than 700 litres. In practice Canadian distillers normally use barrels much smaller than that, with a capacity of about 200 litres.

Ageing processes

Generally, new spirit is diluted to 68 to 72 percent alc/vol (alcohol by volume – also written as abv) before it is put into barrels to mature. As water and alcohol evaporate through pores in the oak, the concentration of the congeners, including those drawn from the oak itself, increases. Losses in volume due to evaporation are commonly known as the "angels' share." In addition to water and alcohol, the angels' share may also include some other volatile congeners. The warmer the warehouse, the greater is the angels' share, although water and alcohol are not lost in the same proportions. In humid climates, such as in Ontario or Nova Scotia, more alcohol than water is lost and the proportion of alcohol in the maturing whisky slowly decreases. In dryer locations, such as Alberta, more water than alcohol is lost, causing the proportion of alcohol in the whisky to increase during maturation.

Air moving in and out of the barrel is part of the maturation process, and this is why temperature changes in the warehouse affect the rate of maturation. As it becomes warmer, the new spirit expands into the wood. As it cools, it contracts, drawing more and more flavours out of the oak and into the whisky. As well, warmer temperatures increase the rate at which fruity congeners called esters are created in the spirit. Generally, the warmer the warehouse the faster the whisky matures.

Detail barrels in warehouse.

However, some reactions happen very slowly, so rapid maturation produces a different flavour profile than slow maturation. Whisky makers will often select barrels from different parts of the warehouse to blend together, taking advantage of differences in the mature whisky caused by temperature differences from floor to ceiling. This increases the complexity of the final whisky. Canada's harsh winters mean that the warehouses need to be heated at least enough to ensure the fire sprinklers don't freeze, should they ever be needed.

In Canada, most whisky is matured in barrels made from American white oak harvested in Missouri and Kentucky. Oak is especially well suited to making barrels as it is very strong, and is porous to air but not to liquids. It is also pliable and when heated can be bent into the familiar curved staves of a barrel. Raw new oak contains tree sap, resins, and harsh tannins that can quickly impart astringent and unpleasant flavours to the whisky. Coopers, the craftsmen who make barrels, overcome this "greenness" by charring the inside of newly made barrels with a gas flame.

Some wood science

Five different processes that take place in the barrel work independently and synergistically to create an array of whisky flavours, both strong and subtle, and to impart colour to the spirit. First, as the new spirit sits in the barrel it slowly extracts flavours out of the oak. Like any organic substance, wood is made up of various chemical compounds. Most of the mass of oak is composed of large, complex carbohydrates. The most important of these, for making whisky, are lignin, cellulose, and hemicellulose. These substances are important sources of the simpler compounds that give whisky much of its flavour and its colour.

While the barrel is being charred, some of the components of the oak will melt and break down into simpler compounds, turning the inside of the barrel into an active layer of flavourants. Lignin, for example, breaks down into vanillin and various similar compounds, while cellulose and hemicellulose, when heated, produce caramels along with many other flavourful compounds. Another important result of heating oak is that more coconut-flavoured oak lactones and

"Red line" on used staves at Gimli Distillery show how far alcohol has soaked into the barrel.

clove-like eugenol are available to dissolve into the maturing spirit. Eugenol's spicy flavours reinforce the rye-like qualities of some whiskies that actually contain only small amounts of rye grain.

Generally, the deeper the char the more flavours that are created or released. All of these compounds seep into the whisky as it matures, adding significant flavour and colour. These flavours are so powerful they can soon overwhelm flavours derived from the grain. Bourbon is always matured in new charred oak barrels and it does not take long for the strong flavours to become the dominant characteristic of the whisky. That is one reason that younger bourbon can be so flavourful. Because these primary wood flavourings impart the characteristic rich vanilla notes and hints of perfume to bourbon, Canadian distillers often use new charred oak barrels when they are maturing corn spirit to make bourbon-like flavouring whiskies.

For the most part, Canadian whisky is matured in barrels that have already been used once to mature bourbon. These are sometimes referred to as "new bourbon drains" or "bourbon dumpers." Knowing the source of these barrels – their "pedigree" – tells Canadian distillers what qualities they can expect from them. Nevertheless, often they will smell, or "nose," the barrels to ensure they are "sweet." A sound barrel may be refilled several times until it gradually loses its ability to mature whisky. Even then it is possible to extend the life of the barrel by scraping it inside and recharring it. At first it may seem odd to reuse barrels when much of the flavour has already leached out while maturing bourbon. However, with the concentration of those primary flavours reduced, more subtle and complex ones can now emerge without the strong primary flavours masking them.

Canadian Club Classic 12 Year Old
40% alc/vol

Juicy oak caramels, ripe dark fruit, warming gingery pepper, spices, herbs, and lilacs. A sweet creamy indulgence of toffee, caramel, fudge, and rum-soaked Christmas pudding. HW

Canadian Club Sherry Cask 8 Year Old
41.3% alc/vol

Redolent of dark fruit, leather, hot candied ginger, and pipe tobacco by a crackling fire. Waxy cream sherry resolves into fresh peaches. Sweet spring flowers and bitter black breakfast tea subdue searing hot pepper. HW

Chemical reactions in the wood

A second process that takes place in reused barrels helps set the Canadian whisky style apart. New flavouring elements slowly develop through two chemical processes that take place after the barrel has been filled with spirit: hydrolysis and oxidation. In hydrolysis, large molecules in the wood are split into shorter more flavourful ones. Oxidation changes the structures and thus the flavours of smaller molecules. Essentially, oxygen dissolved in the spirit, and the ethanol itself, react with certain oak compounds to create a whole range of new flavours. Although these products of hydrolysis and oxidation can be quite flavourful, it often takes years for them to reach the threshold where they can be tasted. This is one reason why long-aged Canadian whisky develops very flavourful crisp woody notes, almost like maple syrup, without the bitterness sometimes expected in whisky that has spent a long time in new barrels.

Chemical reactions in the spirit

The third influence of oak derives from its porous nature. Pores in the oak allow small amounts of water and alcohol to evaporate from the barrel and small amounts of air to come in. In addition to reacting with constituents of the wood, the oxygen in the air also reacts slowly with some elements of the spirit itself, creating additional new flavour substances, primarily fruity esters.

Char removes off-notes

A fourth contribution of charred oak is that charcoal, often simply referred to as char, is a cleansing agent. This char is particularly effective in removing less desirable flavours,

Charring barrels at now-defunct Seagram cooperage in Waterloo.

including sulphury grain components that are prevalent in new spirits. This is one of the keys to making palatable whisky. Many immature elements are adsorbed onto the charcoal and thus are removed from the whisky. Before the practice of ageing whisky evolved, many Canadian distillers filtered their raw spirit through charcoal to remove some of the harsher notes and mellow the spirits. This practice is still used with great success for some fine American whiskies. Nowadays, Canadian whisky makers rely on char inside the barrel to take care of this.

Ghosts of whiskies past
Fifth and finally, the previous contents of used barrels can also have some effect on the flavour of Canadian whisky. A freshly emptied barrel may have as much as six or seven litres of the previous contents soaked into the wood. Residual flavours from the bourbon or rye that was in the barrel carry over as nuances into the new spirit that is filled into these used barrels. Canadian distillers occasionally

augment this effect by using an assortment of cognac, brandy, sherry, and other barrels to mature whisky. This provides a wide range of different whiskies to choose from when it comes time for final mingling. However, this practice is not nearly as common with Canadian whisky as it is with some others.

Canadian Hunter
40% alc/vol

Hints of spirit soon develop Canadian rye spices, rich vanilla fudge, and creamy sweet toffee. Richly flavourful with luscious mouth-coating butterscotch, hot ginger, and a sizzling peppery burn. ND

Canadian LTD
40% alc/vol

Butterscotch ice cream quickly gains a tartness followed by zesty grapefruit acerbity and a peppery warmth. Simple and straightforward and feels good on the tongue. ND

Canadian Peak
40% alc/vol

Initially closed nose opens to baking spices and steely rye. Caramels and wonderful candied citrus peel gradually give way to tingly ginger and hot pepper. Calls for ginger ale. ND

More than a container

Whisky makers have learned how their various spirits interact with different barrels and are able to predict when certain whiskies, stored in specific barrels in particular parts of the warehouse, will be ready for bottling. Even so, maturing whisky is not an exact science. As the whisky gets closer to maturity, samples are taken to ensure that things are progressing as expected until finally the time is right for the barrels to be disgorged, a process called dumping. This is when the contents of many barrels are mingled together according to carefully guarded recipes to produce another batch of fine Canadian whisky.

That white oak barrel in which the whisky rests for all those years turns out to be much more than a container.

Barrels stacked on pallets at Canadian Mist.

Wood, in fact, is the third ingredient of whisky. Although water and grain contribute most of the volume to the whisky, it has been estimated that as much as 60 percent of the congeners found in whisky come from the wood in which it is matured.

With the grain, the water, and the barrels at hand, the distiller can now begin to make whisky.

HOW CANADIAN WHISKY IS MADE

Chapter 4

Processes

Each Canadian distiller has his or her own approach to making whisky, and each distillery may use significantly different and highly guarded processes. Essentially, whisky making begins with the receipt of quality grain, which is ground into a meal and cooked. Then its starches are converted to sugars by enzymes. Next, yeast is used to convert these sugars into alcohol by fermenting them into a weak beer-like liquid. This "beer" is passed through a series of stills to separate out and concentrate the alcohol and desirable congeners. The recovered spirits are then filled into oak barrels for a period of maturation. Once it is mature, whisky from many different barrels is mingled to produce the final whisky that will be bottled and sold. It sounds simple, but each step includes many challenges to ensuring a consistently high-quality product.

Cooking and Mashing

Mashing is the process of converting grain into sugars and making these sugars available for yeast to ferment. This is done by cooking the grain, and treating it with enzymes called amylolytic (or diastatic or saccharifying) enzymes. These enzymes can be derived from malted grain, but more commonly they are harvested from microorganisms. Most distillers grind the grain into coarse flour called grist before cooking. Some prefer to cook, mash, and ferment this grist in batches to feed the stills, while others employ a continuous cooking and mashing process. Most use both approaches, depending on the specific spirit they are making. Usually the different types of grain are mashed separately, although sometimes some malted barley is blended into the mash.

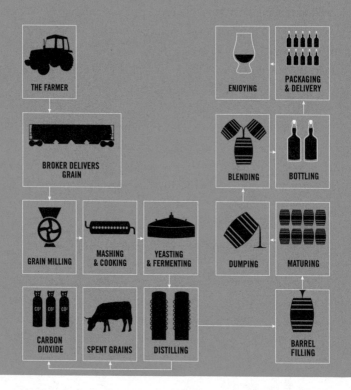

FROM FIELD TO FLASK

THE FARMER

ENJOYING

PACKAGING & DELIVERY

BROKER DELIVERS GRAIN

BLENDING

BOTTLING

GRAIN MILLING

MASHING & COOKING

YEASTING & FERMENTING

DUMPING

MATURING

CARBON DIOXIDE

SPENT GRAINS

DISTILLING

BARREL FILLING

Malted grains release amylolytic enzymes of their own making, which convert starch to sugar within the grain. With unmalted grains, however, the conversion happens in two stages. Liquefaction, the conversion of starches into dextrins, takes place by enzyme action in the cookers, while saccharification, conversion of these dextrins into sugar, happens after the grain has been cooked and cooled. In a batch process, the mash of unmalted grain is cooked at high temperatures in pressurized tanks to make the starch more easily accessible to the enzymes. Each type of grain requires a slightly different cooking time and temperature. Cooking also kills any bacteria that could contaminate the mash.

Corn is often mashed in a continuous process. The corn grist is mixed in slurry with hot water and cooked at 100° Celsius while moving steadily through a long pipe. Most starch becomes a viscous porridge-like gel when it is cooked.

Canadian Supreme
40% alc/vol

Mashed grain, green hay, sweet and fruity caramel, raspberries, barley sugar, and an advancing peppery glow. The bitter, pithy finish of a great mixer. ND

Cape Breton Silver
50% alc/vol

Unusually complex new spirit, resplendent with sweet ripe fruit, pepper, citrus pith, and clover blossoms. Earthy clay, Juicy Fruit® gum, and hard peppermint candy ease slowly into a citrusy finish. GB

This is why distillers will often add enzymes to the mash before cooking it. It liquefies the mixture and keeps things flowing smoothly through the system. While in the cooker, starches continue to be converted into dextrins by this enzyme action. After the mash is cooked, saccharifying enzymes are quickly added to convert these dextrins into sugars, and the mash is pumped into a fermenter, where it is cooled to between 20°C and 30°C, ready for yeasting. Adding saccharifying enzymes right away prevents the cooked, liquefied starch from returning to a more complex, less convertible state. When microbial enzymes are used rather than malt, most of the conversion of starch into sugars takes place in the fermenter.

Loading mash into a fermenter.

Although corn is the most commonly used grain for Canadian whisky production, wheat is the main ingredient in several popular Canadian brands. Cooking and processing wheat can be a bit tricky, as it contains sticky glucans that can gum up the works in a distillery. Distillers who use wheat take considerable care to prevent the lines (piping) from becoming clogged. At Highwood distillery the wheat is cooked whole until the kernels become swollen, gelatinous masses and burst like soggy popcorn to release their starch-rich contents. Rye, like corn,

Fermenter NO.
CAP. 60,859 LITRES

Checking a closed fermenter at Canadian Mist.

may be cooked in batches or it may pass continuously through cooking tubes before being fed into fermentation tanks.

The end product of mashing is a sweet slurry ready for fermentation. For malt whisky, the leftover solids from the grain are separated from the mash by filtering before it is sent to the fermenters. In the case of continuous processing for column stills, typically the grist remains in the mash when it is transferred to the fermenters and the spent grains are removed later during distillation.

Over the centuries distillers have designed and modified all kinds of machinery, tools, and devices to improve yields and quality. However, conversion and fermentation, two processes central to the creation of whisky from grain, are biological processes carried out by microorganisms, so in the end distillers must rely on nature to complete the most crucial steps.

Caribou Crossing Single Barrel
40% alc/vol

Crispy oak in creamy vanilla, stewed prunes, baking spices, and a bursting citrus zip. Soft creamy corn with hot pepper and baking spices develop citrusy elements. A cigar box bursting with peppery spice. ND

Centennial 10 Year Old
40% alc/vol

Begins dry with an aura of lemon oil and gunpowder, then develops rich caramels, red cedar, and searing pepper. Feels good with an oily middle and a tart cleansing finish. HA

Chinook 5 Year Old
40% alc/vol

Sweet woodsmoke, smoldering chili, dusty roads, and pulling tannins bolster sap-heavy grapes, rose petals, and butterscotch. Finishes cleanly with slight bitter lemon, smatterings of oak, and citrus zestiness. ND

Chapter 5

Microorganisms: Enzymes and Yeast

Grain is cooked and mashed so that yeast (*Saccharomyces cerevisiae*) can convert it into alcohol. Yeast feeds on simple sugars, but it cannot consume starch. Since grain stores carbohydrates in the form of starch, the distiller's first job is to convert these starches into sugars.

Enzymes

Liquefaction and saccharification may be initiated by adding enzymes from malted grain to the mash. Generally, though, Canadian distillers prefer microbial enzymes because they are more versatile and less expensive. At one time, distilleries made their own microbial enzymes; today all but one purchase them from specialist enzyme plants. Alberta Distillers is the last Canadian distillery to produce its own enzymes on site. These homegrown enzymes are unrefined and include a broad array of other helpful enzymes that induce some side reactions during mashing. They break down a broad range of carbohydrates and other grain components in addition to starch. These enzymes also generate a number of yeast nutrients and flavour precursors. "Using homegrown enzymes is the secret to making 100 percent rye whisky," says whisky microbiologist Rob Tuer.

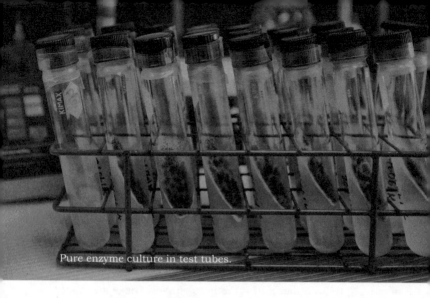

Pure enzyme culture in test tubes.

Enzymes are grown in small fermenters.

Enzymes are grown in a sterilized mash, generally made from corn. This mash is inoculated with spores from a selected strain of *Aspergillus awamori* fungus, and over a period of four to six days the *Aspergillus* grows, creating a lumpy, buttermilk-like mixture with a characteristic musty aroma. When it has reached maximum enzyme concentration, this whole-culture enzyme preparation is added to a mash, sometimes along with some commercially produced enzymes.

Yeast

Yeast is a tiny, single-celled organism, a fungus really, that consumes sugar and converts it into ethanol and carbon dioxide in a process called fermentation. It then excretes these products, in roughly equal amounts, along with a large number of minor by-products that contribute significantly to the flavour of whisky. These by-products include esters, ketones, and an assortment of alcohols including fusel oils. Some of the flavour of whisky thus begins with fermentation.

Once the grain has been mashed and the fermentable sugars extracted, distillers cool the mash to between 26° and 38° Celsius and often dilute it and adjust the acidity with thin stillage. Then they add yeast in a process they call pitching. Canadian distillers often use considerably less yeast than whisky makers in other major whisky nations, as the side products of saccharification using natural microbial enzymes nourish the yeast, stimulating it to begin fermentation very quickly. Over about three or four days, the yeast will consume all the available sugar, producing a beer with an alcohol content somewhere between 6 and 8 percent for rye and small-grains mashes, and about 10 to 14 percent for corn mashes. Often the yeast is added to the mash well before all the starch has been fully converted to sugar, allowing fermentation to proceed in parallel to conversion. This not only speeds up the process, but because saccharification is occurring at the same rate as the sugar is being consumed by the yeast, it helps keep the bacteria in check. This same approach is used by Japanese distillers when they make sake, a process which also uses *Aspergillus awamori* enzymes.

Gibson's Finest Sterling
40% alc/vol

Soft yellow apples, pears, grape juice, and blackberries. Crème caramel with a slightly nutty orange liqueur. Waxiness moderates a growing peppery burn that carries long into a citrusy finish. HW

Gibson's Finest Rare 18 Year Old
40% alc/vol

Sweet-scented lumber in creamy, spicy, vanilla caramel with flickering hot pepper and zesty bitter lemon. Butterscotch and fresh sweet corn; the very essence of luxury defined. VA

While commercially produced yeast is most often used for making base whisky, for flavouring whisky great care is taken to use yeasts that contribute specific flavours. Many Canadian distillers hire specialist companies to produce unique proprietary yeasts from their own well-guarded yeast strains. Among other things, these special yeasts generate unique esters from which come many of the fruity aromas and flavours. While some of these esters smell distinctly of specific well-known fruits, others are not found in common fruits and so bring a generic sense of fruitiness to the whisky. Some distillers, like David Dobbin at Canadian Mist, go so far as to check the yeast's DNA fingerprint before entrusting their fermentations to it.

These pure-strain yeasts are grown in a special yeast-propagating, sterile, grain mash, seeded with yeast from previous batches. Pails of new yeast are collected from each yeast mash and stored carefully to keep the strain pure. The mash used to grow yeast is similar to that used to make whisky. However, before the seed yeast is added to the yeast tub, the mash is tweaked to maximize the growth and viability of the new yeast. There is a school of thought that says yeast is an ingredient of whisky, because yeast is added to the mash to begin fermentation. But yeast is more of a processor, much as the stills are. During distillation the yeast is removed from the beer along with the spent grains and is sold as animal feed.

Bacteria

Yeast is not the only organism feeding on the sugars in the mash. Bacteria (primarily *Lactobacillus*) also thrive in the fermenters and produce other congeners that add to the flavour, though not necessarily in a good way. In small quantities, their effect can be quite pleasing, producing esters and fatty acids that contribute complex fruitiness to the whisky. For this reason distillers occasionally allow some fermentations to go on for longer than the normal three to four days, to encourage the bacterial contribution to flavour. However, in all but the smallest quantities these effects are generally negative. This is why distillers work very hard to keep fermentation times as short as possible and to ensure that all vessels, pipes, and lines are kept scrupulously clean, to prevent the bacteria from gaining a disruptive foothold anywhere in the process.

The product of fermentation, however, is not whisky; it is distiller's beer. It is the next step in the process, distillation, that transforms this beer into whisky spirit imbued with that beguiling range of Canadian whisky flavours.

Glen Breton 11 Year Old Cask #62
64.1% alc/vol

Prune juice and peaches with sweet Akwesasne tobacco and hints of black licorice. The earthy fug of the dunnage warehouse edges in with allusions to wealthy men's clubs. GB

Glen Breton Ice 10 Year Old
40% alc/vol

Tropical fruits with flowery wet mash and dusty dry grain. Awash in floral perfume, hot pepper, and wet clay. Mashy notes overpower citrus bitterness and vaguely astringent oak. GB

Chapter 6

Distillation

ater boils at 100° Celsius, ethanol at 78.5°C. Long ago someone figured out that when a mixture of water and alcohol was heated, the alcohol evaporated before the water did, so capturing and cooling the early vapours concentrated the alcohol. This simple observation is the basis of distillation. Ethanol itself is essentially flavourless, but the beer created during fermentation includes all manner of other more flavourful ingredients known as congeners. Fortunately, distillation is not an entirely efficient process, so traces of these congeners distill along with the ethanol and they provide the basis for some of the flavours found in Canadian whisky.

The speed of distillation affects the concentration and mix of these congeners and so has a considerable effect on flavour. A slow distillation often produces more flavourful spirit, and this is why some distillers will occasionally dilute their beer or their high wines in order to slow the distillation down. As well, the size and shape of the still will tune the spirit it produces so that it is richer in some congeners than others. The distillation process in Canada is specifically designed to take full advantage of the differences among stills.

THREE-COLUMN DISTILLATION

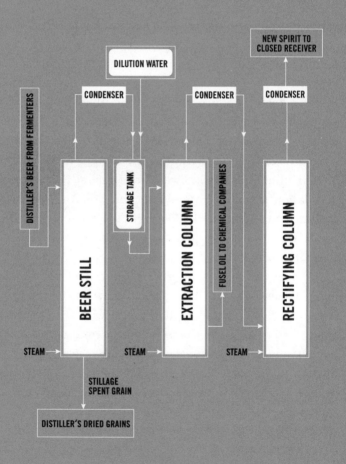

NEW SPIRIT TO CLOSED RECEIVER

DILUTION WATER

DISTILLER'S BEER FROM FERMENTERS

CONDENSER

CONDENSER

CONDENSER

STORAGE TANK

BEER STILL

EXTRACTION COLUMN

FUSEL OIL TO CHEMICAL COMPANIES

RECTIFYING COLUMN

STEAM

STEAM

STEAM

STILLAGE SPENT GRAIN

DISTILLER'S DRIED GRAINS

PRODUCTS OF DISTILLATION

77 METRIC TONNE RAILCAR

DISTILLERY

BY WEIGHT

1/3	1/3	1/3
CO ^{2} (CAPTURED AND SOLD)	SPENT GRAINS AND YEAST DISTILLER'S DRIED GRAINS (CATTLE FEED) 23-26 METRIC TONNES	WHISKY

HOW MUCH WHISKY IS PRODUCED FROM A CARLOAD OF GRAIN?

- One railcar load of grain weighs 77 metric tonnes
- This produces 7,700 litres of absolute alcohol
- After diluting to barrel strength this fills 212 barrels
- When mature this yields 35,400 litres of cask-strength whisky
- When diluted to bottle strength this gives 62,000 litres of whisky
- At bottle strength this produces 82,685 bottles of whisky
- So, one railcar load of grain produces 82,685 bottles of whisky

ALL FIGURES ARE APPROXIMATE

Glen Breton Rare 8 Year Old
40% alc/vol

Delicate soft fruits and grainy mash in a floral, almost soapy perfume. This first release, although bottled too young, foretold of the apples and lupines that infuse older versions. GB

Grand Grizzly
40% alc/vol

Citrus zest, dark fruits, and pickles settle into blue agave mud after a peppery assault. Round and weighty but youthful and zesty, it alternates between tingling hot spirited pepper and wet muddy slate. ND

Harwood Canadian
40% alc/vol

Slowly awakens to rye spices, fruit juice, dry grain, milk chocolate, barbecue spices, and spirit. Light, mild, simple, and subdued for mixing. Awaits ginger ale. ND

Types of stills

Essentially two types of stills are used in Canadian distilleries: the traditional pot still familiar to the earliest Canadian distillers, and a carefully tuned column still, which removes water and impurities while concentrating the ethanol and various congeners. Pot stills have been used by whisky makers for many centuries. However, in

London, on June 10, 1826, the *Register of the Arts and Sciences* carried an illustrated description of a new kind of still designed and patented by J. J. Saintmarc. His still was ingenious because it allowed beer to be added continually to the top of a distilling column in order to replace the escaping whisky vapours. Suddenly distillers could produce spirit non-stop. The following year, Robert Stein developed an improved column still that used steam rather than direct fire to heat the beer. Then, in 1830, an Irish excise man, Aeneas Coffey, patented yet another version of the column still. Though modern column stills are often called Coffey stills (which has been confusing to the ear ever since), early leading-edge Canadian distillers Thomas Molson and John McLaren seriously considered buying the earlier Saintmarc version. But in the end, McLaren chose to stick with the traditional copper pot still, while Molson had another idea. He constructed his own square, wooden, steam-heated adaptation of the column still. Later distillers, such as Hiram Walker, used tall, round, three-chambered wooden charging stills with copper doublers attached, developed by the Hoffman, Ahlers & Company in Cincinnati.

Column distillation

Today, several Canadian distilleries use some form of pot still for specialty whiskies, but the majority of Canadian whisky is distilled in column stills. Column stills work like a series of interconnected mini pot stills. Warmed beer is added near the top of a tall column and flows in thin layers across many tiers of perforated horizontal metal plates to the bottom of the still, where it is discarded or recycled as stillage. Meanwhile, pressurized steam is introduced at the

Hirsch Selection 8 Year Old
43% alc/vol

A youthful eye-opener with crisp clean wood, intense gingery pepper, and a thick, vibrant fruity core. Hints of motor oil interrupt cinnamon toast before all slowly dissolves away. ND

Hirsch Selection 20 Year Old
43% alc/vol

Flavourful, oaky, and surprisingly simple, its lavish fruitiness dusted lightly with cinnamon. Very hot gingery spices lead into pine pitch with pleasant hints of varnish climaxing in unctuous caramel. ND

bottom of the still and, as it rises through the perforations in the plates, it heats the descending beer, causing the alcohol to evaporate. This alcohol then condenses on the plate above, losing its heat to the beer as it flows across that plate and enriching it with alcohol. More alcohol then evaporates from that plate and the process repeats as the spirit rises up the still. Steam bubbling up through the perforations prevents the beer from flowing through the holes, forcing it instead to run to the end of the tray, where a short pipe, called a downcomer, carries it down to the next tray. Here it flows back across the perforations in the opposite direction. As the beer descends the column, tray by tray, more and more alcohol is stripped out, and as the steam ascends it becomes richer and richer in alcohol. Of course, as the water is stripped out and the alcohol enriched, most of the congeners are also depleted, meaning that the spirit that is being produced is often quite light in body and flavour.

To be fully effective, column stills would need to be very tall and this is why, for practical purposes, most are split into two adjacent columns, called an analyzer and a rectifier. The analyzer, more commonly referred to as a beer still, produces a distillate, or high wine, of about 65 percent alc/vol. Since this is quite rich in congeners, the product of the beer still is often put directly into barrels and matured to make flavouring whisky. For base spirit though, the high wines are redistilled in a further series of columns. Each distillery uses its own combination of stills. At Highwood distillery, for example, a tall rectifying column is mounted directly on top of a pot still to take advantage of both processes in a single run. Specific distillation practices are described in the chapters about the individual distilleries, but all are based on a fairly generic process.

Generally, all the grain solids are left in the distiller's beer when it is fed into the beer still. The beer enters the column about three-quarters of the way up and as it passes down the column, the alcohol and congeners are stripped out as vapour and exit through the top of the still. Meanwhile, the depleted beer and grain solids exit through the bottom of the still. Often water is added to the product of the beer still to dilute it down to about 15 percent alc/vol. Then it undergoes an extractive distillation in a fusel column. Fusel oils are natural by-products of fermentation that provide specific flavour characteristics to whiskies. However, Canadian whiskies generally contain lower levels of fusel oils than other whisky types, and most fusels are deliberately removed during column distillation. Because they are not soluble in water, they can easily be separated out of the diluted spirit. Normally, fusel oils are extracted part way up the fusel column and the diluted spirit is drawn off the top and sent to a third column known as a rectifying column. In the rectifier the alc/vol will be raised to as high as 94 percent before the spirit is collected in a large receiving container to be sent off later and put into barrels for ageing.

Distilling then diluting

Canadian distillers think long and hard about how they spend money on production, as each dollar they spend increases the price a consumer must pay for a bottle of their whisky. Distillers have found that spirit that is put into barrels at about 70 percent alc/vol (with a big plus and minus) develops the most desirable flavours while in the barrel. It seems odd then that they would go to the rather high expense of distilling to 94 percent alc/vol when they are just going to add water back before they finally put the spirit into barrels. However, to paraphrase the Bard, there really is method to this madness.

Spirit that has been distilled to a lower alc/vol is a soup of congeners, some of which are more soluble than others and some of which are quite reactive with flavour elements found in the wood. By introducing spirit with a high congener level into some barrels, and spirit with a low congener level into others, Canadian distillers take advantage of the benefits of different kinds of interactions with the wood. Some of these interactions are mutually exclusive. Some reactions happen with greater intensity when the chemicals in the wood are not competing with other congeners in the maturing spirit. Chemical reactions tend to favour an overall equilibrium. With the congeners derived from the grain and fermentation largely removed, that equilibrium shifts in favour of activity within the wood itself.

Pot and batch distillation

In some distilleries – Hiram Walker, for example – some spirit from the beer still will be further distilled in a large copper pot still rather than continuing through the multi-column stills that are used to produce the majority of the whisky spirits. A pot still is most commonly used when making flavouring whisky that has a high content of rye grain. A pot still, quite simply, is a kettle with a pipe leading out of the top and through a water-cooled vessel called a condenser. The pot, which is usually made of copper, is filled with high wines from the beer still, and then heated with steam coils until these high wines boil. The resulting vapours condense as they flow through the condenser. These vapours include most of the alcohol from the high wines,

Top of the beer still at Highwood Distillers.

quite a healthy volume of congeners, and some water. Except for Glenora, which filters its mash before fermenting it, Canadian distillers do not distill beer directly in a pot still because the grist that is left in Canadian distiller's beer would burn in the pot. Because pot stills are quite inefficient, the final distillate, which comes off the still at about 65 percent alc/vol, contains a lot of impurities. This is a good thing, as these impurities give some Canadian whiskies much of their flavour when mixed with the lighter product of the continuous column or batch base still.

In addition to the desirable congeners, high wines also contain some less desirable ones such as highly volatile ketones, often called heads or foreshots, and less volatile heavy alcohols, called tails or feints. In the pot still or batch base process, the foreshots are the first spirits to come from the still and the heavy feints distill off near the end of the run. Only the middle portion of the distilled spirit is matured into whisky. Foreshots and feints are usually collected separately and recycled into the next batch of beer to ensure that all the ethanol and desirable congeners are finally extracted. Meanwhile, the watery leftovers in the pot still, called pot ale or thin stillage, are sometimes added to the next mash to increase the acidity in sour-mash processes, or they may be dried and sold as cattle feed.

Essentially, distillation takes the distiller's beer and separates it into components. In some distillations a large amount of water and congeners is left in the distillate to create flavouring whisky. Flavouring whisky draws much of its flavour from the grain, from fermentation by-products, and from maturation in charred new oak. In other distillations, the percentage of alcohol is raised to a much higher level, which allows other, more subtle congeners to be more fully expressed. Once all these various whiskies have been distilled and matured there is only one step left in creating the final product – blending.

Chapter 7

Blending

When you take a sip of Canadian whisky you taste a beverage that is the sum of many influences that have come together slowly, naturally, and deliberately over a period of many years, or even decades.

Initially, a distiller and a blender will sit down with an idea in mind for a new whisky. They decide on the taste, the smell, and the feel they want, together with the emotions the whisky should evoke. They may also discuss how much it will sell for. Then they decide how they will create the various components. They also may consult their library and inventories of existing whisky, looking for new combinations to bring new flavours to your glass.

The Canadian approach to making whisky is to develop the different flavour elements separately and then bring them together to create a final product that is new and unique, while at the same time evincing the brand's house style. A new Gibson's whisky will always be creamy and voluptuous; Crown Royal will always have elements of bourbon and vanilla; Canadian Club will always be known for its fruitiness, as Black Velvet is known for its dusty rye. Yet within these defined house styles there are many possible approaches to achieve different feels and flavours.

Modern Canadian blending practices continue the basic approaches that Wiser, Seagram, and others introduced in the nineteenth century: highly flavoured rye whiskies and bourbon-like corn whiskies are mingled with elegant base whiskies. To emphasize those wood flavours that are often masked in new charred barrels, base whiskies are aged in used oak barrels. As well, residues from the previous maturation that have spent years absorbed into the wood interact with the new base spirit. Base whisky contributes both flavour and mouthfeel to the final whisky.

Some distilleries make only a single base spirit that they mature into different base whiskies by using a variety of barrels and maturation times. Others distill several different base spirits to start with, and then mature these in various ways to further expand their blending options. Most distilleries make their base whisky from corn. An exception is the exclusively wheat-based Highwood Distillers of High River, Alberta. Alberta Distillers, located in Calgary, uses rye grain for theirs. Alberta Distillers now has more than sixty years of production experience making rye-based spirit. However, for his new whiskies Alberta Distillers' master blender and distiller, Rick Murphy, has begun to scratch his creative itch by distilling some base whiskies from corn, wheat, barley, and even triticale when the price of rye is high.

Flavouring whiskies are distilled to a lower strength. In addition to corn and rye, the Hiram Walker distillery and Diageo's Gimli plant, where Crown Royal is produced, also distill flavouring whisky from barley. Only Hiram Walker makes flavouring whisky from malted rye. Usually flavouring whiskies are matured in new charred oak barrels, once-used bourbon barrels, or rye refill barrels. The use of distilled rye for flavouring distinguishes Canadian whisky from that made in other countries. To qualify for the name "Canadian whisky" the liquid you pour into your glass must always exhibit some of these signature rye notes. But that's not the only thing that sets Canadian whisky apart.

Today there are eight traditional Canadian whisky distilleries operated by seven distillers. (A ninth distillery makes single malt whisky.) Each distiller works independently and they do not share whisky with each other. However, for a time in the mid-twentieth century, several whisky distillers owned several distilleries, each with its own specialty. Sometimes those distillers created new whiskies by blending whiskies from their various distilleries together. Today, for the most part, all of the component whiskies for an individual brand are distilled in a single distillery, by a single distiller who has crafted them to be mingled together. The distiller tunes the fermentation and distillation processes, while the maturation practices are designed with specific whiskies in mind. When all of the different component whiskies have reached their maturity, they are mingled to create a final product. In Canada this product is simply called "Canadian whisky." However, despite the fact that these Canadian whiskies may more accurately be described as "single distillery whiskies," certain American regulations require that in the United States almost all Canadian whiskies be referred to as blends.

Canadian blending is similar in concept to the practices used to blend Scotch, except that in Scotland the products of many different distilleries are mixed together. However, Canadian blending does not resemble the American practice of mixing mature whisky with grain neutral spirits (GNS). Let us dispel the "GNS myth" right now. Canadian whisky is *never* made with grain neutral spirits. Tiny amounts of young rye or base whisky may occasionally be used skillfully as top dressing to brighten or enhance certain flavours, but neutral spirits? Never.

When Scotch single malts began to gain popularity in the 1980s, the reputation of blends declined in certain circles. There were some pretty dreadful blended Scotches for sure, and Canadian whiskies too, but for the most part the disdain for blends was based on serious misconceptions. Most single malts are themselves blends of a sort – blends of malt whiskies, all made in the same distillery and, like Canadian whisky, matured using different kinds of barrels and ageing regimens. Bourbon too is often a blend of corn-based whiskies that have matured in different parts of tall warehouses where gradations in temperature lead to noticeably different whiskies despite the fact that they all begin with essentially the same grain.

Blending history

Early Canadian whiskies were not blended. The first deliberate blending of whisky flavours happened in the first half of the nineteenth century, not with the whiskies, but with the grains, when distillers began to add as much as 10 percent rye grain to their mashes. Long before Canada's ageing law came into effect, Canadian whisky makers were already ageing their whisky. Often the barrels they used were made in their own cooperages, making it common to age whisky in new charred white oak. It did not take long for people to notice that when they reused these barrels, although the whisky was not as robust, it displayed flavours not found in whisky that was matured in new barrels. In the latter half of the nineteenth century, innovative distillers such as

Joseph E. Seagram and J.P. Wiser began to mingle these two types of whisky. The result tasted better than either one alone.

At about the same time, the newly established international network of railways brought competitively priced American corn to Canada, and distillers began to experiment by using a variety of grains in their mashes. Essentially three types of spirit resulted: corn spirit, which was matured in new wood to make bourbon; corn or wheat spirit with rye in the mash that matured into "rye"; and corn or wheat spirit that was matured in used wood to make common whisky. Blends of these whiskies found ready markets.

Later in the nineteenth century, Hiram Walker came up with the idea of mingling the various spirits he produced before they were matured, and then putting them to age in new and used barrels. He called his approach "barrel blending." Once they had matured in various types of barrels, he would bring these barrel blends together in batches, according to a specific formula, and bottle them for sale. Essentially, barrel blending became the secret recipe for Canadian Club, a recipe in place to this day. Barrel blending, incidentally, is not to be confused with the "blending at birth" process introduced in the 1950s by the makers of Black Velvet whisky. Blending at birth involves mixing two-year-old rye whisky with base spirit then putting this mixture into barrels to mature.

Blending practice

Blending starts with consistent distillates that are matured in a consistent manner, so the first job of the blender is to sample the maturing whiskies regularly to see how they will fit into the house recipe. One of the blender's goals is to use that recipe to produce a consistent product that customers have come to recognize. Each whisky has an identity of its own, and because it is made of components, it should be possible to ensure that this identity remains the same from one batch to the next by adjusting the proportions if an individual component changes. This is exacting work, as whisky drinkers tend to be very loyal to a favourite brand and will notice the slightest change.

Distilling is not a strictly automated and mechanical process. Different growing seasons affect the way the grain matures and these variations require skillful adaptation by expert distillers. Each year the maturing whiskies are tasted and categorized based on flavour profiles and textures, and each year the recipes are tweaked to take any differences into consideration. Sample blends are then prepared and after a marrying period are compared to standards. It's

James Foxe
40% alc/vol

Toffee and warming pepper with hints of pencil shavings, gingery rye spices, and maple syrup. A carefully balanced whisky that's just begging for ginger ale. ND

McLoughlin & Steele
40% alc/vol

Watery, fruity, and loaded with oak and pepper. Loosely integrated cherries, apricots, and peach juice are overtaken by a certain misplaced bitterness that slowly fades to caramel, fruit, and dust. ND

Blending tanks at Highwood Distillers.

delicate work requiring an excellent sense of taste and smell and a lot of confidence. Most distilleries use a trained tasting panel to be sure they get the flavours right. One method the taster may use is to put two samples of this year's recipe and one of a reference blend in separate glasses, then see if the panel can determine which is the odd one out. If they can, more work is needed. Close is not good enough, and the formulas are adjusted until the flavour of blends made using the new recipe matches the standards exactly. Once the exact formula is found, the recipe used in the lab is adjusted to production size.

Barrels of each component of the whisky are then withdrawn from the maturing houses (warehouses). In the past, and occasionally today, the requisite number of barrels of each component, also known as a maturate, were dumped directly into the dumping trough, creating the blend as the process proceeds. More commonly, the various components are dumped into separate holding tanks. When the correct amounts of each maturate are in the tanks, samples are drawn from each tank and nosed to ensure they match the expected profiles. Once everything is sampled and approved the blender begins to mingle the various maturates together. Sometimes they all enter the blending tank at the same time. At other times certain components are mixed and allowed to marry for a while before additional ones are added. David Doyle, who is Wiser's master blender, commonly blends the base whiskies in one tank and the flavouring whiskies in another and leaves them to marry for a while before bringing them all together in the final batch. Once all the maturates have been combined in the correct proportions, they are again left in the tank to marry. The more complex the final whisky the longer this marrying period. For high-volume whiskies new batches might be blended nearly every day, which explains why the blenders at the Hiram Walker distillery complain of having only 114 tanks to work with. Most of these tanks at Walker's, incidentally, hold 80,000 litres of whisky.

Once it has been blended, the whisky will be reduced to bottle strength with demineralized or de-ionized water. Usually a tiny amount of spirit caramel is added to adjust the colour. Although the amount of caramel is below any taste threshold, adding spirit caramel is said to have the added benefit of improving the marriage among the various maturates. The caramel-like flavours often tasted in Canadian whisky are natural flavours that have been extracted from the wood in the barrel and do not arise from the few drops of spirit caramel added by the blender.

After processing is complete the final whisky is checked for its colour, strength, pH, and flavour. If it passes all of these tests then it goes on to the bottling department, where it is filtered to remove any residue of charcoal or debris left behind from the barrels and also to make sure it is crystal clear. Often the whisky is chilled to about 10°C before it is filtered to ensure that any components that are not very soluble will drop out of solution and be caught by the filter pads. Some blenders feel that whisky that has not been chill filtered feels just a little bit richer in the mouth.

Mountain Crest
40% alc/vol

Simple but expressive caramels, butterscotch, tingling pepper, pleasingly bitter burnt sugar, and creamy maple fudge. Warming pepper wallows in soft vanilla ice cream. ND

Mountain Rock
40% alc/vol

Long and hot as the eternal flame, it begins with sweet fruit, becomes creamy like corn chowder until a crescendo of cloves, cinnamon, and ginger signal an approaching earthy, bitter zest. KR

Pendleton
40% alc/vol

Big, round, expressive caramels with hints of ripening fruit and building waves of tingly hot pepper. Bitterish rye grain balances the sweetness, leaving spices to entertain the palate. ND

Different formulas for different markets

In the decades following Prohibition, producers could barely keep up with sales of Canadian whisky, but in the 1980s a trend towards white spirits put all categories of whisky into decline. A huge surplus of maturing whisky, called the "whisky lake," developed around the world, and particularly in Scotland. Dozens and dozens of distilleries went bankrupt. In Canada the pressure was on to cut costs and to improve profitability. One way to do that was to take advantage of tax incentives offered by the U.S. government to incorporate small amounts of American spirits or wine into Canadian whisky. There were various reasons for these subsidies, but one was introduced when the Florida orange crop failed in the 1980s. Unsaleable oranges were fermented and distilled into what was called orange wine but was effectively neutral spirits. Since taxes constitute the largest portion of the cost of making whisky, for brands that were selling millions of cases in the United States these tax savings could be quite substantial. Retired Seagram's chief blender Art Dawe remembers those days. Although Seagram's management and Dawe himself did not like the idea, sometimes as a cost-saving measure he made adjustments to the formula to include some of these American wines or spirits.

However, this tax incentive only applied to whisky exported to the United States. Whiskies produced for Canada and the rest of the world were made according to their long-established recipes. Blending wine or other spirits added for the U.S. market did have an effect on the flavour, and so other adjustments had to be made in the blend of component whiskies to compensate. The debate became academic, according to Dawe, because the Canadian version was used

In the 1970s legendary Seagram's chief blender, Art Dawe, was known as "The Nose." Pouring the sample: M. McClenaghah.

as the standard and the American version was adjusted until quality panels could not tell the difference.

But how could they add American spirit and still call it Canadian whisky? The answer to this question dates back to the mid-twentieth century. The expense of ageing whisky contributes significantly to its final cost. Not only must warehouses be maintained and financed, capital is tied up while the whisky is maturing. Moreover, as it sits in the warehouses it slowly evaporates, so that when the time comes for it to be withdrawn less whisky remains in the barrel than was put away to age. Punishing Canadian tax rates that keep profit margins close to just 18 percent make every penny count.

Canadian economy brands faced stiff price competition in the United States from American blends. This was because

U.S. regulations allowed up to 80 percent unaged neutral spirits in their blends, while Canadian regulations insisted all components of Canadian whisky be fully matured. To help address the additional costs Canadian distillers incurred compared with distillers in other countries, regulations allowing the addition of small amounts of wine or other spirits to whisky were implemented. This did not subsidize distillers or reduce taxes, but it did allow them to add unaged wine or spirits as young as two years old to make up as much as 9.09 percent of the final volume. (The regulation is exacting: it says they can add an additional 10 percent to the existing volume of whisky. As an example, they could add 10 litres of young spirit or wine to 100 litres of whisky, so 10 litres in a total volume of 110 litres is one-eleventh or 9.09 percent.) There was no advantage for high-end whiskies or for low-volume whiskies, but for very high-volume, low-margin whiskies – called "value brands" – this meant that not all of the alcohol had to be stored for years in warehouses. This reduced overall costs significantly. This new regulation effectively altered the definition of what was permitted within a blend, which in turn allowed Canadian distillers to price their high-volume "mixing" brands much more competitively in the U.S. market. However, for the most part, this practice was not adopted for deluxe and premium brands. Several distillers did choose to take advantage, but only when blending their value brands, while others simply decided not to.

There were other benefits as well to this new regulation. Rye spirit is particularly vibrant when it is young. Three-year-old all-rye-grain whisky races around on your palate like a puppy with a toy. Some creative blenders began to add small amounts of young rye-grain whisky to some blends in order to recapture those untamed rye notes. Others, noting the benefits the Scots achieved by using "rejuvenated" wine or sherry casks – that is, barrels that had been deliberately impregnated with sherry or wine – began to experiment with adding small amounts of wine to their blends. Sometimes this was done to stretch out the more expensive aged spirit and other times to develop new flavour profiles.

If distilling whisky is a science, blending it is an art, an almost alchemical art at that. The whisky artist's palette is the range of mature whiskies in the warehouse. The canvas is the base whisky to which the artist adds a broad range of bourbon maturates and rye maturates that have been fermented using a variety of yeasts, and that have been matured for different periods of time in different types of barrels. In the end what the whisky artist creates can be quite a masterpiece, one critic and connoisseur alike can appreciate, with its balanced, robust and delicate flavours that come vividly to life on the palate. Canadian whisky is made to be enjoyed and when given the chance it can actually dance on the tongue.

THE PLEASURES OF CANADIAN WHISKY

Chapter 8

Flavour, Taste, Aroma, and Texture

"Taste" can refer to style and connoisseurship. Most often, though, taste is that mix of flavour and texture experienced in the mouth. When we talk about whisky, these flavours and textures are referred to as the "palate." Usually even before we taste a whisky, we smell it. The aromas, which often predict what we will taste when we take a sip, are called the "nose." Almost anyone can take a sip of whisky and tell you what it tastes like, and when they do they are describing the palate as they perceive it. Similarly, almost anyone can describe the nose as they perceive it. There is no mysterious process involved. But when we know what whisky is made from, when we know how it is made, and when we know where the flavours come from and can recognize them in the whisky, we advance from tasting to appreciating and we are on our way to connoisseurship.

Whisky is made up of ethanol and water, plus minute amounts of flavourful chemicals called congeners. And congeners have a profound effect on the final whisky. There are two Groups of Seven in Canada. The more famous are painters; the more applicable to the subject at hand are the seven main sources of flavour in Canadian whisky. These are: 1) the grains; 2) the way they are mashed (cooked, uncooked); 3) the type of yeast; 4) the length and temperature of fermentation; 5) the type of still; 6) the type of barrels and how long the whisky spends in them; and 7) the way the whiskies are blended.

Each of the grains brings its own essence to the flavour. Corn is most commonly detected by its smooth, creamy, and voluptuous mouthfeel. It also is responsible for a faint but pleasant musty note, sometimes found in long-aged whisky. Wheat also has a certain creaminess, but without the oiliness or the richness of corn. Unmalted barley is known for the signature nuttiness it imparts to Irish whisky, but when distilled for Canadian whisky its contribution is quite minimal. Glen Breton, being single malt whisky, derives all of its grain-based flavour from malted barley. However, malted barley is not used in sufficient quantities to impart much flavour to most Canadian whisky, with the possible exception of Canadian Mist, which picks up some of its characteristic cereal notes from it. Rye contributes unique mineral notes such as flint, floral notes including some that are close to lilac, undefined but clearly detectable notes of sweet ripe fruit, and of course, spices. These spices revolve around cloves, but also include allspice, nutmeg, ginger, and cinnamon. Together, these are sometimes called baking spices or simply rye spices.

In addition to the sugar created during mashing, grain also contributes proteins to the mash. Proteins are made up of amino acids, and when amino acids are heated in the presence of sugar they react, in a process called a Maillard reaction. These reactions, also known as browning, are the source of the familiar aromas of toast, baked bread, and roasted meat. Grain for Canadian whisky is dried carefully, taking care not to roast it. Nevertheless,

MATURING WHISKY

GRAIN AND FERMENTATION FLAVOURS
WOOD FLAVOURS

IMMATURE
GRAINY + SPIRITY

MATURE
BALANCED + COMPLEX

OVERAGED
WOODY + BITTER

some Maillard browning does occur while the grain is being cooked during mashing. This contributes some of the malty, toasty, grainy, nutty, caramel, and toffee notes to Canadian whisky regardless of the type of grain used. Additionally, when two of the amino acids from the grain (cysteine and, especially, methionine) break down in the high processing temperatures, they become important sources of sulphur, which also makes contributions, both positive and negative, to the flavour of whisky. Add to these the vanilla, caramel, spices, and so on from the wood and there is a lot of potential flavour in that glass of whisky.

Pendleton 1910 12 Year Old
40% alc/vol

Butterscotch and maple fudge glisten with lime juice, gingery hot pepper, cooling mint, and charred oak. Glowing hot pepper and menthol tobacco turn to red cedar. Fresh, vibrant, bright, and weighty. ND

Pendleton Directors' Reserve 2010 20 Year Old
40% alc/vol

Sweet, peppery, pleasingly oaky wisps of smoke suggest bacon and beans on an open campfire. Balmy resin, dusty aged leather, and rousing peppermint. Ripe dark fruit in a creamy full-bodied rye. ND

Some flavour science

Flavour scientists have worked hard to identify specific chemicals responsible for individual flavours, and to some extent they have succeeded – if you agree that those little yellow candy bananas actually taste like banana. They may be reminiscent for sure but, in truth, most flavours are not the result of a single chemical, but of a pattern of scents and tastes that when combined evoke, say, oranges, cigars, cognac, or whisky. Thus it is possible to detect many aromas in a glass of whisky, and these actually change as the whisky sits in the glass and some components evaporate, while others are released with the addition of water.

The tongue can detect just five flavours, and of these only three – sweet, sour, and bitter – are commonly found in whisky, yet whisky has so many extraordinarily subtle nuances. This is because the nose can differentiate thousands of aromas and, even without our intentionally smelling them, vapours from the whisky enter the back of the nose when we take a sip. This too is part of the whisky's palate.

Modern research on the molecular basis of smell suggests that recent estimates of 10,000 distinguishable aromas are very conservative indeed. And these smells, difficult though they may be to describe, often evoke deep personal memories. This is one reason why no individual whisky tastes exactly the same to any two people. This is also why whisky competitions and quality panels always use a number of experienced tasters and then aggregate their comments.

Whisky writers often prepare tasting notes that list other things the whisky reminds them of, be it oranges, coffee, cloves, pipe tobacco, black pepper, barbecue-blackened pineapple, the beach, and so on. New whisky drinkers may feel inadequate when they are not able to detect these flavours, but since each person's olfactory experiences are so personal this is to be expected. That cigars can remind us of cognac and cognac of cigars does not mean there is a single flavour called "cigar" and another called "cognac." So it is with whisky. The fun is in the nuance, and the more you taste the better you will become at detecting that nuance.

Almost every whisky book includes a picture of a tongue neatly divided into sections, each of which specializes in a specific flavour. Although flavours do tend to be detected mainly by specific parts of the tongue, these regions are not nearly as distinct as some would have us believe. On the tip of the tongue, the taste buds focus on detecting sweet flavours: caramel, toffee. On the sides, just behind the sweet area, and also way at the back of the tongue, the taste buds tend to work hardest detecting salty flavours. Saltiness is rare in Canadian whisky, leaving these parts of the tongue to focus more on their secondary interests: sweetness and sourness. Behind these receptors, though still on the edges of the tongue, are concentrations of sour receptors that sense any acidic or citrus notes in the whisky. And way at the back, the tongue's bitterness sensors detect the pithy rye notes and tannic elements of the wood. To talk of bitterness, though, is to oversimplify, as there are actually several different kinds of bitter and these are not detected uniformly or all by the same receptors. Some of these are more enjoyable than others, particularly to a mature palate.

In addition to the four basics, there is a fifth flavour, umami, which is rarely found except in the oldest whiskies, where it gives a distinct richness that can be very enjoyable. Umami is detected across the tongue, but unless you have special access to whisky from some ancient barrels, you'll never come across it in Canadian whisky. Recent research on the molecular basis of taste has led some observers to talk about a sixth flavour, astringency. In proper balance this certainly can contribute pleasant feelings in the mouth, just as grape tannins do in red wine. Oak tannins, one source of astringency, sometimes can lend a sense of elegance to long-aged Canadian whisky.

More than just taste

There are two other key components of flavour in Canadian whisky. The first is the ubiquitous pepper. Pepper ranges from flavoursome black pepper through white pepper (hot but less flavoursome) to volcanic cayenne. The flavour of pepper is more than just a combination of tastes and aromas; it also includes stimulation of pain sensors on the tongue by the alcohol. While this sensation can become painful, the tingle of moderate amounts of alcohol on the tongue is pleasant in small doses. Think of peppermint or spicy food. The sensation of pepper can be accentuated by gingery flavours and smoothed over by creamy sensations, especially from corn or long-aged rye.

The other component of flavour is mouthfeel. This takes two forms, the first being a creaminess or buttery feel associated with corn whisky. Mouth-coating whisky that feels syrupy is often said to have "weight." Quite the opposite of creaminess is the pleasantly bitter sensation that sometimes emerges when other flavours have subsided. Because it is aged in reused barrels, Canadian whisky accumulates significant woody notes without becoming bitter. Rather, it develops a slight pulling feeling, much as red wine does. In addition, some rye congeners almost feel like grapefruit pith. This pithiness has a salutary effect on the mouthfeel, as it refreshes the palate.

Knowing where whisky's flavours come from and how you taste them enhances your enjoyment whether you are a casual but curious whisky drinker or a budding connoisseur. If the latter, though, you may want to take the next step and learn some techniques to discern, differentiate, and describe all the subtleties you find in your glass.

proof whisky
42% alc/vol

Lemon drops and floral perfumes mingle with maple syrup, white pepper, and sweet gingery spices. Fragrant sandalwood, saffron, and spearmint in a bright, simple, and engaging mixer. ND

Rich & Rare
40% alc/vol

Butterscotch, sultanas, pepper, and smatterings of oak in a rich, mouth-filling nectar – quintessentially smooth whisky sprinkled with fresh cedar sawdust, ripe fruits, and hot, hot pepper. ND

Rich & Rare Reserve
40% alc/vol

An oakier, fruitier, spicier Rich & Rare enhanced with dusty dry grain and lemony roses. Succulent and lusty with tingling pepper, cinnamon sticks, and spicy rye, subdued by earthy amber maple syrup. ND

Chapter 9

Tackling Tasting Techniques

here is nothing more refreshing than a good rye and ginger and no better segue from a demanding day to a relaxing evening than a great Manhattan. That said, Canadian whisky has so much more to offer those who make even the smallest effort to understand it. This means starting with the most basic: tasting it neat or with a few drops of water in order to learn about the nuances, the subtleties, and the house styles of each brand and distillery.

Although the pleasures of good whisky are pretty much self-evident, there are approaches (techniques if you like) to tasting that will amplify that pleasure. Yes, you can simply throw the whisky back, shooter-like, wipe your mouth on your forearm, wince and gasp, and everyone will know you're a real tough cowboy – or cowgirl. A little bit of flavour will linger on your tongue, but your mouth will be anaesthetized, your eyes watering, and you will have missed 95 percent of what you could be enjoying. Better to take a somewhat more structured approach, based on what it is you taste and smell. It's called "sippin' whisky" for a reason.

There are many theories on the proper way to taste whisky – so many theories that you will quickly surmise that none can be entirely correct. Indeed, people who conduct whisky tastings love to inject a bit of showmanship and certainly a bit of ego into the event. Some will have you take a mouthful of whisky, then lean forward and chew it with your front teeth, the so-called Kentucky chew. Others will have you tilt your head back and gasp for air like a carp in a summer pond. Some want you to warm the glass in your hands so the most volatile elements evaporate. Others insist that you taste at room temperature, as the typical consumer would.

Adding water

About the only factor most experts tend to agree on is that you should add water to truly appreciate the subtleties of whisky. They say it "opens up" the whisky to reveal all kinds of hidden flavours and aromas. Many explanations are given for this, some fanciful, others more sound. Whisky scientists tell us that whisky is not a homogeneous solution of alcohol and water, but that "clumps" of pure ethanol form within the whisky, and congeners that are not soluble in water dissolve in these microscopic regions of pure alcohol. They tell us the clumps get smaller as water is added and, as they do, the "hydrophobic" congeners are expelled, adding new aromas to the nose of the whisky. Of course, once these are released into the air they are lost to the palate and this may explain why professionals who "nose" but don't taste whisky prefer to add water, while many aficionados who simply enjoy drinking it do not. No doubt adding water, especially to high-alcohol whiskies, can enhance the flavour, even if only because it reduces the anesthetic effect of the alcohol on the nose and tongue.

You can start by adding just a few drops of water and see for yourself what happens. It won't be the same with every whisky. To amplify this effect you may want to cover the glass for a few minutes to let the hydrophobic vapours collect before you smell them. Some people prefer to taste a whisky first and decide if it needs water at all. Some very old whiskies, for example, lose their delicacy and fragility when water is added.

Royal Canadian
40% alc/vol

Caramel, fresh white cedar branches, mounting pepper, rye spices, hints of wood and grapefruit rind. Barley sugar and bitter citrus pith fade to lingering pepper. Sweet, pleasant, and uncomplicated. ND

Royal Canadian Small Batch
40% alc/vol

Sweet winey fruit with earthy rye, hints of fresh oak and cedar, hot pepper, cinnamon, cloves, pickle juice, spirit, and refreshing bitter notes. A slight oily-waxy feel, then a touch of tannic grip. ND

Professional whisky tasters, not drinks journalists or marketing representatives, but quality assurance people who are employed by distilleries, usually dilute whisky before assessing it. According to distiller Rick Murphy of Alberta Distillers, experience has shown that when it is diluted to 23 percent alc/vol the flavours in a sample of whisky are the easiest to detect and, more importantly, so are any flaws. Most whisky judges will nose and taste the whisky at bottle strength and then again with a splash of water. Some even go so far as to pour two glasses of the same whisky so they can nose one with water and the other without it before tasting either. For the casual whisky aficionado and the budding connoisseur who wants to understand whisky better, nosing and tasting first at bottle strength and then diluted with a few drops of water is probably the best approach.

One thing for sure is that mixing water and alcohol causes what is known as an exothermic reaction; that is, it produces heat. This warms the whisky, causing some of the more volatile elements to evaporate. Try this experiment. Take a small amount of water into your mouth and hold just a little bit of it on your tongue. Then draw a small amount of whisky into your mouth and let it mix with the water. See how warm it gets?

Professionals usually taste at room temperature, but if your booze-hound father-in-law is on his way over and you fear for your most precious bottles, take the worst bottle of Scotch you can find and place it in the refrigerator. The cold will disguise most of the harshness (along with most of the flavour, of course) and you can make points with dad-in-law by pouring him giant drams, all the while using him to dispose of that bottle you knew at first taste was a terrible waste of money. Add a few ice cubes as insurance that any flavour will be masked until the very last sip.

Outside influences

One thing that really does affect the tasting experience is glassware. A glass that is narrow at the top will concentrate or focus the aromas. An ISO tasting glass is quite effective for this. For rich sipping whiskies, the Glencairn glass favoured by single malt drinkers maximizes the pleasure. Canadian whisky can be comparatively sweet, so some people prefer to introduce the whisky a little deeper into the mouth first. This ensures the nuances and complexities are not swamped in sweetness. A glass with an out-turned lip helps, but if you don't have one take a sip anyway. Just wait and everything will reveal itself. For cocktails or mixing whiskies with a spirity overtone, a wide-mouthed glass is preferred because it helps dissipate the spirit. However, spirit is an important part of the drinking experience with mixing whiskies, so if you are using a wide-mouthed glass, don't wait too long to take that first smell or you will miss it altogether.

For analytical assessments, it probably works best to assemble flights of four or five whiskies in identical glasses, then nose or taste them one after another. The order in which they are nosed and tasted will affect the flavours, so it helps to do this several times, changing the order or even the line-up of whiskies. Analyzing more than five or six whiskies at a sitting can be difficult because of a phenomenon called sensory-specific satiety. When you have smelled the same aroma many times in a short period, you come to enjoy it less. This is similar to the effect of eating a large meal and being unable to take another bite, yet still having room for dessert and

Glencairn tasting glass.

coffee. As well, smelling the same aroma repeatedly can make you much less aware of its presence. This can throw off the balance in a flight of whiskies that have both common and differing aromas. It can also have benefits, as it tends to help you forget any background odours and just smell the whisky.

The label on the bottle can also have a large influence. People often taste what they expect to find in a whisky. This is why, when possible, analytical assessments are best done blind, thus preventing tasters from detecting what they think they should rather than what is actually there.

Some people like to comment on the colour of the whisky first, believing it will tell them something about the whisky itself. However, often the colour of the whisky has been adjusted so that customers who know what they want and demand consistency will not be put off by any minor colour differences between batches. Other people will comment first on the "legs" or "tears" that run down the inside of the glass. Larger and slower moving legs are said to indicate a weightier body. This seems kind of pointless when you can simply taste the whisky and actually feel the body firsthand, but people do tend to follow rituals.

Analyzing whisky's flavours

The whisky tasting begins with smelling the whisky's bouquet. Swirl the whisky slightly in the glass and then smell it.

Very simple. Think about the different aromas that emerge, how they emerge, and the order in which they emerge. If you like, you can jot down notes of some the aromas you smell in the whisky. Then perhaps smell a second whisky and note the differences. Deep breaths are not necessary. Your nose quickly becomes attuned to the smell of the whisky, a factor called olfactory fatigue. Refresh it by smelling something else now and then. Some people will keep a glass of water handy to smell between whiskies to refresh their noses. Others simply smell their arms.

It can take some time for a whisky to reveal all its complexities, so the nosing may last for a few minutes, but eventually you will want to taste the whisky and assess its palate. As with nosing, begin with a small sip. Some people like to aspirate a small amount of air with the whisky to help spray it in tiny droplets around their mouth. Because much of the flavour comes from aromas that drift up from the tongue, it also helps to savour the whisky with your mouth slightly open to increase airflow. This is not necessary, though. Right away you should be able to recognize the special spiciness of fermented rye grain, and detect notes from the barrel – vanillas, caramels, tannins. For palates used to single malts or bourbon, Canadian whisky can be a bit difficult at first. After a little practice you'll be surprised how quickly you detect the different flavours from the other elements of the whisky-making process as well. Remember it's finesse, subtlety, nuance, balance, complexity you're looking for, not a firewater kick in the face.

Research with wine tasters has shown that most people are unable to detect reliably more than about four flavours or aromas in an individual wine at a single sitting. For this reason, published tasting notes, when they are not entirely fanciful, are often composites of several tasting sessions. Of course, each person brings different olfactory experience to the table, and so will put different names on the flavours and aromas they find. Few flavours in nature are pure, as they are the result of specific and sometimes complex combinations of many chemicals. Mango, for instance, includes elements of melon and pine needles. Different tasters may find different associations and use different descriptors for it. The best approach is to write down the various things you taste and smell and not worry about what other people find.

But there's more to tasting than just the flavour. Let the whisky roll around in your mouth and feel it. Is it rich, creamy, and weighty, showing lots of corn whisky, or is it watery, perhaps even a bit thin? A luxuriant mouthfeel is one of the characteristics that helps set the great Canadian whiskies apart. And if it ends with a cleansing feeling of grapefruit pith, not only have you experienced one of the unique pleasures of Canadian whisky, you are also ready to taste it again. This time add a dash of water and take particular note of any new aromas.

Structured tasting

There are tens of thousands of flavour nuances in whisky, so your notes could quickly become voluminous. As your tasting experience grows, you will want to be able to refer back and compare your notes. This implies the need for more than just simple random jottings. Using a structure helps. Some Canadian whisky makers have simplified this process by categorizing these nuances using an 8/2/3 system based on the interplay of eight key aromas, two base flavours, and three aftertastes. As you will quickly note, these do not

Royal Reserve Canadian Rye Whisky
40% alc/vol

Subtle but complex brittle rye, with glowing pepper, creamy toffee, and lemon zing. All is nuance as cinnamon and cloves meet pickles, pine needles, and hints of walnuts. Pulling and slightly tannic. ND

Silk Tassel
40% alc/vol

Quite dusty, with inklings of cloves and ginger. Spirity with sweet and sour fruit, chocolate-covered caramel, and spicy hot pepper. A pleasing balance of bitter pith and hot pepper. ND

correspond exactly with the three primary tastes and almost infinite number of aromas described earlier. Rather, this is a simplified way to classify the flavours of Canadian whisky, the interactions of taste and smell, and how they are perceived. Using this system you can pretty much describe and compare any number of Canadian whiskies, and if you find something that doesn't fit you can just call it "other." Of course, if you are going to write tasting notes you will want to add a bit of flourish, but this approach provides the basic building blocks. Systematically describe each whisky as you taste it, and over time you will have built up a catalogue within which comparisons can be made. The best way to do this is to quantify each of the 8/2/3 descriptions and sketch a graph, as in the accompanying illustration.

So what are these eight aromas, two flavours and three aftertastes? The aromas are simple. Although you will encounter

MAPPING AROMAS AND FLAVOURS

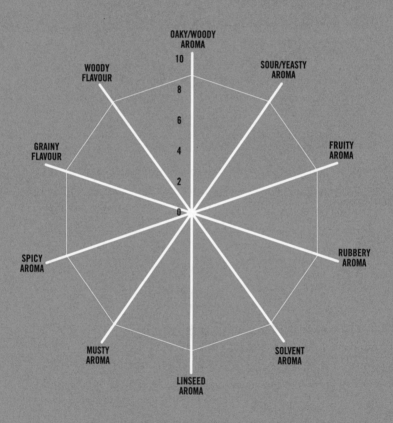

thousands of nuances, these are the eight basic aroma groups: 1) *oak*: ranging from tannic, astringent dry wood to fresh-sawn lumber; 2) *sour/yeasty*: from bread dough to sour pickles; 3) *fruitiness*: including fresh fruit, dried fruit, apples, plums, and so on; 4) *rubbery*: bike tires or a lit match; 5) *solvent*: sweet nail polish or acetone; 6) *linseed*: flaxseed, or oily linen; 7) *musty*: a hint of earth, river water, or old books; and 8) *spiciness*: cinnamon, cloves, ginger, and pepper.

When nosing a whisky it is helpful to use a tasting sheet or run through these categories in your mind. Ask yourself, are there any oaky tones here? Any sourness? What about fruitiness? The trickiest one is solvents, because these very often smell fruity, so if you've already covered them off under fruitiness, don't worry about it. When you focus on these one at a time you enhance the likelihood that you will discover more of the characteristics of the whisky.

The two basic flavours are not what you might expect. These are not two of the primary tastes, sweet, sour, and bitter. Rather they are the flavours of the two ingredients, grain and wood. Yes, you can smell a thousand variants of these, but remember grain and wood are the two fundamental flavours of Canadian whisky around which everything else revolves. Oak, you will notice is also one of the key aromas.

After nosing the whisky and tasting it, there is one final characteristic worth noting. This is the finish, the flavour that lingers long after you have swallowed the whisky. Generally a long finish is considered preferable to a short one. As well the actual flavours of the finish are important. For this kind of analysis, the three flavour elements of the finish are caramel, vanilla, and pepper. Caramel includes similar flavours such as fudge and toffee. Vanilla can range from vanilla pods to delicate flowers, perfume, and "bourbon" notes. Pepper is hot or hotter.

For each of these characteristics jot down a ranking based on its presence, from 0 to 10. Very complex whiskies will show something in every area, simpler ones in only three or four. Balanced whiskies can be complex or simple but will either have similar scores in each of the areas where they score, or will have one element balanced against another. Once you have assigned numerical scores, these can be plotted on a bar graph or web diagram using a simple spreadsheet program. Using the same categories each time will provide you with easy-to-compare pictures of the individual whiskies and will quickly let you sort them into your preferred styles or classes. It's kind of fun, and a really good way to train your palate.

Whether you are used to tasting other kinds of whisky or not, the process may take a bit of getting used to. Whisky judges know that the most important qualities are that a whisky be balanced and true to its type and character. Unless it comes from Glenora distillery or Shelter Point, we wouldn't want a Canadian whisky tasting like single malt. Best of all, these classifications are based on *your* assessment and not that of a whisky marketing department or writer.

Whether you choose to focus hard on your tastings or to have fun with them, you will, with practice, learn to differentiate among whiskies and you will also learn what kind of whisky you prefer. In all likelihood you will also modify the 8/2/3 system to make it conform with your own tastes and preferences. You may even develop your own approach. This, in turn, will give you confidence in your own opinion. After all, you have only one person to please – yourself.

A CONCISE HISTORY OF
CANADIAN WHISKY

Chapter 10

Canada's First Distillers

Exactly who made the first Canadian whisky, and where or when they made it, will never be known. Canada's original inhabitants did not distill alcohol, but when European immigrants began arriving en masse, whisky and whisky stills arrived with them. By 1767 James Grant was operating a rum distillery with a capacity of 70,000 gallons in Quebec City. Within twenty years this output had grown nearly six times to 400,000 gallons distilled in four copper pot stills. Almost certainly dozens, if not hundreds, of small home distillers had preceded Grant. Throughout the eighteenth century, stills arrived in Lower Canada (Quebec), from England via the Hudson's Bay Company, and then eventually in Upper Canada (Ontario) with the earliest European settlers and later with United Empire Loyalists fleeing the American Revolution (1775-1783).

In 1794, when Métis fur trader Nicolas Montour bought the derelict Montreal Distillery Company from Isaac Todd, Canada was still seventy-odd years away from being a country in its own right, but already some distilling businesses had flourished and failed along the way. At the same time, 480 kilometres west in York (Toronto), John Graves Simcoe, who was Upper Canada's lieutenant governor, reported that residents were distilling their excess grain into spirits. And he encouraged this effort. By 1801, fifty-one licensed stills

Twenty-two men and boys from Seagram's early 20th century cooperage.

served a population of fewer than 15,000 residents in Upper Canada. The tiny size of these "distilleries" well into the 1850s is illustrated in Port Hope, where eight distilleries served a population of 2,500. That's one distillery for every 300 residents, regardless of age. Sadly, none of these distilleries left behind even a trace. Although we assume that many other Upper Canadian stills operated unofficially, several hundred people did the Canadian thing and bought distilling licences. Many of these stills were operated as adjuncts to gristmills, but others were simply household appliances.

Some certainly did try their hand at commercial distilling, but for most success was short-lived. John McLaren and Spalding & Stewart, for example, each had some success with Scottish-style malt distilleries in Perth, Ontario, but they eventually could not compete with rye whisky or column stills. These column stills, incidentally, were developed in Canada using European and American designs. Hundreds of other small distillers followed McLaren and

Spalding & Stewart into bankruptcy, especially after the 1890 ageing law came into force.

Contrary to popular supposition, it was largely English and continental European immigrants who successfully introduced commercial whisky making to Canada and who later developed Canadian whisky into the distinctive sweet and spicy spirit it is today. Scottish and Irish

Snake River Stampede 8 Year Old
40% alc/vol

Silky caramel envelops peppery spice and velvet tannins in a mealy, milky, enticingly mouth-watering temptation. Spicy, dry rye grain, butterscotch sweetness with vague herbal tones, and newly split firewood. ND

Tangle Ridge
40% alc/vol

A fresh, sweet cigar evolves into rich, dusky, overripe fruit, massive vanilla, and blistering pepper, with odd overtones of camphor, wine gums, and candy floss. Herbal, creamy, and slightly fruity. AD

WhistlePig Straight Rye Whiskey
50% alc/vol

A walloping bouquet of fragrant vanilla pods, lilacs, and a fruitiness especially rich in cognac-cured pipe tobacco. This hugely voluptuous whisky just brims with cloves, nutmeg, cinnamon, and eye-watering chilies. ND settlers were, in effect, sidebars to the larger story. It was Molson, Gooderham, Worts, Corby, and Seagram – all of them English – who set the foundations for Canadian whisky. Wiser and Hespeler were of German descent, while Randall and Walker were from New England. The Scots and Irish who first settled the Atlantic provinces took advantage of ready access to Caribbean molasses and consequently distilled rum, as did settlers along the St. Lawrence River as far inland as Montreal. Indeed, Canada's first known whisky still was built for making rum in a small distillery just outside of Montreal. No doubt, early Canadian distillers learned sour mash techniques from their American counterparts. American distillers were themselves influenced in their selection of grains by those Dutch and German settlers who, since the fifteenth century, had been distilling rye to make alcohol in their homelands.

Revolution in the mid-eighteenth century convulsed the territory that was to become the United States. People loyal to the British crown trekked north. These United Empire Loyalists have been credited with introducing whisky making to Canada. However, beyond this mythology, no record has been found to confirm anything close to production at a commercial level. By 1890, the Loyalists' tiny mill- and farm-based operations had disappeared entirely. Other immigrants brought the skills of whisky making on a commercial scale with them. Indeed, if the United Empire Loyalists had any influence at all, it was probably the Dutch and Germans among them who influenced Canadian distillers to add a few shovelfuls of rye to their mashes, marking the turning point for Canadian whisky.

White Owl Spiced Whisky
40% alc/vol

Subtle vanilla and butterscotch flavours dissolve into
Highwood's unique clear rye whisky, emphasizing its
creamy smooth custard, baking spices, and kindling-
dry oak before finishing in traces of cloves. HA

Wiser's Reserve Special Edition
43% alc/vol

Big, bold, and spicy with pickle juice, rich, lush toffee,
and smoldering pepper. Butterscotch and vanilla glaze
oaky tones and fresh pine sawdust while simmering
heat balances bitter pith. HW

To better understand the evolution of Canadian whisky
we need to explore the roles of the key players. Let's begin
with Thomas Molson, the second son in the first Canadian-
born generation of Molsons.

Chapter 11

The Dynasty:
Thomas Molson (1791-1863) and
Molson Distillery (1821-1867)

O n June 10, 1791, King George III of England gave royal assent to the *Constitutional Act*, splitting the Province of Quebec into Upper and Lower Canada. Several weeks later, on September 1, 1791, in Montreal, with neither royal fanfare nor public notice, an English immigrant named John Molson and his American housekeeper, Sarah Vaughan, celebrated the birth of their second child. They named the infant Thomas. John had sold the Lincolnshire estate he inherited from his father to invest in a new life as a brewer in Montreal, an enterprise he began even before reaching the legal age of twenty-one in December 1784. In time, his son Thomas would turn his brewery in the east Montreal suburb of St. Mary's into the largest distillery in the Commonwealth.

Although 1786 is generally accepted as Molson Breweries' founding year, the young Englishman was likely familiar with brewery operations long before he arrived in Canada. His family, or their tenants in Lincolnshire, grew grain, and operated a craft brewery on the property. John Molson with his partner, Thomas Loid, another Lincolnshire native, had begun brewing beer in Montreal as early as 1783. Even before he mashed his first Canadian bushel, Molson was familiar enough with the process to recognize that Canadian farmers were growing the less favoured six-row barley rather than traditional two-row barley used in England. Molson decided to import the two-row seed barley from England to distribute among local farmers.

In 1801, while visiting rum distillers McBeath and Sheppard at L'Assomption, Molson bought an old copper pot still. Molson could not have known the significance of his decision to purchase that particular still from McBeath and Sheppard. The copper pot turned out to be Canada's first known whisky still and the significance of its provenance was auspicious. Another McBeath, an Irishman, (who spelled his name "MacBeath") has been credited by whisky historian Charles

MacLean with bringing the first whisky still to Scotland some four centuries earlier. However, except for a £334 sale in 1803, Molson remained a trifler, distilling only small amounts of whisky during those early years.

In all likelihood, Montreal-based North West Company agents used the little whisky Molson did produce to fuel the dying days of their notoriously exploitative trade in furs with Canada's indigenous peoples. Their plan to wrest control of the fur trade from the Hudson's Bay Company ended ignominiously in 1821 when the English firm absorbed them, but

Molson imported malting barley from England.

their introduction of alcohol as currency in the fur trade left a long and appalling legacy. But Molson, of course, was far from their only source.

By 1811 John Jr. and Thomas had joined their father in operating the brewery. Their younger brother, William, later joined them. Although as partners they shared in the operating profits, John Sr. retained ownership of the brewery and received an annual rent from the partnership for its use. The brothers had a new copper pot still shipped from England, and the next year John Bennet arrived from England to build a distillery for the Molsons and to provide them with basic instruction. Nothing seems to have come of that undertaking.

Young Thomas Molson had an insatiable curiosity and a fascination with distilling not shared by others in the family. He was forever experimenting with processes and recipes, never missing an opportunity to discuss his trade with other distillers or travel to learn more about brewing and distilling. While visiting England and Scotland in 1816, Thomas toured as many breweries and distilleries as he could and brought back notes and sketches. Unable to draw to scale, he was careful to record dimensions on these sketches.

Molson learned his lessons well, jotting down notes in a diary so he wouldn't forget. In January 1820 he wrote: "A still and heads of copper with pewter worm containing a charge of 180 gallons to 200 gallons. First charged with stale beer, run off 12 gallons low wines and sometimes 20 gallons but the spirit will not be so good but generally run off altogether 64 gallons from one still. It takes 5 half bushels of sea coal, better than 1 half bushel for to get the still down the worm, there is a small piece of soap put in wash every still full."

Already he had the whisky bug, but it wasn't until almost two years later, October 19, 1821, that Thomas began his own first distillation. He used eight hogsheads and half-hogsheads of stale mild ale to charge the 200-gallon direct-fired copper pot still six times over two days. To the second and subsequent charges he added feints from earlier distillations. To reduce surface tension and thus prevent the still from boiling over into the lead and copper worm, Molson added a one-and-a-half-inch cube of soap to each charge. He sealed the still using rye flour and heated it directly with a wood fire.

On November 17, 1821 Molson exported his first two puncheons of high wines, also called spirits of whisky, to London merchants Grayhurst & Hewatt. The following year he shipped another 1,385 gallons of rectified spirits (whisky) to London, but a year later the London agents ran into difficulty trying to sell Molson's whisky. Despite this setback, Thomas was keen to continue, but without a reliable export market the rest of the family wanted out of the distilling business.

A family divided

There were further complications for Thomas, who by many accounts could be quite difficult. On a trip to England he had impetuously married his cousin and, either unthinkingly or unaware of Quebec's succession laws, had neglected to have his wife sign a prenuptial agreement. This meant that should he predecease her at least half of his share of the brewing business would pass to his wife, who could then leave it to whomever she pleased. This greatly worried John Molson Sr., who saw the business as his family legacy and did not want part of it bequeathed to Thomas's in-laws back in England, even though they were John's own nieces and nephews. As a result, John Molson prepared a will leaving his entire estate to his eldest son, John Jr., and so his son Thomas, the only Molson with a passion for distilling whisky, was effectively, and it turns out unnecessarily, disinherited. Thomas outlived his cousin-wife.

With his brothers' loss of interest in distilling and his own long-term future in the family business seemingly bleak, Thomas Molson left Montreal late in 1823 to seek his own future. At first he investigated opportunities in England, but his passion for whisky won out and he returned to Upper Canada to settle some 275 kilometres west of Montreal, where he set up his own brewery and distillery in Kingston.

Early in 1824 Thomas Molson had acquired land for his Kingston operations and by September he was advertising to purchase barley. The Montreal whisky operation went silent even as Thomas Molson was quickly becoming Canada's largest whisky distiller at his new location. In 1832 Thomas licensed a single steam-heated still with 910 gallons capacity, just under 20 percent of the 5,138 gallon total licensed still capacity for all of Upper Canada. This was without doubt the largest still in Upper Canada.

Molson's was not the only distilling operation in Montreal. In 1821, William Wilson was also busy making whisky there. His distillery was close enough for him to rely on Molson's to grind his malt and provide his yeast. That they were neighbours is not surprising. At a time when transportation in Canada was very difficult, businesses tended to serve their local market or cluster around transportation links, and St. Mary's Current, where Molson's and, later, Handyside's and Harwood's distilleries were located, was the highest navigable point on the St. Lawrence River. In 1834 and with fourteen years of experience behind him, Thomas Molson's brother William decided the Montreal firm should once again fire up the still. He had grown tired of watching from the sidelines as increasing numbers of new distilleries flourished right on the Molson doorstep. But William was a brewer and it was his disinherited brother, Thomas, who knew how to make whisky. Their father, encouraged by William, took the first step and invited Thomas to make what would surprisingly turn out to be a joyful return to the family business in Montreal. Amidst this new-found harmony in the family, the old man also realized a respectable profit on the £802 worth of whisky that Thomas produced in the old copper pot that very first year.

To further secure these lucrative family bonds, John Sr. devised a plan that allowed Thomas and his descendants to share in the future of the business. By willing his assets not to Thomas, but to Thomas's son "named John," the elder Molson avoided the unpleasant prospect of his life's work falling into the hands of Thomas's in-laws in England. The formerly impetuous Thomas seemed to like the idea too – he liked it so much, in fact, that he named a second son, born shortly thereafter John as well, as a kind of double insurance policy. How very Canadian. Always the entrepreneur, when Thomas decided to return to Montreal he didn't sell his Kingston distillery. He leased it instead to James Morton, who also enjoyed considerable success with it. Morton and Molson did very well under this arrangement.

Increasing profits emboldened the company. By 1835 Molson's whisky sales had jumped to £4,460, so the firm invested £1,000 in new equipment including a 700-gallon steam-coil-heated wooden still. Molson used the large wooden still to make low wines. which he then brought up to strength by redistilling them in the copper pot still. This enabled him to increase the level of production and it was not long before whisky sales far surpassed the income from the brewery. In those days, distilling, like brewing, was a seasonal business that shut down during the hot Montreal summers. Molson's production for just the first half of 1836 reached nearly 31,000 gallons. Ever curious, in May 1836, with the distilling season over, Thomas Molson spent two weeks in New York City and Brooklyn to learn more about distilling.

Some Thomas Molson whisky science

Back in Montreal, Thomas, who had an accountant's eye for precision, puzzled over a seeming loss in volume when he added fourteen gallons of water to 376 gallons of over-proof spirits and got only 386 gallons of whisky rather than the 390 he was expecting. We know now that water and ethanol molecules insert themselves among each other in solution, so the volume of a mixture of alcohol and water is always a little bit less than the sum of the volumes of the two separately. Molson had yet to learn this, which is why he repeated this experiment over and over for years, most likely shaking his head each time it didn't add up, but attributing the loss to "concentration" – presumably of the solution, although he might have been referring to his own.

Europe's war: Canada's boon

The early success of Molson's distillery operations had as much to do with international politics as with the quality of their whisky. Between 1792 and 1814 there were frequent brandy and wine shortages in England, the result of the

Napoleonic Wars with France. These shortages helped awaken the British palate to the pleasures of grain spirits. Thus, it was recurring British–French hostilities that actually kick-started Canadian whisky making as an industry. At the time, Scottish Highland distilleries were largely craft operations, restricted by law to the use of a single small still. These distilleries were permitted to mash no more than 25 tons of grain annually, making them

"Dumping" mature whisky.

woefully unable to supply the growing English demand for whisky. An interim option was the product of Lowland distilleries, but these were operating under outrageous taxation pressures. All they could offer was a rapidly made, unpalatable product, and many simply went out of business. Consequently, Britain turned to its North American colony to meet demand.

To get some sense of the scale of this activity, let's look at some numbers. Thomas Molson distilled his first whisky in 1821. Business was so good that within a year he was able to export 1,385 gallons of whisky to England. By 1827 there were some thirty-one known distilleries in Lower Canada. By 1831 that had more than doubled to seventy. And it was Molson's that continued to dwarf all the others. Indeed, Molson's has the double distinction of being the first industrial-scale distillers in both Upper and Lower Canada in the decades prior to Confederation. Having just been weaned off French brandy, British tastes weren't forced to undergo yet another complete transformation. This early Canadian whisky was almost certainly blended with Scotch malt whisky and British spirits once it reached England.

Strength in numbers

Canadian whisky of those days, like Scottish or English whisky of the time, would not be recognized by today's connoisseur. At best, it was little more than rectified spirit, straight from the still. With the addition of flavourings, it could be sold as any of a number of beverages, including gin, rum, brandy, cognac, and even whisky. At that time, rectifying was the process of filtering the raw spirit through charcoal to remove any off-flavours. Sometimes even this step was skipped, so what was sold as whisky was really what today we would call new distillate.

In addition to flavour there was also the issue of strength. Back then, the whisky was often much weaker than today's potation. What was commonly sold to Canadian drinkers in the early days was what is known as low wines, the product of a single distillation, with a strength of about 20 percent alc/vol or less, about half the strength of today's whisky. Barkeeps and retailers would often further dilute these low wines before selling them to consumers as whisky, explaining to some extent at least why our ancestors were able to drink so prodigiously and still do an honest day's work.

The precise alcohol content of the earliest whisky Molson's sold in Canada is not known, but Molson's preference to use double distillation would certainly increase its strength. When Toronto's Gooderham and Worts began making whisky in 1837, it was probably low wines that were reduced to as little as 11 percent alc/vol by the time they reached the consumer. The whisky Molson's exported to England was distilled twice to concentrate it to 34 degrees over proof for shipping. This whisky was made from barley malt, and rectified using fine-rolled pine charcoal. For the Canadian market Molson's used a mixture of grains, often including some rye, in a sour mash recipe. Whether distilled for England or for Canada, whisky was generally sold without any ageing. This was a time when whisky that had spent as little as a month in wood was considered old and commanded a premium price. By 1840, though, the quality and consistency of Canadian whisky in general was improving and whisky was now sold at a standard 12 over proof.

Developments in Upper Canada

Molson's first serious competitor, Gooderham and Worts, entered the market in 1837, a turbulent year in Canadian politics, with insurrection in Upper Canada and outright rebellion in Lower Canada. Undeterred, Gooderham and Worts set about distilling whisky at their gristmill near Toronto harbour, some 500 kilometres west of Montreal on Lake Ontario. Unimpressive early production levels and a relatively weak spirit gave no indication that the Toronto distiller would come to dominate the industry before eventually fading away. Gooderham and Worts must have seemed like just another of the small distillers when in 1839 Molson's produced about 150,000 gallons of whisky (proof spirits), while Gooderham and Worts managed to turn out a mere 28,863 gallons, and these were most likely 35 degree under proof spirits.

Molson's and Gooderham and Worts faced competition from other lesser Canadian distillers as well, Harwood and Sons, Handyside Brothers, and William Dow in Montreal, John A. McLaren in Perth, and James Morton in Kingston. And long before Manitoba became a province in 1879, distilling had also begun in earnest there. As early as 1837, Manitoba's Governor and Committee had authorized the establishment of a distillery at the Red River Settlement, the place we now know as Winnipeg.

Molson's annual production for 1845 climbed to 250,000 gallons, but the following year the British export market collapsed. Scottish production capacity grew as a railway boom brought commercial distilling to formerly inaccessible places. It took Molson's nearly a decade to recover lost trade by developing new markets in the Maritime provinces, eastern United States, and Canada West. Other distillers weren't so lucky and by 1853, only William Dow's and Molson's distilleries remained in Montreal. Upper Canada's distillers, who had never relied on the export trade, were much less affected, but their numbers too were in decline. Canadian whisky making was becoming organized as an industry with the larger distillers trading supplies and firmly adhering to mutually agreed prices, making it difficult for small producers to compete. The days of the microdistiller were clearly ending.

Changing of the guard

As directed in his grandfather's will, when he came of age in 1847, Thomas's son, John Henry Robinson, or JHR for short, inherited the brewery and the next year also became a partner in running the enterprise along with the distillery. JHR did not share his father's enthusiasm for distilling.

Moreover, with improved transportation links, a growing population in Upper Canada to support economies of scale in distilling there, and the loss of the export trade, Molson's whisky sales had plateaued, while Gooderham and Worts's slowly grew stronger. Gooderham and Worts were joined as serious competitors by Philip (J.P.) Wiser, who took over Charles Payne's Prescott-based distillery in 1857; William Hespeler and George Randall, who built the Waterloo Distillery, also in 1857; and Hiram Walker, who began making whisky in 1858. Despite production of nearly 350,000 proof gallons in 1863, when Thomas Molson died that year the demise of his distillery was all but certain. While JHR had inherited the brewery from his grandfather, Thomas had left the distillery to his other son named John – John Thomas – who, probably influenced by the growing temperance movement, had no appetite for the liquor business. He sold the distillery on to his older brother, John H.R. Molson who, in turn, consolidated it with the brewery.

In 1867, almost exactly seventy-six years after King George III assented to the *Constitutional Act*, Queen Victoria gave royal assent to the British North America Act, creating the Dominion of Canada. But 1867 also marked Molson's withdrawal from the whisky business. Until 1848, taxes on alcoholic beverages were the largest single source of revenue for the nascent nation. In 1867, when the tax on whisky was increased to sixty cents a gallon, JHR Molson, perhaps in part because he was grief-stricken over the recent death in childbirth of his young wife, finally closed Molson's distillery, despite record profits. It had been a great run and a family business was created that is still going strong five generations later. Faced with stiffening competition from elsewhere in the country, a growing temperance movement coupled with the family's own strong Protestant faith, increasing taxes, and declining market share, the Molsons turned their focus back to brewing beer. The family returned to the business eighteen-year-old John Molson Sr. had begun eighty-four years earlier when he first arrived in Montreal.

But just as Molson's was leaving the whisky business, others were enjoying its burgeoning success. And the success of those distilleries was such that, in time, whisky drinkers in nearly 200 countries around the world would also be able to appreciate their production. But before we jump too far ahead, let's take a look at the development of Canadian whisky making as a fully integrated industry, beginning with the phenomenal success of Toronto's Gooderham and Worts.

Chapter 12

Gooderham and Worts

I n May of 1831, James Worts, accompanied by his fourteen-year-old son, James Gooderham Worts, arrived by boat at "muddy York." Worts, a Yorkshireman who had been a miller in Suffolk, England, immediately set about looking for a site on which to establish a gristmill. The Town of York had been founded on the northern shores of Lake Ontario less than forty years earlier by British colonists. By 1831 it had become a thriving town of 4,000. Worts's arrival coincided with, and some have argued was eventually responsible for, the transition of York from a backwoods outpost to a rapidly expanding industrial centre. In 1834 York was renamed Toronto.

Despite his experience as the proprietor of Kirtley Mill in Bungay, Suffolk, Worts's trip to Canada was almost certainly a scouting expedition on behalf of his brother-in-law, William Gooderham, who underwrote Worts's expenses. Why he would abandon his mill in England and rely on Gooderham to re-establish him in business in Canada is a matter of speculation, but Worts was a bit of an oddball, occasionally described as troubled, and known to carry on loud conversations with himself. That he lived but forty-two years and died by his own hand, leaving five children orphans, may provide some insight. Fortunately his eldest son did not share Worts's troubles and grew to become a driving force in what would one day be the largest distillery in Canada, and for a brief period, reputedly the world.

Personality quirks aside, Worts was nothing if not effective. By November of 1831 not only had he found a site for his mill, on the Lake Ontario waterfront near the mouth of the Don River, but he had advanced construction of the twenty-two-metre-tall red brick structure to the point that work moved to interior finishing when winter's storms arrived. In Suffolk, mills were commonly powered by wind and that was Worts's plan in York. However, he would have to wait until the following April, when the ice had broken up and navigation could resume on Lake Ontario, to receive delivery of the main mast, the millstones, and other workings for the mill. Transportation in Upper Canada at that time was largely by water.

Family and misfortune

On July 25, 1832, Worts's brother-in-law, William Gooderham, arrived with their two families, several servants, and eleven orphans he apparently had picked up along the way – fifty-four people all told. Gooderham, it seems, was quite happy to share his own good fortune with others less fortunate. Two days after he first set foot in York, on July 27, he invested a further £1,823 in Worts's venture, and the flour-milling business, Worts and Gooderham, was formally established as a partnership. Just a few days later the partners bought their first load of wheat and by early October the mill was in full operation. By year's end they had milled 2,991 bushels of wheat into flour. At that time, wheat was the primary cereal crop grown in Upper Canada and York was right at the centre of the wheat-growing region.

In Suffolk, the wind was steady and reliable, but as anyone who has landed at Toronto Island airport can attest, the winds coming off of Lake Ontario can be quite gusty. At other times the air is too calm to turn a windmill. The partners quickly realized that they would need supplementary power. And so, in 1833, they installed an auxiliary engine that was powered by steam. It was good timing, for not long after the sails of the windmill blew away in a storm and steam power supplanted wind entirely.

In 1834, with their families well settled in a large nearby home, and the seeming success of the flour mill assured, Worts looked forward to the birth of a sixth child. But the birth was difficult and his wife, Elizabeth, died. Worts was despondent and two weeks later was found, drowned, in the company well. In the space of a fortnight his family of two boys and three girls lost both their parents. At fifteen, James Gooderham Worts was the eldest.

True to form, and although they already had six children of their own, William Gooderham and his wife assumed responsibility for their orphaned kin, raising them as part of their own family. At the same time, Gooderham took over full ownership of the mill and renamed it the William Gooderham Company. As wheat production expanded in Upper Canada, Gooderham's business prospered and by 1837 he decided to add a distillery.

Milling and distilling

The distillery was housed in a frame building beside the mill and went into production right away. However, distilling was clearly intended simply to dispose of wheat middlings, a course mixture of flour, bran, and wheat germ left over from milling. It was not until some years later when Worts's son joined the firm that distilling became a business activity of its own. As well, the whisky Gooderham was selling was low wines, the product of a single distillation, with an alcohol content of about 22 percent alc/vol. There was no indication that great distilling success awaited Gooderham and Worts.

Yet from the start Gooderham found a ready market for his whisky, selling the first day's production of 128 gallons to Joseph Lee, a grocer on nearby King Street. Lee returned the next day for another 156 gallons and for a full month bought all the whisky Gooderham distilled. Soon other grocers joined Gooderham's clientele. The mash bill for Gooderham's very first batch of whisky included thirty-six bushels of wheat, 304 bushels of middlings, and twenty-seven bushels of malt. That first year Gooderham purchased malt from the Cull brothers. However, in 1838 he incorporated a small maltings into the distillery. This was step one in making the distillery self-sufficient. However, he continued to buy yeast from nearby breweries, of which there were many.

In 1842 Gooderham added a rectifying column to the distillery. Not to be confused with modern rectifiers, in the early days of Canadian whisky making typically the new spirit was slowly trickled through tall wooden columns that had been filled with charcoal. This removed some fusel oils and other impurities, producing a much more palatable product. The charcoal would be renewed at regular intervals. As well, Gooderham began adding small amounts of caramel to the final product to give it the colour of wood-aged brandy, which was considered to be a higher-class beverage than whisky.

In the 1820s and 1830s considerable work was being undertaken in New York to remove the constraint of batch distilling in pot stills and to develop new distilling technology that allowed beer to be added to the still continuously. The ingenuity early American engineers applied to distilling technology is largely lost in the stories of how Scotch whisky developed, and the fact that much of the evidence of their work fell victim to Prohibition. The concept of using rising steam to drive alcohol vapour up the still was well known, but compared with modern sieve plates and bubble caps, mechanisms for doing so effectively were still very crude. Gooderham's still consisted of a large, square wooden box that was packed with stones. Steam injected at the bottom would strip the alcohol out of beer descending from the top, with the stones providing surfaces on which the alcohol and water could exchange heat. It was primitive, but it worked.

If whisky making was a way to profitably recycle the waste from flour milling, feeding cattle took it one step further. Turning the middlings into whisky depleted them of their starch but left a protein-rich grain residue, known as spent grains, behind. These spent grains were highly digestible by cattle and because they were rich in grain proteins and yeast residues contributed to rapid weight gain. Gooderham had been selling this distiller's waste to William Lumbers, a local feed broker, but in 1843 he decided to build his own feedlot right next to the distillery. Although the neighbours came to complain of the smell, and eventually he moved the feedlot across the Don River, Gooderham's cattle business soon became a lucrative enterprise in its own right.

William Gooderham seems to have been a man of incredibly generous spirit, for in 1845 he brought his nephew, James Gooderham Worts, into the business as a partner. He had previously helped young James set up his own gristmill, but the enterprise did not succeed. Nevertheless, Gooderham felt that his nephew was ready to assume his father's place in the partnership and so Gooderham and Worts, millers and distillers, came to be on the site of James Worts's original mill. Time would prove this to be the most profitable of reunions.

Gooderham had been a successful merchant and miller in England and had used those skills to turn the York mill into a resounding success. He had recently expanded his wheat receiving facilities, adding a company wharf and lakeside elevator. Wheat now arrived at the mill not just from Upper Canada, but from the American Midwest as well. Whether it was the energy of youth or simply gratefulness for his uncle's confidence in him, young James threw himself into the business wholeheartedly. In particular he took the lead in turning the distillery from a waste-disposal plant into a going concern of its own. This was exactly the sort of complementary leadership the firm needed. Though he does not seem the type to keep score, Gooderham must have been very pleased to see his own generosity so amply rewarded.

It was Worts's nature to deliberate carefully before making a decision. Then he would spare no effort in carrying it out. Young Worts soon had two copper pot stills installed in the old windmill so he could redistill the low wines into full-strength whisky. At the same time he took steps to improve the flavour of the whisky by adding small amounts of rye grain to the mash, as Gooderham too had done occasionally. Worts, however, made the use of rye a practice. It would be some time yet before the distillery really hit its stride, but with these two giant steps it was well on its way.

Worts involved himself in a number of other ventures as well, including banking and especially railways. It seems inevitable that early Canadian distillers would dabble in politics, and in 1867, the year of Canada's Confederation, Worts considered running for Parliament in the riding of Toronto East. Vociferous opposition at his nomination meeting revealed simmering resentment towards the powerful influence wielded by Gooderham and Worts, and convinced him to withdraw. Worts was not a people person and the Toronto *Globe* had already given him little chance of success. Perhaps this disappointment influenced his later philanthropy, which included making a major donation to the expansion of the Toronto General Hospital.

The stone distillery

In 1856 the real driving force behind the distillery arrived in the form of William Gooderham's son George. George joined the growing business as a partner, and as his cousin had done before him, immediately seized on the potential in making whisky. He actively lobbied his partners, and by 1859 the firm had embarked on a major undertaking – to build a $200,000, five-storey dedicated distillery that would be at the leading edge of industrial technology. It was to be a distillery where grain passed from railcar to whisky barrel with barely any intervention by human hands.

Gooderham's Bonded Stock
40% alc/vol

Fresh air after a rain then heavy oak caramels and a generic spiciness. Sweet but herbal with hints of licorice root, spearmint, and savoury herbs. A peppery mixer. HW

The distillery today.

The citizens of Toronto had never seen such an undertaking, and given that the Canadian economy was in depression it was a godsend. Four lake schooners were engaged to bring limestone in from Kingston and fully 500 men worked on the construction. The new stone distillery, complete with thirty-metre chimney and a new twelve-metre wooden still, really was an accomplishment. Forty-two tall wooden rectifying columns, each filled with charcoal, received the new spirit, which slowly percolated through the charcoal before being put into barrels to mature. Two 1,500-gallon pot stills were installed in Worts's original millhouse. In addition to deliveries at the lakeside elevator, grain arrived at the distillery's private fourteen-car siding, on the Grand Trunk Railway, and was carried to the top floor by a modern bucket elevator. A 100-horse-power steam engine powered eight sets of grindstones.

With annual production capacity boosted now to 2.5 million gallons, suddenly Gooderham and Worts dwarfed Molson's distillery in Montreal and became the key player in Canadian distilling. In 1861, despite its advanced automation, the new distillery provided work for 150 people and paid excise duties exceeding $100 a day. It soon became the largest source of tax revenues for both the Government of Canada and the City of Toronto. The Gooderham and Worts feedlot was feeding 400 contented milk cows and fattening 1,000 beef cattle annually. Operations at the flour mill continued as well.

However, distilling had become the primary business of Gooderham and Worts, and although the distillery produced fully half of the whisky distilled in Canada West, time would demonstrate that Gooderham and Worts, and their successors, were not whisky men, they were distillers. As long as the stills were operating they were just as happy to make industrial alcohol, acetone, antifreeze, or rum. For the time being, however, whisky was their only product and they produced both rye and common whisky. With actual annual production of over 2 million gallons of whisky, export markets were soon expanded in the United States, Europe, and South America. At one point, according to the Montreal *Gazette*, Gooderham and Worts had become the largest distillery in the world.

Once distilling became the focus of the business, numerous ancillary activities were centralized on site. Maltings were constructed and a cooperage, which kept forty coopers busy, was put in place. Oak for making barrels was harvested locally and further inland. As if to seal the transition from incidental distillers to distilling magnates, in 1864 the partners had Worts's old windmill demolished. What had been a city landmark since 1832 became a mere stepping stone to bigger things.

The walls of the new limestone distillery were more than a metre thick at the base, and interior beams were set onto protruding stone mounts rather than embedded in the walls. So when, in October 1869, the distillery caught fire and the interior was gutted, the walls continued to stand, as they still do today. The partners took the fire in stride, perhaps finding some solace in the fact that large quantities of grain stored in the top of the distillery had fallen through the burned floors, smothering the fire before it could destroy the equipment. Within two days the firm was calling for tenders to rebuild, and within four months, early in 1870, at a cost of $100,000, the distillery was back in production.

On August 21, 1881, nearly fifty years after he arrived in Canada, ninety-year-old William Gooderham died. His nephew, James Gooderham Worts, followed him, less than a year later, on June 20, 1882, at age sixty-four. William's son George was left to run the distillery on his own. Although he maintained the Gooderham and Worts name, George Gooderham bought Worts's interests from his family, making himself the sole owner of the distillery he had been instrumental in building.

The business continued to prosper, and expanded significantly during the following decade or so. When the government passed legislation requiring that by 1890 whisky must be aged a minimum of two years before it could be sold, twelve additional warehouses were added. This law strongly reinforced the already good reputation for quality enjoyed by Canadian whisky around the world, and particularly in the United States. Canadian distillers had long been barrel-ageing their best spirits; now the government of the Dominion of Canada was prepared to certify it.

In 1902, directly across the street from the five-hectare distillery site and in partnership with Hiram Walker and Sons, George Gooderham established a new enterprise, the General Distilling Company, to distill industrial alcohol. It would not be long before non-beverage distillates would be the firm's primary products.

Gooderham's well-tempered enthusiasm

When William Gooderham brought his son George into the business, he still had his mind clearly set on milling flour. His nephew, James, had seen the potential in distilling, but it was George who really propelled the firm to become an industry leader. George's enthusiasm for distilling never waned. However, when he died in 1905, at age seventy-five, and the distillery passed to his three sons and six daughters, the temperance movement had exactly its desired effect: it tempered the Gooderham enthusiasm for whisky. Production continued, but the younger generation behaved more like caretakers than industry leaders.

World War I offered a reprieve from the disapproving gossip of the temperance fold, as the distillery switched production to making corn-based acetone for the war effort. Management of the plant was taken over by British Acetones, which turned Gooderham and Worts into a major supplier to the Allied effort. In addition to producing acetone, the firm launched a very successful business distilling and canning antifreeze. This experience demonstrated the viability of distilling products other than whisky.

The Hatch years

The war ended in 1918; American Prohibition commenced in 1920. Not all Canadian distilleries benefited from increased sales during Prohibition, however. Indeed, Gooderham and Worts struggled. One that did profit enormously was the Corby distillery in Corbyville. Its owner, Mortimer Davis, engaged Harry Hatch, a top sales manager who Davis knew had good connections in the United States. Hatch succeeded in generating enormous sales volumes for Corby. In 1923, however, Hatch left Corby, disgruntled, and purchased a now floundering Gooderham and Worts from the Gooderham family. He soon set himself to building a whisky empire.

The network he had established to sell Corby whisky switched to selling Gooderham and Worts almost without skipping a beat, leaving Davis to scramble. Without Hatch's American connections it is doubtful that Gooderham and Worts would have survived Prohibition. Low Canadian sales volumes, coupled with the Gooderham family's lack of interest, were not enough to sustain operations. However, Hatch made such profits with Gooderham and Worts that within three years he was able to buy Hiram Walker's distillery as well. In 1927 he merged the two firms to form Hiram Walker-Gooderham and Worts.

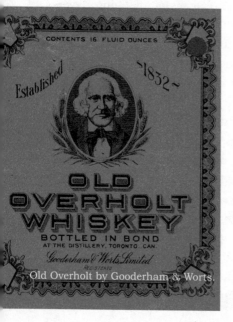

CONTENTS 16 FLUID OUNCES

Established 1832

OLD OVERHOLT WHISKEY

BOTTLED IN BOND
AT THE DISTILLERY, TORONTO, CAN.

Gooderham & Worts Limited
REGISTERED

Old Overholt by Gooderham & Worts.

Although a few individuals profited immensely from Prohibition, sales of Canadian whisky to smugglers could not match lost sales to legitimate distributors. When Prohibition was repealed in 1933 and legal channels of distribution were reactivated, Hiram Walker-Gooderham and Worts expanded rapidly. At the same time, American whisky makers restarted production. However, with updated equipment and new production methods, the bourbons and ryes of the pre-Prohibition era were diffi-cult to recapture. American producers found themselves in competition with established Canadian producers and their well-loved product.

In recent decades extensive research has been conducted on the architecture of the Gooderham and Worts complex with an eye to maintaining its historical integrity during rede-velopment. However, details of its whisky-making operations remain vague. Perhaps this absence of documents confirms stories that following Prohibition Hatch, seeking to distance himself from that lawless era, ordered all records of pre-1933 dealings destroyed.

In 1957, the last grain alcohol flowed from the stills at Gooderham and Worts. The new owner's success making whisky at an expanded Hiram Walker plant in Walkerville made the Toronto distillery redundant. To maintain an active distillery licence and thus keep its bonded warehouses open, the firm continued to distill some rum at the Toronto site, but for the most part production there switched to antifreeze and other industrial products. The end finally came in 1986 when a British firm, Allied-Lyons, bought Hiram Walker-Gooderham and Worts from Hatch's heirs. Within four years all production ceased at Gooderham and Worts. Decades later

The stone distillery.

the gloom that accompanied Allied-Lyons's disinterested takeover is still felt bitterly by former employees.

The Gooderham and Worts distillery has been identified as a national historic site in recognition of its extensive and unique Victorian architecture. It truly is a beautiful location. In 2005 the old distillery was purchased by real estate developers who converted it to retail and residential units. Its status as a national historic site ensures many of the old buildings, including the stone distillery, will survive. However, it has not become the tourist magnet the developers must have hoped for and, in truth, other than beautifully preserved facades, little remains of the old distillery but simulacra. The streets are paved with cobblestones imported from the United States, and its several bars serve a range of Scotch whiskies, but only the most mundane of Canadians. Nevertheless, what is now called the Distillery District is the last of Canada's original distilleries to remain at least superficially intact, and the only place in Canada where a grateful whisky lover can sit, eyes closed, and breathe in a legacy that for the most part has been forgotten.

Chapter 13

Henry Corby:
A Man, a Plan, a Town,
a Distillery

enry Corby was born in 1806, one of twenty brothers and sisters. His father, James Corby, was a baker. His mother, Anne, was clearly focused on children, lots of them. When he was twenty-six Henry Corby left England for Belleville, Ontario with his wife, Alma. Belleville, on Lake Ontario's Bay of Quinte, was a growing town of some 2,000 residents at the time. Although Corby was born in Hanwell, England, and was later described as "a thorough Englishman," his family descended from French Huguenots who went by the name Corbil. Legend, almost certainly apocryphal, says that Corby arrived in Belleville with a single sovereign in his pocket. Shortly after he arrived in the small Upper Canada lumber town, Corby opened a small grocery shop, where he quickly demonstrated at least one of his father's attributes: he became a baker.

On December 24, 1835, with thoughts of a warm and joyous Christmas celebration with friends, Corby, his wife, their three young children, his wife's sister Matilda, and a friend set off by sleigh across the frozen surface of the Bay of Quinte. Just off Massassaga Point the sleigh plunged through thin ice. Alma and the three young children died.

Alma Mills

In response to this tragedy Corby immersed himself in his business and his bakery did well. So well that he was soon able to buy a steamboat and move into the grain trade, which in turn led him to purchase a gristmill. Corby married Matilda and started a new family with her. In a tribute to his first wife he renamed the gristmill Alma Mills. Her tragic death never faded from the family's memory and three decades later Corby's son (by Matilda) would successfully promote an iron bridge across the Bay of Quinte, ending the need to run the risk of crossing on the ice.

It's hard to imagine a lovelier site for a distillery than this spot on the Moira River, but Henry Corby had really wanted to locate his new business venture six kilometres

Corbyville Distillery circa 1900.

downstream in Belleville. For that he needed to dam the river to power a mill but local politicians were not supportive. With the thumbs-down from the Conservative city fathers, in 1855 Corby, at that time a Liberal, bought Silas Reed's 1812-vintage flour mill just upstream on 1.6 hectares at Hayden's Corners in Thurlow Township. It took Corby two whole years to get the mill working. Two years after that he was ready to start distilling. And it was whisky that Corby distilled, whisky that soon brought him fame and fortune.

While Corby commuted daily from Belleville to Hayden's Corners in a horse and buggy, a settlement soon grew up around the distillery. Eventually the settlement would be named Corbyville after its founder. Although this was his first venture into distilling, Corby was not entirely unfamiliar with the process. He had been partners with Silas Reed's brother Robert in supplying the Hastings Rifle Company, which fought against the Upper Canada Rebellion, led by William Lyon Mackenzie. The rifle company troops camped in Belleville for the better part of 1838. At the time Corby was a baker and Robert Reed operated a large distillery, now lost to time, in Belleville. The rebellion quashed and politics being what it is, Corby went on to become mayor of Belleville, then a Conservative member of the Provincial Legislative Assembly. His confidence, large stature, and booming voice made him a natural leader.

Harry takes the reins

In August 1881 Corby was seventy-five and frail, and ready to sell the mill and the distillery. For the sum of $10,000 his twenty-one-year-old son, Henry Corby Jr., became the new owner. Within three months the old man died and Henry Jr., better known as Harry, closed the flour and feed mill to focus his efforts on making whisky. He began selling whisky in bottles, as well as the pails, jugs, barrels, half-barrels and kegs that his father had favoured. Harry had big plans for the distillery and began expanding the market and the plant, adding new buildings and establishing an ageing warehouse and a modern bottling line in Belleville. He also had track laid for a rail spur from Belleville to the distillery. Harry not only expanded production at the distillery, he also modernized its methods. If Henry founded a distillery, Harry created an industry. Harry Corby had a theory about the popularity of his whiskies in the United States: "The fact that the extremely cold weather of Canadian winters adds a peculiar quality to Canadian cereals in the form of certain esters and aromatic compounds which Canadian distillers have learned to preserve. It is these esters which make the 'bouquet' of Canadian rye and bourbon whisky so distinctly pleasant."

Like his father, Harry had a great interest in politics. In 1888 he was elected to represent Belleville as a Conservative member of Parliament. In 1912, Harry Corby's civic mindedness and political career were formally recognized when he was appointed to the Senate of Canada. The town was proud of Harry Corby and thereafter he was referred to exclusively as Senator Corby. Nevertheless, it is Henry Corby Sr. who is best remembered for his distillery. The legacy of his son Harry is the contribution he made to his community.

Prohibition to the rescue

By 1905, it was Harry Corby's turn to think about the future of the business. With three daughters and no sons to take it over, he decided to sell the distillery to Montreal businessman Mortimer Davis for $1.5 million – quite a tidy profit. Davis did well with his new acquisition and further expanded exports to key markets in the United States. When fire destroyed the original distillery in 1907, Davis not only rebuilt but expanded the distillery on the same site. Then, after a great start under Davis's management, whisky making came to a sudden halt in 1916, by government order. For the balance of the First World War the firm's output was restricted to industrial alcohol. When the war was over, whisky sales had declined to a measly 500 gallons a month. This was nothing like the 9 million gallons that would soon lie sleeping in fifteen rack warehouses under the watchful eye of ten government excise officers when American Prohibition (1920–1933) intervened to resuscitate Davis's failing distillery.

Davis also owned the late J. P. Wiser's distillery in Prescott, having purchased it in 1918, a year after the death of Wiser's treasurer and successor, Albert Whitney. In 1920 Mortimer Davis reorganized these two firms as Consolidated Distilleries Limited, a division of Davis's distributing agency, Canadian Industrial Alcohol Company Limited. The name was predictive of further consolidations to come.

Within a year Davis hired one Harry C. Hatch to handle sales. Hatch had begun his liquor-industry career as a bartender in various Ontario locations, first at the Oriental Hotel in Deseronto, then the Shannonville Hotel in the Tyendinaga Mohawk Territory near Belleville. He soon moved on to operate his own package liquor stores in various places including Whitby and Toronto in partnership with his brother. However, Canada has its own history of prohibition. The *Ontario Temperance Act* of 1916 made it illegal to sell liquor in Ontario, but not to import it for personal use. Hatch immediately seized this opportunity to open a mail order liquor business based in Montreal. A persuasive salesman, Hatch was soon bringing Ontario whisky into Montreal then "exporting" it by the case to Ontario residents and, with the arrival of American Prohibition in 1920, by the truckload to bootleggers in the United States. Harry, his brother Herb, and a partner, Larry McGuinness, had established an extensive underground sales network there.

American Prohibition was not an instant bonanza for Canadian distilleries. Sales at Mortimer Davis's Corbyville distillery were lagging badly in 1921 and the interprovincial mail order trade had just been shut down when Davis persuaded Hatch to join as Corby's sales manager. Or did he? The terms of this "arrangement" would later become hotly disputed. At the same time Davis offered Harry and his partners a dollar for every case of Corby's whisky they sold south of the border. Hatch immediately used his American connections to Corby's benefit, tapping into the steady demand created by Prohibition. It was Hatch's efforts that saved Davis's distillery.

The *Volstead Act* of 1920 made the sale of whisky for other than medicinal, sacramental, and baking purposes illegal throughout the United States. In Canada, however, export of whisky out of the country was not illegal, as long as the proper Canadian duties were paid. Canadian authorities were not responsible for what happened to the whisky after it left the country. Corby's was in a perfect location to dispatch whisky by boat across Lake Ontario to small ports such as Oswego in New York State. Hatch, along with partners, quickly established "Hatch's Navy" – a loosely organized but highly effective flotilla of wharf rats and fishermen. Some used their own craft, others used one of Hatch's fleet of forty-two boats, to carry whisky across the lake to a country willing to pay almost any price to quench its thirst.

Sales surged to 50,000 gallons a month and the distillery grew to become one of the world's largest. In 1923, Harry Hatch moved to exercise his option to join Mortimer Davis as a partner in his now thriving whisky business. Davis, however, could not remember having made such an offer when he first hired Hatch. The two, who came from very different strata of society, had never really been friends, and they parted on bad terms. Hatch left Corby's later that year and set his eyes on another distilling opportunity: Gooderham and Worts's then-silent distillery in Toronto. This put a serious dent in Davis's sales. If Prohibition had closed Gooderham and Worts, Hatch was about to revive it.

Mortimer Davis had become Sir Mortimer in 1916 when King George V knighted him. In light of his elevated status, doing business with bootleggers was somewhat beneath his dignity. Though his office in Montreal accepted their telephone orders and, of course, their cash, Davis had never deigned to deal directly with smugglers, delegating that task to Harry Hatch. When much of Hatch's Navy followed Hatch to Gooderham and Worts, Davis had to seek out other means to move his whisky. Demand was great, though, and even with the serious blow of losing Hatch, Corby's sales actually doubled between 1923 and 1926. Soon trains carried Corby's whisky west to Vancouver and east to Halifax for forwarding, with much of it transiting the French islands of Saint-Pierre et Miquelon in the Gulf of St. Lawrence. From there it was dispatched by ocean-going ships to the eastern seaboard – America's "Rum Row," stretching south from Boston to New York. *Ahh,* the pillars of today's American society who rose from scoundrels by bootlegging Corby's whisky on the eastern seaboard! But Sir Mortimer was clean. Despite enormous whisky profits, his real wealth came from another product with huge sales returns and tax revenues for governments: tobacco. He was the president of Imperial Tobacco Company of Canada.

In 1932 Consolidated Distilleries Limited moved production of Wiser's whiskies from Prescott to the Corbyville plant. That same year, Hatch purchased a controlling interest in Corby's from its parent company, Canadian Industrial Alcohol. If the late Mortimer Davis had not remembered his promise to bring Hatch into the Corby fold then Hatch would simply buy out his successors, setting Corby's, Wiser's, Gooderham and Worts, and Walker's on the long but ineluctable path to a single, shared, multipurpose distillery.

Corby products

National styles were neither well established nor government protected at that time. By 1935, along with 2 million gallons of Canadian whisky, 7 million gallons of Canadian-made bourbon and rye sat maturing in Corby's rack warehouses, waiting to be bottled, clearly labelled indicating that they had been made under Canadian Government supervision, and sold as William Penn American Rye Whiskey, Twenty Grand Bourbon, Twenty Grand Straight Rye Whiskey, Old Crow Bourbon Whiskey, Stewart Old American Rye, and Wiser's Old Rye Whisky, as well as Corby's own brands. Throughout the 1930s, Consolidated Distillers Limited was the registered owner of these brands. And, with similar disregard for national origins, by 1941 production of Corby's Special Reserve Canadian Whisky had shifted to Hiram Walker's new American distillery in Peoria, Illinois. The American plant did not always follow the original Canadian recipe though, and substituted raw alcohol for aged Canadian base whiskies.

The Second World War forced operations at Corbyville to switch once again to industrial alcohol. Once the hostilities were over, the 400 staff at the eighty-building, 9.3-hectare complex returned to producing beverages – whisky and gin – from grain. They also continued the production of industrial alcohol distilled from molasses in a newly installed column still with 4 million gallons annual capacity. In the 1970s the future looked bright indeed. Corby's, in partnership with Dutch distillers DeKuyper, purchased the Meagher's distillery near Montreal. In this move, the Corbyville distillery

In customers' eyes, bonded warehouses guaranteed the quality of Corby whiskies.

was expanded, the plant modernized, and a new up-to-date distribution centre was added.

1980s consolidations

Alas, the boom was temporary and in 1987 distilling ceased at the Corbyville distillery. The company moved its maturing processes and new production to Walker's. A glimmer of hope appeared when Corby's bought the McGuinness distillery in 1988 and moved the bottling and blending operations to Corbyville, installing a modernized bottling line in March 1989. That did not last long, and in May 1991 the company announced all operations would cease within five months. An abandoned sign left on the derelict site gives the story: at its peak, operations at the plant included the distillery, dry house, barrel handling, blending and filtration, bottling, finished goods warehousing, yards, garage, mechanical, a boiler room, and office. The complex also included a blacksmith shop for the draught horses, a cooperage, and barns to house cattle fattened on the spent grains.

Twenty-five years ago, people driving between Toronto and Ottawa would pass a sign for Corbyville and a large, tin-hat water tower painted with the words "Corby's London Dry Gin" that stood just north of Highway 401 near Belleville. Just off the highway, on River Road, the last two warehouses of the abandoned distillery today sit vacant, awaiting redevelopment. Signs on the front claim these are Government of Canada bonded warehouses, and a peek in through a vandalized window reveals the wooden bases of four mash tubs. The rest is a shambles. Across the road, the old brick buildings have been demolished and the new metal-sided warehouses and distribution centre built when

Hiram Walker's took over management of Corby's in the 1970s have been sold. All that is left today of Henry Corby's once-thriving distillery are a brick-built stable, a few ramshackle shells of warehouses, a banquet hall decorated with assorted Corby paraphernalia, and the hope of some form of redevelopment.

Corby's brands are now owned by the French multinational Pernod Ricard, and administered from corporate offices in Toronto. Wiser's original distillery has disappeared without a trace as has McGuinness's. And now the last few bits of Corby's are on the market for development. The laboratory, built during modernization, is one room of the River Inn banquet hall. Only the regal stone house, home of the company president, maintains its original purpose as a residence. Corby's whiskies, as well as Wiser's and McGuinness's, all of which once flowed from the stills in the Corbyville distillery, are now made in Walkerville at the Hiram Walker and Sons distillery. That illustrious distillery is now operated by the successors to Corby, a firm that maintains the name of its founder, as Corby Distilleries Limited. As departing Corbyville distillery worker Bill Nicol opined presciently in 1991:

Now we're here: now we're gone,
But, Corby's Spirit will live on.

Chapter 14

Hespeler and Randall, Joseph E. Seagram, and Mr. Sam

eemingly destined for a new life across the Atlantic, Octavius Augustus Seagram of Bratton, in Wiltshire, England, was no ordinary settler. When he arrived in Galt, Upper Canada, he was greeted by a family friend, Dean Boomer, who was an Anglican clergyman. The year was 1837 – a turning point in the life of Canada. The eighth son of a wealthy landowner, Seagram received an ample endowment from his father before leaving Bratton. Seagram's destination was a mostly English settlement in what was then a largely German-speaking area of Upper Canada about 100 kilometres west of Toronto. The official record is incomplete, but it is likely that Seagram's wife, Amelia Stiles, accompanied him.

Seagram arrived in Galt with visions of owning his own estates and so, on the advice of Dean Boomer, he bought a farm in Fisher Mills, north of Galt. There, on April 15, 1841, his first son, Joseph Emm Seagram, was born, followed a few years later by Edward Frowde Seagram. The Seagram boys attended Dr. Tassie's Galt Grammar School, where they joined other privileged boys from across Canada and the United States. It was a very good education. Sadly, tragedy soon befell the family. When Joseph was just seven, his father, Octavius, died. Then, when he was eleven, Amelia, his mother, died, leaving the two brothers orphaned and in the care of the Anglican Church. Joseph applied himself to his studies, and when he graduated from Dr. Tassie's School at the age of eighteen he travelled to Buffalo, New York, to study commercial law at a business college.

After a year of studies Seagram returned to Galt as a bookkeeper. Seagram was an excellent worker, but he was dismissed over a disagreement with a more senior employee whom he threw out of the building. Before long, Seagram was keeping the books at Cowan's mill in Galt. Cowan was impressed and in short order he had Seagram running the business.

Granite Mills

While Joseph Seagram was still busy with his studies at Dr. Tassie's school in Galt, in nearby Berlin (now Kitchener), William Hespeler, an Alsatian-German merchant, and George Randall, an American-born contractor for the Grand Trunk Railway, formed a business partnership. They built a steam-powered flour mill and distillery in the 500-person-strong German settlement of Waterloo, right next door to Galt. Although they called their business Granite Mills, at first they earned most of their income selling dry goods and liquor from a shop within the mill.

Joseph Emm Seagram.

By 1861 their four sets of millstones produced 12,000 barrels of flour and enough grist to make 2,700 barrels of whisky for a total value of $100,000. "Can't make whisky fast enough," a census taker commented that year. With $6,000 invested in the mill and $10,000 in the distillery, it was clear that distilling was no sideline. Fifteen workers could distill 50,000 gallons of proof spirits annually. Unlike other Upper Canadian distillers who mashed wheat, Hespeler and Randall catered to the largely German population and used rye. They called their product *Alte Kornschnapps* (Old Rye) rather than whisky.

Business was brisk and by 1863 Hespeler and Randall invited Randall's brother-in-law, William Roos, to join their expanded firm, forming Hespeler, Randall and Roos. Hespeler likely had other intentions in taking on Roos, as in 1864 he left Waterloo for an extended visit to Europe. Before leaving, he hired the young Joseph E. Seagram to look after his interests. This would become a life-changing opportunity for Seagram. As part of his remuneration, Seagram was to live in Hespeler's house during his absence. It was a fateful perquisite, for there he met Hespeler's niece, Stephanie Erbs. In 1869 Stephanie and Joseph were married, making him Hespeler's nephew. His impending nuptials had given Seagram the inside track when, earlier that year, Hespeler decided to sell his shares of the business. Thus Joseph E. Seagram became a partner in the new firm of George Randall and Company.

By 1875 Randall's whisky was being shipped to Great Britain as well as to New York, Cleveland, Detroit, Toledo, and Chicago, and by the turn of the century the United States would become the distillery's primary market. In

DISTILLERS SINCE 1857

WATERLOO, ONTARIO, CANADA

Seagram's Waterloo Distillery.

1878 Seagram and Roos bought out George Randall's interests. Seagram made another critical move five years later when he bought out Roos and registered the firm under his own name: Joseph E. Seagram Flour Mill and Distillery. In eighteen years he had become the sole proprietor.

Seagram operated under the name Waterloo Distillery, reflecting his focus on distilling. His staff had grown to almost forty men, and his mill to a production capacity of a hundred barrels of flour a day. The mill serviced the distillery's 1-million-gallon annual output of whisky. Seagram sold distillery waste to local farmers for cattle feed, and himself kept large numbers of hogs and cattle in sheds adjacent to the distillery. His market had long since ceased to be just local, so he renamed *Alte Kornschnapps*: Seagram's Old Rye. He also started distilling a white wheat whisky for sale in Quebec. In 1887, to commemorate having bought the distillery outright, Seagram introduced

the first whisky distilled and matured under his sole ownership. He called it Seagram's 83. The whisky had spent four
years maturing in thirty-seven-gallon sherry casks he had
imported from Spain. He continued to use sherry casks
until supplies dried up with the start of the First World War
in 1914. Seagram's 83 continues to this day, although it is
now called Canadian 83 and is distilled by Diageo in
Valleyfield, Quebec, and Gimli, Manitoba.

Other ways to serve the public

There's a recurring pattern in the lives of most of the
major Canadian distillers: parallel to their business
careers and their expensive personal hobbies they were
blessed with a vocation to political life. Like J.P. Wiser

Crown Royal Cask 16
40% alc/vol

Peaches, grapes, and Porto engage rye spices, lumber,
singeing pepper, peach pits, and bitter lemon. Hot
figs, candied citrus rinds, and flaming brandy with
pleasantly pulling tannins and floral vanilla. GI

Crown Royal XR
40% alc/vol

Elegant, creamy, and understated with rye spices,
cooked fruit, vanilla, toffee, brisk citrus zest, and pepper.
Hugely complex and skillfully structured with the
gravitas of maturity and the refinement of nobility. GI

and Henry Corby, Seagram ran as a member of Parliament. From 1896 to 1908, he sat as a Conservative MP, eventually finding his role in Her Majesty's Loyal Opposition to be less influential than he'd originally hoped.

Also like Wiser, in addition to distilling, Seagram developed a passion for horses. When he arrived at Hespeler's mill in 1864, Seagram negotiated care and keep for a horse as part of his terms of employment. Within ten years he was racing thoroughbreds and by the time of his death had built a very successful racing stable using the best British bloodlines. His son Edward continued the tradition, taking the Seagram stable to the greatest heights in the annals of Canadian horse racing: a string of wins at the Queen's (later King's) Plate that began with a first victory in 1891. By 1935 Seagram's stables had garnered twenty wins and the distillery soon began using his black and gold racing colours on the ribbons that for decades decorated bottles of Seagram's V.O.

Seagram's success came at the expense of his health. When he reached seventy it was time to secure the future of the business. In 1911, he invited his sons Edward and Thomas to join him, and renamed the business Joseph E. Seagram and Sons Limited. In 1914, Thomas Seagram asked distiller William Hortop for a good barrel of whisky to celebrate his upcoming marriage. Hortop responded with a special blend that so impressed the Seagrams that they felt they had to bring it to market. When it was first introduced to the world in March 1917, Seagram's V.O. – the meaning of the initials has been lost in time – was a ten-year-old blend rich in rye spirit. It went on to become Seagram's biggest seller.

Although he drew little attention to it, Seagram gave significantly to local churches and schools, and provided six hectares of land where the Kitchener-Waterloo Hospital was built. His grandson, J. E. F. Seagram, later donated Joseph's sixty-five-room house to the town to be used as an orphanage.

The Bronfman era begins

Following Joseph's death in 1919, at age seventy-nine, Edward F., Norman, and Thomas W. continued to operate the family firm, but found it tough going. In 1916, prohibition, in the guise of wartime restrictions, was instituted in Ontario and seriously cut into their business. Four years later when Prohibition was declared in the U.S., the firm suffered badly. The Seagram brothers branched out into furniture making and also bought a cooperage, which under their guidance soon became the largest in Canada. Still, times were tough, and in 1927 the Seagram sons decided to take the Waterloo Distillery public. A year later, they agreed to merge the firm with Samuel Bronfman's Distillers Corporation Limited, of Montreal.

Although under the merger the Seagrams nominally retained their power and position, it soon became clear that Sam Bronfman was really in charge. Prohibition was an opportunity rather than an impediment to Bronfman, and instead of closing the distillery, as had seemed inevitable, he increased production. One hundred and fifty men made 1 million gallons annually of V.O., Seagram's 83, White Wheat, Canadian Rye, Paul Jones Bourbon, and Old Quaker American Rye for thirsty Americans still coming to terms with the *Volstead Act*. The Seagram distillery was now firmly in Sam Bronfman's hands, and despite Joseph E. Seagram's great success in the early years its best days were still ahead.

The story of the Bronfman family is layered in mythology. Some official versions describe a prosperous tobacco farmer and his family fleeing Russian pogroms to arrive in Saskatchewan in 1889. Two years later, a son, Samuel, was born and the family's fortunes were assured. Sam, they say, was the motivation and the brains behind a series of successful ventures in the hotel business, whisky rectifying, distilling, and blending, and later in building a worldwide distilling empire. Considerable resources have been used to shape a Bronfman family hagiography that casts Samuel Bronfman as a respectable, philanthropic, and visionary businessman. That story begins to break down, though, even before the family arrives in Canada. Naturalization papers filed in 1937 show that the individual destined to become "Mr. Sam" was born on February 27, 1889, in Bessarabia, which was in Russian Rumania at the time and is today part of the Republic of Moldova. In all likelihood the family lived in a small Bessarabian market town called Soroki. The family landed in Canada several months thereafter. It would appear, too, that at least well into his thirties Sam rode the coattails of his older brothers.

The facts: In 1889, Yechiel and Mindel Bronfman, fleeing anti-Semitic pogroms in Bessarabia, arrived in Canada with their four young children in tow. The family made their first Canadian home on the prairies in Wapella, in what is now Saskatchewan. Yechiel Bronfman, who had indeed been a thriving tobacco farmer in Bessarabia, hoped to repeat his success. He quickly learned that the harsh prairie climate was quite unsuitable for tobacco. In 1892 the family moved to Brandon, Manitoba, where Bronfman supported them by selling scrap wood, frozen fish, and later horses. The

Bronfman boys eventually joined their father in breaking and selling horses.

Creating the Bronfman fable

Continuing efforts by Mr. Sam to deny his foreign birth, to minimize his involvement in supplying rum-runners, and to belittle the accomplishments of his brothers suggest someone ashamed of his origins. His constant self-aggrandizement, his need to hobnob with the elite, and his desire for a royal warrant if not a knighthood tell of a man with a desperate need of validation by others. He could be foul-mouthed, cruel, and ruthless, yet he inspired loyalty, respect, and perhaps even love in those who knew him well. Despite many shortcomings, Samuel Bronfman was one of the most brilliant business-men Canada has ever known and perhaps will ever know. Moreover, he was principled, determined, and above all he really knew good whisky and how to make it. Here was a man who created one of the greatest whiskies of all time – Crown Royal Fine De Luxe – then waited twenty-five years to export it to his largest market, the United States. This man turned his back on untold millions while he waited two and a half decades

Sam Bronfman.

until he could produce enough long-aged whisky to maintain the quality should sales increase. And yet, one of the greatest whisky men who ever lived felt the need to create an even better whisky man as his lasting legacy.

Meanwhile, the Bronfman "facts"

When Abe Bronfman was twenty-two and Harry was eighteen, the family bought the Anglo-American Hotel in Emerson, Manitoba. It was a profitable venture and they soon added the Balmoral Hotel in Yorkton, Saskatchewan. Before long Sam arrived in Yorkton to learn the hotel business from Harry. Then, when Sam turned twenty-two, Harry and Yechiel bought the Bell Hotel in Winnipeg for him to run on his own. Meanwhile, as penance for his gambling, Abe was banished to the Mariaggi Hotel in Port Arthur (now Thunder Bay), Ontario. The habit – perhaps it was an addiction – was an encumbrance he never shed, and one that Sam often referred to with contempt. Harry, on the other hand, soon became a very successful Yorkton hotelier and prominent real estate investor.

When wartime prohibition laws were passed in Manitoba in 1916, business at Sam's Bell Hotel in Winnipeg began to dry up. Every Canadian province except Quebec implemented prohibition at one time or another, but with laws that applied only to sales within the province. Provincial governments did not have the power to regulate the manufacture (or transport) of alcohol or its sale outside the province. Abe cleverly moved to Kenora, Ontario, from where he could readily service the Winnipeg whisky market. Not long after, he relocated again, this time to Montreal to set up a mail order business from Quebec, exactly as Harry Hatch did at about the same time from Ontario. Whether these two entrepreneurs knew each other at that time is doubtful. At about the same time Harry Bronfman set up a bonded warehouse in Ottawa. Here he imported Scotch, which he sold by mail order or forwarded to Yorkton for distribution. From his headquarters in Winnipeg, Sam set out on the road, buying and selling whisky. While he covered the country from Ottawa west, Abe did the same to the east.

Working within the law – for the most part

For nearly two years, until the end of the First World War, the manufacture of alcohol, except for medicinal and sacramental purposes, was illegal. Harry built a one-storey building next to the Balmoral Hotel and created the playfully named and deliberately misleading Canada Pure Drug Company. Sam began shipping whisky made in eastern Canada and Scotland to his brother in Yorkton, to the tune of about $50,000 a month. But this was just the beginning.

Next, Harry and Sam bought ten 1,000-gallon wooden vats and a bottling machine Suddenly they were distillers. With one hundred gallons of aged rye whisky, 318 gallons of over-proof alcohol, some flavour, some colour, and enough water to top it up, Harry could produce 800 gallons of whisky daily. An assortment of labels turned a single batch into a variety of brands. Their first efforts were not successful as stray metal in the wooden vat turned the whisky black. Undeterred, Harry blended it away, little by little, in future batches, but he refused to pay for the vats until the supplier took him to court. During the proceedings the court learned that Harry's medicinal whisky business was bringing him a cool $390,000 a month. Harry was finally ordered to pay for his vats.

Harry soon opened warehouses, known as boozoriums, along the Saskatchewan border to supply rum-runners from the northern United States. It was perfectly legal to sell whisky for export. No law was broken until the rum-runner crossed into the U.S. Similarly, Saskatchewan boozoriums on the Alberta and Manitoba borders were exporting to those provinces in a perfectly legal manner. It was profitable and even exciting – but everything changed on October 2, 1922. Masked gunmen robbed Harry's brother-in-law, Paul Matoff, of the night's take, and shot him dead in the process. Harry never really got over Matoff's death. Shortly thereafter the federal government closed all the export warehouses.

In 1923, the Saskatchewan government took control of all liquor sales in the province and the $390,000-a-month Saskatchewan adventure was finally over for the Bronfmans. The Bronfman adventure itself was also almost over for Harry. He had been charged with bribing a federal customs agent. The trial dragged on for over four years before the charges were finally dropped. In the meantime Sam moved to sideline him. Again, in 1930, Harry faced new charges of tampering with a witness, and although he was acquitted he never again had a prominent public role in the family business. No, from that point on it was always "Mr. Sam."

Starting over – again

In the early 1920s, as provincial governments across Canada took over the sale of alcohol, Sam and Harry had a new idea. They would open their own real distillery. In May of 1923 the brothers bought the Greenbrier Distillery of Louisville, Kentucky and had it shipped to LaSalle, near Montreal, to be reassembled. Harry managed the construction and, by virtue of his experience in Yorkton, was made responsible for operations. The brothers, together with younger brother Allan, named their new enterprise Distillers Corporation Limited. The spirit began to flow, but rather than sell it the brothers put it in warehouses to age. It was Mr. Sam who insisted on quality. Even then it was more important for him to be known for quality than to make a quick dollar. This was the policy that would bring him and his family billions of dollars of business.

To keep the cash flow positive the brothers entered into partnership with the world's largest whisky corporation, Distillers Company Limited of Scotland, and they began importing Scotch, gaining exclusive rights to several top brands. Then, in 1928, the merger with Joseph E. Seagram and Sons sealed their future as they formed Distillers Corporation-Seagram's Limited.

Among the greatest assets of the new firm were the Seagram's brands, 83 and V.O. Mr. Sam was acutely aware of the success that Harry Hatch, his rival, was having in the U.S. with Walker's Canadian Club brand and quickly adopted V.O. and 83 as his own. Bronfman worked very hard to promote these whiskies, making them the keystones in a growing empire. Sensing that Prohibition could not last, he correctly predicted a huge market for well-aged whisky. He expanded and upgraded both distilleries in anticipation. When Prohibition finally ended in 1933, quality Seagram's Canadian whisky instantly and legally filled American whisky bottles for the first time in nearly fourteen years. Success only made him more determined than ever to put Prohibition-era instant whisky behind him.

Seagram's LaSalle Distillery.

Although ownership was shared, Sam Bronfman was the president of the company and on the force of his personality Distillers Corporation-Seagram's Limited rapidly became his personal enterprise. Bronfman alone made almost all significant decisions, including buying up distilleries in the States. He started in 1933 with the Rossville Union plant in Lawrenceburg, Indiana. Next, a distillery in Relay, Maryland, where raw alcohol was being bottled as Lord Calvert American blended whisky. Bronfman put a quick stop to that practice, shipping well-aged Canadian whisky to Relay to bolster the blend until supplies of mature U.S.-distilled whisky became available. The acquisitions continued until Seagram's owned thirteen distilleries in the U.S.

Polishing up the image

Bronfman's desire to erase any memory of his Prohibition beginnings was manifest in an almost pathological obsession to establish a new reputation, one based not on himself but on the quality of his products. His first new whisky came out of Lawrenceburg in 1934. It was an American blended whisky called Seagram's 7 Crown. Despite regulations that allowed him to include cheap neutral spirits in the blend, he used a Canadian formula and created the new blend using aged base whisky instead. It was a phenomenal success. To this day there are people who believe 7 Crown is Canadian whisky, but of course it is not.

The best-selling Canadian whisky in the world is Crown Royal. This was Sam Bronfman's legacy, a blend he personally developed to mark the visit to Canada in 1939 of King George VI and Queen Elizabeth. Bronfman was wealthy and well connected by that time and managed to have the whisky placed aboard the trains carrying the royal couple across Canada. It was billed as whisky fit for royalty, but there is no evidence that either of them ever tasted it. Still, it was an instant success with Canadians. The early bottlings included whiskies as much as thirty years old. The rare few that survive demonstrate that it truly was the height of the blender's art.

Late in the 1930s Bronfman acquired the Jordan Wine Company. That was just the beginning of even greater diversification to come. Over the next few years the distillery acquisitions continued, the best-known being Four Roses in Frankfort, Kentucky, in 1943. At about the same time he also purchased the Reifel's British Columbia Distillery Limited, and with that came another pre-Prohibition bourbon distillery that had been dismantled and moved to Canada, this time, to Amherstburg, Ontario. By 1945 the Amherstburg distillery was the home of the Calvert Canadian and V.O. brands. To increase shelf space in liquor stores and competition within the company, Bronfman introduced the Thomas Adams brands under the leadership of his son, Charles. His other son, Edgar, took the lead with the Calvert line. The House of Seagram introduced distinct house styles for both, to differentiate them from all the other Seagram brands. Essentially, Seagram whiskies featured bourbon notes, Adams featured rye, while Calvert was a synthesis of the two.

Seagram's fortunes in the United States called for a landmark building there and in 1952, the company engaged architect Mies van der Rohe to design and build a headquarters suitable for the House of Seagram. When Sam's hardheaded and creative daughter, Phyllis Lambert, saw the original plans, before van der Rohe was hired, her withering dismissal convinced Sam to turn the entire project over to her. The result is a stunningly beautiful thirty-eight-storey, bronze-coloured tower set amid pools and fountains at 375 Park Avenue in New York City. The interior and the decor, also under Lambert's control, made an equally favourable impression on all who entered the building, reflecting the same aura of quality that Sam sought for his whiskies.

Success in the U.S. was overshadowed by tensions back in Canada when, in 1953, Bronfman decided to close the Waterloo distillery and the Amherstburg-based Calvert distillery, and to replace both with a single new plant in Oakville. The atmosphere was charged when Bronfman, the so-called heartless businessman, finally entered the old Seagram plant in Waterloo. He fell in love with it and dropped the plan. Nevertheless, in the late 1960s Seagram's built a new modern distillery in Gimli, Manitoba, a plant intended to produce V.O., while the production of Crown Royal would remain in Waterloo.

Seagram's also expanded internationally, branching into foreign-made vodka, gin, rum, wine, and other products. By 1970 the firm was a publicly held corporation with 20,000 shareholders and 15,210 employees. The company owned a total of thirty-nine distilleries around the world, seven of them in Canada. In addition to Crown Royal, V.O., and a host of Canadian whiskies, their brands included The Glenlivet and Chivas Regal Scotch whiskies, Mumm Champagne, and a number of other household names. Later, in 1987, Seagram's bought the French cognac maker Martell & Cie for $1.2 billion.

Sam Bronfman was a man of many contradictions. Although solicitously loving to his wife and unquestioningly supportive of his children, he cruelly and systematically eliminated his siblings from the business, despite a death-bed promise to his mother to keep the family together. His brothers, sisters, and their families benefited financially from Seagram's success, but there was simply no room for them in "his" business. They were left to pursue business interests elsewhere and they were successful on their own, to be sure, but the family showed the strain. At the same time, Sam was enormously generous, particularly in the Montreal Jewish community, where he used substantial amounts of his own money to support fundraising campaigns for Jewish charities and for the State of Israel. Indeed, he became a leader within the Canadian Jewish community. Self-centred, yes, but never greedy or selfish, Sam Bronfman may have felt the comparative pittance he bequeathed his siblings and their families was generous enough. In the end, he failed to keep his mother's dream of family unity alive, and indeed his own descendants let the business that might have kept them together slip through their fingers.

Sam Bronfman died in 1971 and the leadership of the company passed to his son, Edgar, who proved to be a steady hand, and profits continued to grow. In 1975 Edgar changed the business name to Seagram Company Limited. The company's original Waterloo Distillery was a going concern in the late 1970s, employing some 250 people and with an annual income of $60,000,000. It processed 650,000 bushels of Ontario Essex County corn annually, paid $4 million in wages, spent $6 million on supplies and generated over $800,000 in local business taxes. In 1978 there were 570,493 barrels of whisky ageing in its warehouses. However, the old distillery was in need of repair and the city was encroaching on all sides. Then, in the 1980s, the unthinkable happened. The bottom fell out of the international whisky market and forced Seagram to consolidate its operations in Gimli and to close other plants.

Waterloo was on borrowed time even as the company struggled to keep Mr. Sam's beloved historic plant in operation, at least to some degree. In 1990, however, the decision finally to close the Waterloo plant was announced amid declining sales, high taxes, and limited expansion opportunities. The last barrels rolled off the Waterloo line in November 1992, and not ten months later the abandoned distillery was razed by fire. A community icon was gone. All that remains today is a rackhouse, now used for offices and a few buildings converted to condominiums.

In 1994 Edgar Bronfman passed the chairmanship of the company to his son, Edgar Jr., in a move that was the beginning of another kind of end. Sam Bronfman had a prophetic saying: "Shirt sleeves to shirt sleeves in three generations." Edgar Jr., who had been raised in luxury, had no passion for the spirits business. Rather, he had his eye set on Hollywood. In the 1980s, in a series of moves and countermoves, an attempt by Seagram's to purchase an oil company ended with Seagram's owning significant shares of the Dupont Corporation. When Edgar Jr. took control, Dupont was Seagram's largest profit centre. To finance his decision to purchase Universal Studios, MCA, PolyGram, Deutsche Grammophon, and several theme parks, Edgar Jr. sold Seagram's stake in Dupont for $9 billion. It was a death blow to company profitability, culminating in 2000 with the sale of the once mighty firm to Vivendi. Pernod Ricard quickly took over the beverage division, marking the break with the Bronfman family and Seagram's. But certain brand names remain.

In 2001, Diageo made a move and acquired the Seagram name and portfolio from Pernod Ricard. Now Seagram's whiskies, Crown Royal, V.O., Five Star, and 83, are distilled in Diageo's plants in Gimli, Manitoba and in Valleyfield, Quebec. Mr. Sam's volcanic temper would undoubtedly erupt to learn that his whiskies are now made in the Valleyfield plant once owned by his arch-rival, Lewis Rosenstiel. Although they were briefly partners, Sam hated Rosenstiel with a passion, accusing him, among other things, of stealing his trademark Seagram's "S." Crown Royal is now bottled in Amherstburg, while bulk shipments of the other brands are sent to the United States for bottling. For the Canadian market these whiskies are still bottled in Valleyfield or Amherstburg. Seagram's 83 is now known as Canadian 83 and Seagram's Crown Royal, the jewel in Mr. Sam's crown, is no longer linked to any family name and is simply Crown Royal.

The Bronfmans today may not wear torn work clothes or walk around in their shirt sleeves, as various ventures by family members, many in real estate, have kept them much more than solvent. In the whisky business, though, the Bronfmans have become little more than a fading memory in a once remarkable saga. Oh, Edgar, say it isn't so.

Chapter 15

Hiram Walker & Sons –
Walkerville, Ontario

anada's largest – and what would turn out to be its longest-surviving whisky distillery – was built near Windsor, Ontario by a grocer, tanner, grain merchant, rectifier, and vinegar maker from Detroit, Hiram Walker. Born not far from Boston in Douglas, Massachusetts on the Fourth of July in 1816, an auspicious day for any American, Walker was a sixth-generation American. His family had played prominent roles in their communities since 1661, when Thomas Walker and his wife, Mary, arrived from Norfolk, England, in the Puritan city of Boston. The death from smallpox in 1825 of Hiram Walker's father, Willis Walker, left nine-year-old Hiram in the care of his mother and his eldest brother, Chandler, who was just thirteen at the time. Hiram remained in school in Douglas until he was sixteen. He later credited his success to good friends who sent him to school and who taught him the value of a penny and the importance of work.

When Chandler married in 1836, Hiram made the seventy-kilometre trip east to Boston, a thriving metropolis of 60,000 people. Within days he found employment as a clerk in a dry goods store. He was twenty-two when he caught "Michigandia fever" and joined the throngs arriving in Detroit from the eastern seaboard. He was the first in his family to leave Massachusetts. From Boston, Detroit was a six-day journey, overland to New York then by boat up the Hudson River to Albany, north through the Erie Canal into Lake Ontario, south through the Welland Canal into Lake Erie, and west to Detroit. The Detroit that welcomed Walker in 1838 was a booming western frontier town of 9,000 people. In one of his first acts of civic duty, shortly after his arrival, Walker joined 190 citizens to stand watch

Hiram Walker.

over the city during the Battle of Windsor. American militiamen attacked the 300-person Canadian town of Windsor, just across the river, successfully bringing Canada's Patriot War, the final throes of Canada's uncertain 1837 rebellion against British colonial government, to an end. If Walker had only known how profoundly Windsor would later change his fortunes, and he Windsor's! Walker's prior experience as a grocery clerk led to similar employment shortly after he arrived in Detroit.

On October 5, 1846, a thirty-year-old Hiram Walker married Mary Williams, who was said to be the first non-Aboriginal child born in the nearby Saginaw Valley. Three years later, after several false starts, he began to operate a soon thriving grocery shop of his own. With an astute understanding of his market, Walker immediately stocked some 500 barrels of wheat whisky. In the mid-nineteenth century, groceries almost always included whisky. Indeed, some Detroit grocer's shops might better have been described as saloons. By 1854 Walker was making his own whisky, but not by distilling. He first purchased high wines from a nearby distiller and filtered them through charcoal, in a process known at the time as rectification.

By 1856 growing prohibition sentiments in the U.S. and conflicting legislation had led Walker out of whisky and into the grain business as a broker, where he quickly found considerable success. At the same time, and for the same reason, he decided to buy land just across the Detroit River in East Sandwich Township on the outskirts of Windsor. However, it was more than anti-whisky agitation that caused him to look to Canada. North American governments have had, almost from the beginning, a love/hate relationship with whisky makers. They love the tax revenues from whisky while at the same time must appear to hate the sin that certain Protestant denominations say accompanies its consumption. This has resulted in some puzzling, contradictory, and outright incomprehensible laws. Thus, at the time that Walker was operating his grocery business in Detroit, and until the U.S. *Internal Revenue Act* was passed in 1868, American distillers were not permitted to make whisky as a finished product. They could not sell whisky, and whisky could not be rectified within roughly 180 metres of a distillery. This led numerous grocers, Hiram Walker among them, to buy new distillate from local distillers, cart it 180 metres from where they purchased it, and filter it through tall columns packed with charcoal. Then they would add water to dilute it, flavouring in the form of prune juice, and colour in the form of burnt caramel or wheat, to turn rough distillate into whisky they could sell, legally, to the public. Walker had already had considerable success cutting out the middleman and making his own vinegar to sell in his grocery store. It was natural for him to think about making whisky as well, by distilling spirits himself rather than buying and rectifying someone else's products. In Canada there was enormous untapped potential for buying and milling grain. Moreover, in Canada Walker would be allowed both to distill and to rectify whisky.

Canada beckons

Although he is claimed as one of Canada's best-known distillers, except for a period of about four years, beginning in 1859, Hiram Walker lived all his life in the United States. He commuted daily from his home in Hamtramck, Michigan, to build and operate his steam-powered flour mill, and distillery on 190 hectares of Canadian riverfront land. Walker's success as a grain merchant in Detroit and the huge unserviced grain market in southwestern Ontario helped draw him to Canada, where he invested $40,000 in his new enterprise. Two modest distilleries operating in nearby Windsor at the time offered little competition. There were no other flour mills in the region. As the name of the enterprise, Windsor Flouring Mill and Distillery, suggests, distilling was more than an offshoot of the mill. From the beginning Walker clearly had his eye on the more accommodating Canadian legal climate for whisky. His distillery, which was built as a part of the four-storey wooden mill, commenced operations in June 1858, within months of Walker grinding his first flour. The distillery had substantial capacity with twenty 4,000-gallon fermenters (some were slightly larger). A five-day fermentation period meant that a total output of

16,000 gallons could be ready for distillation each day. Two of the four sets of millstones in the mill ground grist solely for the distillery.

Walker raised the money for this large-scale operation with help from his friends and the Bank of Montreal: an investment of an additional $60,000. In the early days Walker experienced considerable difficulty servicing that debt and the Bank of Montreal continually pressed him for repayment. Thirty years later, Walker's enterprise had grown to the point that the bank found it profitable to open a branch in Walkerville specifically to service the financial needs of his workers. By 1859, John McBride, one of his key employees from Detroit, was travelling the length and breadth of the United States by train, drumming up business for the two components of Walker's business: whisky and flour. Before long he added a third: hogs that Walker fattened on distillery waste. The distillery could barely keep up with the demand generated by McBride.

From the start, Walker used corn, rye, and barley malt in his mashes, and used wheat strictly to make flour. In 1860, corn imported into Canada from the U.S. made up about 80 percent of the mash bill, rye 14 percent, malt 3 percent, and oats 2 percent. For flavouring whisky he used 94 percent rye and 6 percent malt. The fermented mash was distilled in a three-chambered wooden continuous still and then passed through a single-chambered copper doubler and a 7.5-metre water-cooled copper worm condenser. The wooden still stood over 10 metres tall and 2.5 metres in diameter. It took several redistillations in the doubler before the spirit was strong enough to qualify as high wines.

These high wines were slowly leached through tall columns of charcoal, similar to those then being used in Toronto by Gooderham and Worts. After a dash of burnt sugar was added for colour, the whisky was ready for market. Although some other Upper Canadian distillers had already begun to age their whisky in oak barrels, this practice had not yet been formally legislated, and as a result Walker was quickly able to establish a positive cash flow. He had learned the art of rectification well during his days as a grocer in Detroit. It was 1871 before Walker installed a Hoffman, Ahlers–style continuous copper column still in his distillery. Walker's Old Magnolia whisky, a name curiously reminiscent of the popular Monongahela whisky from Pennsylvania, quickly found a steady market locally and in the U.S.

The success of Walker's distillery mushroomed with the huge demand for Canadian whisky created by the American Civil War. Legal sales continued following the war, but smugglers intent on avoiding tariffs bought volumes equal to those of the Prohibition era. Although Prohibition is often credited with creating the American taste for Canadian whisky, when it was imposed in 1920 the smuggling that ensued was merely a reprise of events that had occurred sixty years earlier. The Civil War also provided another opportunity for Walker. As the war dragged on, the value of the American dollar plummeted, slumping as low as forty Canadian cents. Walker scraped together every Canadian penny he could find and bought up as many American dollars as he could. Once the war was over the value raced back up. Combined with returns from his flourishing whisky sales in the U.S., the profits of this speculation made him, for the first time, a truly wealthy man.

Canadian Club 6 Year Old / Premium
40% alc/vol

Sweet, hot, and peppery with prune juice, apricots, black licorice, creamy caramel, and zesty bitter rye. Fizzy ginger ale tingles while traces of almond skins pull. HW

Canadian Club 100 Proof

50% alc/vol

Beefed-up Canadian Club gushing extra pepper, roasted grain, cinnamon hearts, prunes, and canned peaches. Now add vanilla ice cream, crisp kindling, cooked corn cobs, and fresh peonies. HW

Partnerships and expansions

Hiram Walker was the driving force behind the distillery, but he would have preferred not to be alone in managing the business. In 1863, in recognition of outstanding service, Walker made John McBride a partner in the firm. It is quite possible McBride had been involved from the beginning in establishing some elements of the business. Walker was delighted to have a partner but in 1867, after only four years, McBride decided to leave Walker and Company to revive a small and failing distillery called Rolf and Melchers, recently established about a mile east up the river. Walker thought very highly of McBride and gave him a generous settlement of $12,500, but unfortunately McBride and his two partners could not make a go of it and ended up selling their distillery at a loss, to Walker, who soon closed it down. Walker's next attempt at partnership, this one much more successful, involved his own family. In 1871 he invited his son, Edward Chandler Walker, known affectionately as Mr. Ed, to join the firm. Two years later, his middle son, Franklin Hiram Walker, joined the partnership, followed by the third son, James Harrington Walker.

The year 1867 saw the birth of Canada with Confederation. It also saw the arrival of a new tariff structure that made the flour business less profitable but lowered the price of corn. This was a great advantage to the distillery. At about the same time, Walker began a deliberate and successful campaign to move beyond the U.S. and Canadian markets. He established beachheads in England and Ireland, where the quality of his whisky was quickly recognized, generating consistently growing sales. This ultimately led to a reliable market for Walker's whiskies in 155 countries.

In 1873 a worldwide recession drove thousands out of business. Walker's response was an aggressive – some called it reckless – expansion in the face of the most difficult adversity. He expanded his lumber business and shipped the logs and lumber on two ships, one he purchased and the other which he had especially built. It was a tough few years, and Walker's fortunes wavered between ruin (some weeks he was unable to meet his payroll) and halting success. He pressed on, battered and bruised, emerging from the recession stronger, if not wealthier. The success of the distillery now clearly overshadowed the mill, which ceased operations in 1878.

Walker was an American citizen and prominent in the Republican Party, and he was not able to vote in Canada.

That did not stop him from playing an active role in back-room politics with the Conservatives, however. His close personal friendships with some of Canada's Fathers of Confederation, including two Canadian prime ministers, Sir John A. Macdonald and Sir Charles Tupper, gave him considerable influence. In 1878 he enthusiastically endorsed Sir John A.'s protectionist National Policy of tariffs and made considerable donations to Macdonald's campaign. Similar policies in the United States had reduced his trade there, and he reasoned this approach would benefit Canadian manufacturers in the home market. When Sir John A. was swept back into power in the 1878 election, Walker had not yet introduced his Canadian Club whisky, but there is little doubt that the triumphant prime minister and Walker's own member of Parliament, J. C. Patterson, who was minister of railways and canals, celebrated their victory with Walker's whisky.

While Walker supported tariffs as a means to increase trade within Canada, he did not abandon the idea of rebuilding strength in his primary market, the United States. If tariffs meant he could no longer compete there based on price, he would appeal to people's palates and compete based on quality instead. Walker studied the American market carefully, and in 1882 introduced an aged product that was a blend of corn and rye-grain whiskies. It was expensive and slow at first to gain acceptance. But Walker persisted, and gradually his "Club" brand developed a devoted following. At about the same time Walker began a national advertising campaign to improve sales in Canada. Newspaper ads were placed in every major city from Halifax to Victoria.

As his business grew, Walker built a small company town to house and service his workers. The area where Walker built his distillery had been a mix of rough farmland and solid bush when he arrived. Walker's mill, distillery, and cluster of outbuildings attracted great local interest and were immediately dubbed Walker's Town. As there was already a Walkerton in Ontario, when a post office was established in 1869 the town became officially known as Walkerville. Among many other things, the contribution of Walker's distillery and various other enterprises to the town included subsidized rents, free electricity and water, paved roads, streetlights, and fire and police forces. Eventually Walker also underwrote schools and a hospital. There were great benefits to being a Walker employee.

New regulations

In 1883 the Government of Canada introduced the practice of bottling in bond. This was intended simply as a measure to allow distillers to defer paying taxes on whisky until they actually sold it, and not while it was maturing in a bonded warehouse. Distillers, however, quickly saw the advantages this provided from a marketing perspective and began affixing government seals to their bottled whisky, certifying its age. In 1885 the government responded with new measures, which would take effect over the next five years, requiring that all whisky be aged before it could be sold. Until the United States passed a similar law in 1897, Canadian whisky enjoyed an unparalleled official seal of approval.

Major distillers benefited enormously from having the quality of Canadian whisky be government certified. Small distillers who could not afford to wait as long to sell their whisky quickly went out of business. Walker, however, who began ageing some of his whisky as early as 1869 and had instituted ageing as a practice in 1880, did not bat an eye. He launched a major expansion project in 1886, and by 1890 the thriving distillery included five warehouses, enough to hold 5 million gallons of ageing whisky. Several additional expansions since then have brought an initial output of 700 gallons a day to annual production in the neighbourhood of 36 million litres today.

William Robins who?

In the spring of 1888 Walker hired a mysterious figure named William Robins to help him manage the distillery. It appears that Robins had a significant positive influence on the company's financial affairs. In 1890, due to increasing debt load, Robins recommended incorporating the business with Hiram Walker and his three sons as equal partners. Robins was also instrumental in convincing the Bank of Commerce to assume an $800,000 loan that the Bank of Montreal had decided to call in. Details are scarce, and though Robins saved the day, his friendship with Hiram Walker was severely strained at this time, and it was only on the urging of Walker's sons that he remained with the firm. Robins became a very powerful figure, but following disagreements with Edward C. Walker he left in 1912. After Edward's death in 1915, Robins returned, this time to challenge Hiram Walker's will. He did not succeed. The Walkers' disenchantment with Robins almost certainly led to the company minimizing or simply not acknowledging his contributions to the firm from then on.

Walker's success was not limited to making whisky. Among his many Canadian enterprises were lumbering, farming, oil and gas production, a hotel, steamships, and railways. To shorten his own commute, he also built and ran a ferry between Walkerville and Detroit that soon emerged as a successful business in its own right. Not content with the success of his Canadian endeavours, in 1864, when Walker moved back to Detroit, he opened another vinegar factory in a venture that was short-lived. Undeterred, he moved next into the newspaper business.

Canadian Club

Hiram Walker is best known for his distillery and particularly its Canadian Club whisky, initially introduced as a seven-year-old and now a leading six-year-old Canadian whisky. Walker is credited as the first Canadian distiller to blend powerful flavouring whiskies from a pot still with lighter corn whiskies from a continuous still. As Molson's Distillery and Gooderham and Worts, among others, had done before him, Walker had installed both pot stills and wooden continuous stills heated with steam. But whether Walker himself made that innovation remains uncertain. Although he was an experienced rectifier, Walker never distilled whisky while he was in Detroit, and may not have had the skills to do so. In 1863, distillation in Walkerville was the responsibility of William McManus. The original wooden stills are long gone, but early in the twenty-first century Kentucky's Vendome Copper & Brass Works recreated a large copper pot still from the 1930s to the last detail when the original finally wore out.

Walker's Club whisky first came on the market in 1882 and, as the story goes, was made famous in the United States when distillers there attempted to tarnish its name by petitioning their government to force Walker to label his product as Canadian. The whisky was so good, however, the plan backfired and American customers just bought more Canadian whisky, boosting not only Walker's sales, but those of other Canadian distillers as well. This was a true testament to Walker's marketing acumen. Around the world, the lore of whisky is built on an oral tradition that some-times masks a lack of hard evidence. So it is with this one. The word "Canadian" did not appear on a Walker's label until 1888. In 1886, Walker managed to sell just 616 cases of his Club whisky in the U.S. In 1889, this quadrupled to 3,156 cases for "Canadian Club." Impressive, but still a minuscule amount compared with what American distillers were selling, or indeed, with Walker's other brands. In 1890, his "CC" sales grew slightly to 4,817 cases. Compared with American whisky and Walker's other brand, Imperial, Canadian Club was very expensive. Even the most paranoid distiller could not have felt threatened. Moreover, "Canadian" was not used for any of Walker's better-selling brands. It was, however, adopted by some American distillers wishing to polish the image of their own products. Despite consider-able research, no documentary evidence of an actual peti-tion or the resulting regulations has ever been discovered. It was the 1950s before Canadian distillers were required to display the word "Canadian" on their labels but, contrary to the prediction of protectionists, American consumers responded by maintaining Canadian whisky's place as their country's best-selling brown spirit, by far. And among these, Canadian Club is still a coveted favourite.

Without question, Walker was an innovator and fiercely protective of his reputation. He was the first Canadian

Canadian Club Premium
40% alc/vol

Caramel, whiffs of spirit, prunes, spicy pepper, suggestions of lime, ginger ale, and corn cobs. Refreshing rye bitterness complements the zest and tartness of white grapefruit. HW

Canadian Club Reserve 10 Year Old
40% alc/vol

Hard, flinty rye in sizzling pepper. Sweet with dried grain, dark fall fruits, and bright spring flowers bursting from fresh damp soil. Meaty with bitter lemon peel and mint. HW

distiller to sell whisky in bottles, a practice he instituted as early as 1882, to ensure that customers always knew what they were buying. But canny counterfeiters in the U.S. soon learned to take advantage of this practice and began selling copies of the popular Canadian Club, complete with fake Canadian government tax strips. Some counterfeits were better than others, but almost all achieved some success. However, the diminutive but feisty Walker was not prepared to sit back and watch his reputation be damaged by inferior whisky. In 1892, at the urging of William Robins, he mounted a very successful advertising campaign using print ads and posters to identify the counterfeiters by name and daring them to challenge him in court. None ever did. Other distillers were careful not to copy Walker's label, but the perceived superiority of Canadian whisky did inspire them to display "Canadian process" prominently on their labels. Walker was quick to point out that there was no such thing as a Canadian process, and at the time he was correct. Early distilling practices moved freely, north and south, across the border.

Harry Hatch

When Hiram Walker died in January 1899, management of the distillery was passed, in turn, to his three sons, Edward, who died in 1915, then briefly to Franklin, and in 1916 to James. Then, when James died in 1919, Hiram Walker's grandson, Harrington E. Walker, took over. This third generation of Walkers, raised in luxury, lacked the founder's

Harry Hatch bought Hiram Walker's distillery during Prohibition.

passion for the business. Although the firm had had a heavy and lucrative involvement in smuggling during the American Civil War, Harrington Walker was somewhat queasy about resuming the practice during Prohibition.

Making and selling whisky was completely legal in Canada, but in 1926 lingering temperance sentiments among polite society prompted Hiram Walker's grandsons to sell the family business to one Harry C. Hatch, who had no compunction whatsoever about dealing with small-time rumrunners and organized criminals alike. The official story has the

Walker grandsons fearing for their American citizenship if they sold whisky to rum-runners. The fact is, however, that Harrington was born in Walkerville, Canada, and both brothers had long since established themselves there, having built lavish homes in the company town. Harrington Walker had been in protracted negotiations to sell the distillery to Harry Hatch's archrival, Mortimer Davis, who owned the Corby distillery. However, when Davis blinked, Hatch quickly sealed a deal that turned all the company's assets over to a consortium led by him, for the sum of $14 million. It was a sweet deal for Hatch. More than $14 million worth of whisky alone lay maturing in the company's extensive warehouses, and the distillery complex was worth at least that much again. In 1926, however, servicing rum-runners became part of the corporate strategy and by 1929 profits had reached a peak of $4 million. Improved law enforcement on both sides of the border and the devastation of the Great Depression trimmed profits to a mere $255,000 by 1930. The distillery was not to see such staggering profits again until Prohibition was finally repealed. It is said that from 1929 to 1932 the distillery lost more whisky through evaporation than it disposed of through sales.

Unlike Hiram Walker, Hatch was a very private man, but he was passionate about his distillery. The Hatch years were good years as he spent millions on upgrades, modernization, and expansion. Almost the entire distillery, as it exists today, dates back to extensive modernizations undertaken in the 1950s and 1960s. However, Hatch himself did not witness this growth, as he died unexpectedly in 1946 while still in his early sixties, and the firm was led by others until 1964 when his son Clifford assumed leadership.

Unprecedented demand for Canadian whisky led the firm to build a new distillery near Kelowna, British Columbia in 1971. Called the Okanagan Distillery, it was intended to serve the western market for Canadian Club, among other whiskies. Within a year the Okanagan Distillery had entered into a ten-year contract with Suntory of Japan to make malt whisky for their Japanese blending operations. Suntory had been buying Lowland malt whisky from Scotland, but the Scotch Whisky Association disapproved, so Walker's installed two wash stills and two spirit stills, in typical Scottish fashion. The new add-on malt distillery was called Kel-Whisky. The malt whisky was said to be very good, but it was all sold in bulk exclusively to Suntory and none was ever bottled. Not even one bottle. Elaborate stories of this Canadian single malt, dubbed Glen Ogopogo by a company blender, circulated widely and for a couple of decades collectors searched in vain for a bottle. In 1982, when Suntory did not renew the contract, the Kelowna plant was sold to a fuel ethanol company and production of whisky reverted to Walkerville.

The conglomerates

In 1987, the Hatch family also left the whisky business, selling the distillery to the British-based Allied Lyons, which became Allied Domecq in 1994. Decades later, former employees do not have fond memories of the Allied days. "It was sad, we wanted to be Hiram Walker, we wanted to be Canadian, but all of a sudden we were British and all the profits were going to London," a long-retired employee remembers. "They gave us good packages, but it wasn't family anymore."

Even bigger changes were on the horizon. In 2005, French giant Pernod Ricard launched a takeover bid for Allied Domecq. When the dust had settled it was Pernod Ricard that owned the distillery and all the brands that Harry Hatch had brought into the company. Not Canadian Club, though. No, when the deal was finalized the American conglomerate Fortune Brands (now called Beam Inc.) owned that iconic brand. Allied had been very production oriented, but had never really regarded Canadian whisky as a distinct category; to them Canadian Club was just one more brand in a huge global portfolio.

It feels a little strange to visit Hiram Walker's distillery these days. The gorgeous Florentine palace from which he conducted business in his later years retains its magnificence. The offices are tastefully appointed with artifacts accumulated over 150 years of distilling history. At the visitors' centre a guide tells the Hiram Walker story, and recently the long-hidden chapters from American Prohibition have been reopened. Prohibition is far enough in the past to be romanticized, and the current owners of the Canadian Club brand are proudly reviving the stories of their prominent role in fuelling the Roaring Twenties. However, the tour ends without ever setting foot in the distillery proper.

Profits from Canadian Club whisky built the palace, the distillery, and the brick houses in the town that grew up around it. Canadian Club, one of the first Canadian whiskies ever to make a name in the American market, opening doors for others to follow, is still the major product of this distillery. Today, however, Canadian Club buys its whisky on contract from the new owners of the plant. Indeed, they bottle a new batch of "CC" almost every day. But there is a

Canadian Club sign atop Hiram Walker distillery.

certain melancholy in Canadian Club, the brand born and bred in this distillery more than a century ago, having been relegated to tenancy in the form of a granny-flat "heritage centre." As if to emphasize the end of an era, the giant iconic Canadian Club sign that for decades teased residents of Detroit as it shone across the river has come down, a victim of old age and faulty wiring, and has been replaced with a smaller Wiser's sign on an overhead walkway across Riverside Drive.

The strands of ownership can quickly become tangled so let's recap. Corby Distilleries, the successors to Henry Corby, now operate Walker's distillery on behalf of Pernod Ricard, which currently owns the distillery. Corby's major brand is Wiser's, a brand they bought after the death of J.P. Wiser, and now distill in the Walkerville plant. Wiser's whiskies are very highly regarded by Canadian whisky enthusiasts. Walker's distillery, under Corby's, has also begun to make the highly esteemed Gibson's line of whiskies. Canadian Club itself has expanded from a single bottling to nearly a dozen versions. Somehow though, it engenders a sense of nostalgia to drive past the distillery today and see that the lone acknowledgement of the brand that started it all is a simple image on a black and white flag, flying above Hiram Walker's former office.

Chapter 16

J.P. Wiser – The Mingled Souls of Rye and Corn

On October 4, 1825, just north of Utica, New York, in the small town of Trenton, Isaac Wiser and his wife, Mary Egert, had a son. They named him John Philip. Isaac and Mary were descendants of a widely dispersed group of early-eighteenth-century Palatinate German refugees, the Egerts having settled in Pennsylvania, the Wisers in New York State. From adolescence J.P., as he was called, was industrious and ambitious, with a good nose for business. While still a youth he began buying cattle and travelled as far as Albany, some 160 kilometres to the east, selling them to butchers along the way. As long as he lived Wiser never lost his interest in the cattle business.

J. P. Wiser carved in barrel head.

Amos S. and Charles P. Egert were established merchants in Gouverneur, New York, about 150 kilometres north of Trenton. Like J.P.'s mother, Mary, they were members of the extended Egert family of Philadelphia, and so took an interest in young J.P.'s obvious business acumen. J.P. accepted readily when they suggested that he come work for them in their dry goods store in Gouverneur. Shortly thereafter Amos moved fifty kilometres north to the St. Lawrence port town of Ogdensburg to expand the family business. J.P. remained behind. Before long, Charles had young J.P. buying cattle throughout northern New York State. J.P. excelled at this and soon moved to Ogdensburg to become a partner in the firm.

In Ogdensburg the Egerts had entered into partnership with a prominent local businessman named James G. Averell, who operated a distillery there. Averell wanted to expand his business by using the wastes from his distillery to fatten cattle. As the venture involved cattle, J.P. eagerly joined in. Just across the St. Lawrence River from Ogdensburg, in the town of Prescott (Ontario), four distilleries were producing about 200,000 gallons of whisky a year. In those days people and businesses moved freely back and forth across the border and in 1857 Averell expanded his distilling business accordingly. He purchased Charles A. Payne's distillery, the second largest in Prescott. J.P. moved to Prescott to manage it and immediately began a program of upgrades and expansions that continued for more than fifty years.

When J.P. Wiser took it over, Payne's distillery was selling high wines, proof, and common whiskey – 69,680 gallons of it in 1858 and within a year he managed to increase the output to 84,836. Wiser later added rye whisky to the range. Early grain bills show that, compared with distilleries in other parts of the province, Wiser mashed considerable quantities of rye and corn in his eight pine mash tubs. He imported the corn by boat from the United States and the rye by train from other parts of the province. Before long he was growing his own rye, a crop that a local newspaper reported to be two metres tall. Wiser is said to have "branned" his corn; that is, he removed the unfermentable bran before mashing only the corn meal itself. As well, Wiser was known to use hops in his mashes, as brewers still do, almost certainly to prevent contamination by bacteria.

Prescott was already a bustling community of some 2,500 souls when J.P. Wiser arrived in 1857, and its location on the St. Lawrence River made it a major eastern Ontario transportation link. Rail lines from Ottawa, Montreal, and Toronto passed through the busy border town. Some trains boarded a steam ferry in Prescott for the short trip across the St. Lawrence to Ogdensburg and then on to the American northeast. Prescott was also an active river port, serving steamships and schooners. The comings and goings on the river could be seen clearly from the distillery, which was right on the waterfront at the western end of town.

Averell had been a good tutor, and the energetic J.P. learned all aspects of the distilling business quickly. He also had the good sense to hire a skilled distiller along with an assortment of skilled trades who reported to the distillery foreman, George Lane. Despite the fact that the other local distilleries were in decline, J.P. was quick to grasp the economic potential of the distillery and cattle business in Prescott. He waited just five years before moving to buy out Averell and Egert, becoming the sole proprietor of his own thriving business.

Little is known of J.P Wiser's wife, Emily Goddard of Richville, New York. The facts are limited: she gave him six children and she loved to garden. However, it may have been her family connections that allowed J.P. to gain ownership in such a short time and to expand so rapidly afterwards. It is possible that Emily's mother may have underwritten his investment. However he financed it, J.P.'s attention to detail and his well-honed business sense soon left him the only distiller of any size in Prescott, as one by one the others closed their doors. Not only did the distillery expand; shortly after the Wisers arrived in Prescott, their family also began to grow. A son, Harlow Goddard Wiser, arrived in 1859, followed by two sisters and three brothers over the next few years.

The year 1864 started off badly. A fire destroyed most of the distillery. Undaunted, J.P. seized the opportunity to build an even better plant. He increased its size and incorporated up-to-date equipment. His new storehouses could hold up to 10,000 bushels of grain. He also installed a shiny new copper column still. Ninety metres west of the distillery he built barns large enough to house 2,000 head of cattle. Almost immediately this part of the business began generating profits, but not without a certain impact in the community.

The west end of Prescott had been a good neighbourhood before the cattle barns were erected. To minimize complaints from the neighbours, Wiser built his own home on the distillery grounds adjacent to the barns. He was a commanding figure who walked with a gold-tipped cane. He could be gruff and driven but was known for his ability to find the strengths in people. He was regarded as a benevolent patriarch by both his family and his employees. In particular, Wiser had a good eye and great respect for craftsmen and he soon employed many of the area's top artisans. They worked five ten-hour days, then another half day on Saturday and Wiser treated them generously given the standards at the time. Weekly wages for Wiser's employees of $10 to $15 were supplemented with very generous Christmas bonuses. Cash went home with the men; liquid bonuses sometimes did not make it off the premises.

Although he owned the business and it bore his name, much of Wiser's success can be attributed to his company treasurer, Albert Whitney. Cranky and slightly stooped, Whitney was not as good with people as Wiser but he was just as shrewd. Whitney spent fifty years there, equally dedicated to the firm. Until 1906 it was Whitney, not Wiser, who held the licence to distill. Whitney, who was known for his sarcasm, had a solid build and wore a short sandy-coloured beard. He was prominent in local politics, often accused of ensuring that every political decision would benefit the distillery, but voters still re-elected him to represent them session after session. Accusations of conflict of interest came to a head in the election of 1896, in which Whitney and a group of like-minded councilmen were dubbed the "Distillery Ring." They fought back on the hustings, and when the votes were counted Whitney and his ring were returned to office and the matter was settled.

As dedicated as Whitney was to the distillery he was also committed to maintaining his routine. Days were long at the distillery and Whitney practically ignored his family, choosing instead to spend most of his Saturday afternoons and Sundays playing poker at J.P. Wiser's home. And though Whitney was married and had at least one daughter, he also kept a mistress whom he visited weekly, in full view of the town. When his wife died, Whitney did the socially acceptable thing and married his lover, the long-widowed Anna McDonnagh. Whether the poker weekends continued thereafter is not known.

Wiser's Deluxe
40% alc/vol

Dusty rye, creamy vanilla, and baking spices with a peppery, sweet caramel delivery. Dry grass, hints of sawdust, with sweet ripe fruit and sour citrus. Hints of cloves, cinnamon, and ginger. HW

Wiser's Legacy
45% alc/vol

Fresh gingerbread, tingly cinnamon, mild cigarette tobacco, hard candy, and citrus zest. Sweet powerful cinnamon, ginger, peppermint, and cloves with glowing hot pepper, overlie complex tones of stewed prunes, fresh-cut lumber, soft leather, gently perfumed violets, and sour rye bread. HW

Wiser's Red Letter Rye
45% alc./vol

Newly sawn oak, lacquer, roasted grain, butterscotch, vanilla, sweet tingling ginger, and glowing hot pepper. Creamy sweet corn whisky loaded with Christmas spices – cinnamon, cloves, and ginger. Sour rye bread, black fruits, and earthy rye. HW

Burgeoning sales in the U.S., in part attributed to the Civil War, soon made Wiser a principle supplier of whisky and beef cattle to the border states. Whether it was an intended consequence or not, Wiser's fastidious attention

Staff at Wiser's distillery in Prescott, November 1890.

to quality – he called his whisky "the mingled souls of rye and corn" – kept those markets open to him long after the Civil War had ended, despite stiff postwar tariffs introduced by the Americans. Wiser's mantra, "Quality is something you just can't rush. Horses should hurry but whisky must take its time," was shared by his gifted distiller and blender, Comfort Whitney (no relation to Albert). From the start Wiser aged his whisky in new charred oak and recharred barrels, each one made on site by his own coopers. Settlers in surrounding communities who were clearing forests to make fields provided abundant timber for Wiser's cooperage.

A decade after he had purchased the distillery, excise duty on his production was putting $2,000 into the Canadian treasury daily. The distillery provided employment for sixty workers, supporting forty-six families. In ten short years its more than $1 million annual operating costs had made J.P. Wiser's distillery the most important contributor to the prosperity of Prescott, and J.P. himself had become one of the leading city fathers. He became a Canadian citizen, served on town council for eleven years, and in 1878 was elected as a Liberal member of Parliament, despite his paradoxical agreement to support Canadian prohibition, an act that if it were ever passed would have had dire consequences for the town. Wiser was not much of a drinker, but neither was he teetotal. In all likelihood he realized that prohibition was not on the near horizon and felt safe endorsing it.

Nevertheless, politics was more or less a distraction and Wiser preferred the political backrooms, often financing his favoured candidates. During his term in Parliament, however, he did exercise some influence. Debating Conservative Prime Minister Sir John A. Macdonald in the House of Commons, Wiser persuaded Macdonald to alter his party's plans for development in the west. Wiser wanted to know more about the issue and decided to find out for himself. He toured western Canada and reported back to the House on his conclusions. In the following election a grateful Liberal leader, Sir Wilfrid Laurier, spent a few days visiting Wiser in Prescott. When the campaign was over, Laurier replaced Macdonald as prime minister.

In the late 1860s Wiser purchased a twenty-five-hectare farm just west of Prescott. Every day draught horses would make the short trek from the distillery, bringing barrels of spent mash to the farm. Although distillery waste was the primary fodder for 1,000 head of cattle, this was clearly more than a waste disposal plant. The farm soon became one of Canada's foremost centres for cattle and racehorse breeding, and Wiser was prepared to spend extravagantly to obtain and improve the best bloodlines. Wiser named his farm Rysdyk after a particularly outstanding $10,000 stallion he had purchased in Connecticut. On the farm he also established a brickworks that at its peak employed some forty men.

In 1875 a boat loaded with several hundred distillery-fattened cattle left the dock at Wiser's distillery. This was the first time cattle had been shipped from Canada across the Atlantic. It took little time before Wiser had established steady markets in several British ports. A man interested in knowing the details, Wiser himself accompanied a load of cattle across the Atlantic in 1879 so he could learn how best to care for them on their journey and also to better understand the market to which he was sending them. Wiser's beef exports essentially initiated a new Canadian export business in which many others soon joined.

J.P. Wiser's love of the cattle trade also led him to establish a huge ranch, this time in the American South. He called his Texas ranch the Dominion Cattle Company. Early in the 1880s young Harlow Wiser spent three years there managing the over 4,000-hectare ranch and learning the cattle trade. Wiser then expanded his 12,000-head cattle operations in the U.S. to include another over 60,000 hectares in Kansas. He owned some of the land these ranches occupied, but most of it was free-range, or leased. The ranches provided 2,000 cattle a year to be fattened in Prescott and then shipped to markets in Glasgow, London, and Liverpool. Many more found their way to stockyards throughout the United States.

The gregarious and popular Harlow Wiser returned to Canada to work at the distillery in 1887. The promise of a Wiser legacy seemed assured until one day in 1895 Harlow Wiser was stricken by a heart attack. By the next day the thirty-six-year-old was dead. Although J.P. was now a Canadian, and despite Harlow's birth in Canada, the family buried him across the border in Ogdensburg. His brother, Frank, was dispatched to Kansas to manage the ranch, but he returned a year later complaining that the cowboy business did not agree with his constitution. Harlow's brothers Ike and Frank (a third brother, John, died in childhood) did not share his enthusiasm for the business nor his obvious skill.

Improvements to the distillery were constant and in 1885 the expansion continued with the addition of eight copper tanks each holding 11,000 gallons. These tanks weighed two tons each and were fabricated on site from huge sheets of copper and installed in a new brick building. More improvements followed in 1887 when much of the distillery was again damaged in a fire. Determined as ever not to be distracted by these challenges, Wiser worked hard to ensure that within sixty days the new and improved distillery was back in production.

Prior to 1893 Wiser sold his whisky in kegs, barrels, and other bulk containers. Using the venue of the Chicago World's Fair, Wiser exhibited his first bottles of whisky. Although Hiram Walker's Canadian Club whisky was already popular in the U.S., in all likelihood Wiser's was the first whisky from any distillery to be specifically designated "Canadian whisky." In addition to the Canadian and American markets, by the early 1900s Wiser was also exporting whisky around the world, most notably to China and the Philippines. In an age when quality was equated with purity, Wiser's whisky was considered among the purest. In 1977, Edward McNally, a veteran excise officer who worked at Wiser's distillery, remembered Wiser's Red Letter Rye as "a little too dark in colour but smooth and well matured." It took more than one hundred distillery workers to keep up with demand for that dark, flavourful potation.

On April 30, 1911, John Philip Wiser's long and distinguished career making Canadian whisky ended with his death. His funeral service was held in Prescott and then Wiser's cortege boarded a boat and crossed the St. Lawrence River to New York State, where he had been born. There his remains were interred in the family plot in a shady nook on the banks of the gentle Oswegatchie River.

J.P. Wiser built a thriving distillery in Prescott and earned a stellar reputation for making great whisky, but sometimes stories involving families take a surprising turn. Wiser's distillery, for all its innovations and skilled workforce, languished after his death. His sons lacked the skills – or perhaps the interest – to run it, and when Albert Whitney died sixteen years later, in 1927, its once remarkable run was more or less over. Wiser's heirs sold out to Mortimer Davis, who also owned Corby Distilleries. Corby's maintained Wiser's approach and carefully guarded the recipes.

Despite its strong reputation in the United States throughout the Prohibition years, Wiser's distillery struggled under Davis. In 1932, the year before Prohibition ended, the distillery was closed and production of Wiser's whiskies moved to Corbyville, 132 kilometres west of Prescott. When Corby's distillery was consolidated with Hiram Walker's plant in 1991, operations moved yet again, this time to Walkerville. Today in Prescott, not even a trace of Wiser's distillery, nor his equally successful cattle and horse farm, remain. The Wiser family home, later converted to a retirement lodge, is no more. The radiant stained glass windows that renowned

Wiser's Small Batch
43.4% alc/vol

Christmas cake, cereal, cinnamon hearts, candied ginger, and earthy rye with a crisp flintiness, redolent of cloves and vanilla. Burning hot pepper complements rich toffee and a refreshing bitter zest. HW

Wiser's Special Blend
40% alc/vol

Simple, straightforward ginger ale, rye spices, sweet and sour sauce, and caramel in a rich peppery mustard-like heat. A closing citrus pithiness washes clean an almost oily palate. HW

Prescott glass artist Harry Horwood made for J. P. Wiser's home are now installed at Upper Canada Village in Morrisburg, Ontario.

Based on comparisons with mature Wiser's whisky distilled during the 1940s in Corbyville, Corby Distilleries Limited (which owns the Wiser's name and operates the Walkerville distillery) has done an admirable job indeed of maintaining J.P. Wiser's original flavour profiles, at least as they were reproduced in Corbyville. But of course these could very well be the work not of Wiser, but of his employee, a certain Comfort Whitney.

THE NINE DISTILLERS OF
CANADIAN WHISKY

Dozens of distillery names appear on Canadian whisky bottles, but just nine physical plants produce all of the Canadian whisky sold around the world. Legions of marketing companies, independent bottlers, and private blenders (who would like you to think they are distillers) have made it difficult to ascertain an exact number of distilleries from the first time anyone thought to count. Of the 200 distilling licences sold in 1840, for example, many went to home distillers who sold not a drop of whisky. To say there were 200 distilleries is like calling every home with an oven a bakery.

Consolidations in Canada that began in the 1980s saw the twenty-two distilleries that business reporter William Rannie counted in 1976 reduced to just nine today. Three of these nine were built since he made his count. He included eight in Ontario, four in Quebec, four in British Columbia, two in Alberta, two in Manitoba, and one each in Nova Scotia and Saskatchewan. Since then some, such as Weyburn Distillery, have found new life as fuel ethanol plants, but most have been demolished.

Today there are three distilleries making whisky in Alberta, one in Manitoba, three in Ontario, one in Quebec, and one in Nova Scotia. Government regulation has ensured that the burgeoning craft distilling movement in the United States has not crossed the border into Canada. Nevertheless, several intrepid souls have begun to distill grain spirits, and soon the nine will be joined by several others, including Still Waters Distillery in Concord, Ontario; Shelter Point Distillery on Vancouver Island; Pemberton Distillery and Okanagan Spirits (both also in B.C.); and Last Mountain Distillery in Lumsden, Saskatchewan.

Whisky aficionados keen to see where their favourite whiskies are made are routinely disappointed when their enthusiasm leads them to try visiting a Canadian distillery. As a result of the September 11, 2001 attacks on the World Trade Center, American legislation now requires that all foodstuffs that cross into the U.S. by truck must be made in secure facilities. That means no visitors. In Canada, whisky buffs are restricted to visiting Kittling Ridge, Shelter Point, and Glenora. The rest are strictly off limits. It's the law, and no amount of pleading will change that. Visits, regrettably, must be made through the eyes of the occasional journalist or author willing to take the time to negotiate the layers of security.

Chapter 17

Alberta Distillers

algary sits amidst vast expanses of prime Canadian grain fields, so it is no surprise that in 1946, when the Alberta government offered subsidies to stimulate the struggling economy, someone thought of making whisky. Calgary businessman Frank McMahon, a wealthy petroleum man even before the 1947 Leduc discovery turned him into an oil baron and transformed Calgary from a backwater to a bustling metropolis, saw an important commercial opportunity in those grain fields. So did Max Bell, a rancher and newspaper publisher, and together they developed the idea of establishing a distillery in Alberta. Although McMahon and Bell certainly knew how to make money, they had none of the skills required for making whisky. Thus they began the search for a qualified distiller to build the plant and run the operation – and to make a quality product. Who better to turn to than the Reifels, the B.C.–based distilling family, then in its third generation of whisky makers? And so it was that with the Reifels' skill, whisky knowledge, and passion, the seed of a simple business idea grew into Alberta Distillers, almost certainly the greatest rye distillery in the world.

But who were these Reifels? George C. and Henry F. (Harry) Reifel, the Nanaimo-born sons of German-Alsatian brewmaster Heinrich Reiffel (yes, two *f*s), had been prosperous

Alberta Premium 30-year-old 100% rye-grain whisky.

brewers, distillers, and liquor dealers in British Columbia until the Canadian government introduced prohibition in September 1916, casting a shadow of uncertainty over their business. However, by 1920 Canadians had given sober second thought to prohibition, and only four years after they had been turned off the taps were flowing again in British Columbia. But nothing is simple in public policy. Just as B.C. voters decided to end their dismal experiment with prohibition, the American government introduced it, creating an unintentional and huge business opportunity for Canadian distillers willing to turn a blind eye (or possibly not) to where their whisky might end up.

With distilling legal again in Canada, George C. and Harry Reifel again fired up the stills at their British Columbia Distillery Company in Vancouver. Over the next decade and a half they amassed considerable fortunes supplying West Coast rum-runners in the service of "American drought relief." Details are sketchy at best: the west coast Rum-Runner's Credo, "Don't never tell nothin' to nobody, nohow," was rarely broken. But Fraser Miles, a hand on Harry Reifel's boat, the *Ryou II*, wrote about his experiences in his book, *Slow Boat on Rum Row*. He describes how he delivered tens of thousands of cases of Vancouver-made Coon Hollow Bourbon Whiskey and Kentucky Colonel Rye Whiskey to buyers in American west coast communities from Puget Sound to Baja California. This area was affectionately dubbed "Rum Row," like its equivalent on the eastern seaboard.

Following repeal of Prohibition, the Reifels sold their distillery to Sam Bronfman's Distillers Corporation Limited and invested generously in corporate Vancouver. Whisky, however, was in their blood, and although officially they had long since retired from distilling, when McMahon and Bell came calling in 1946 they quickly jumped back in, helping George's son, George Henry, to establish Alberta Distillers on a sixteen-hectare plot of vacant land in what was then the outskirts of Calgary. At the time, Calgary was home to barely 100,000 people, less than one-tenth of its population today. Calgary, incidentally, was also home to George Henry's wife, Norma.

In 1963, an American firm, National Distillers, launched its first Canadian whisky brand, Windsor Supreme, relying on Alberta Distillers for its supply. Windsor was so successful that just a year later National Distillers bought Alberta Distillers to ensure it would always have a reliable source. In the process, this acquisition put a third generation of Reifels into retirement. Windsor Supreme, now called Windsor Canadian, is still one of the most popular whiskies in the United States. In 1987 Fortune Brands (Beam Inc.), the current owners, bought the distillery and all of its brands and chose to keep the name Alberta Distillers. Now, in addition to what they bottle in Canada, Alberta Distillers ships carloads of finished whisky, including the Windsor Canadian brand, to the Jim Beam distillery in Kentucky, where it is bottled for the American market.

Alberta Premium 30 Year Old
40% alc/vol

Ever-evolving layers of oak, darkest fruit, cereal, bitter chocolate, vanilla, and blistering peppery spice. Sweet violets counter musty rye, and pitchy timber becomes balsam as prairie dust meets cold wet slate. AD

Alberta Springs 10 Year Old
40% alc/vol

Broad hints of clean oak, toffee, vanilla, aromatic spices, and dusty rye resolve in citrus pith. Creamy with a slight oiliness. Rich, hot white pepper, cloves, and ginger. AD

Think local, buy local

The Calgary distillery, the oldest in western Canada, has not changed much in appearance since the early days; in spots there are still polished hardwood floors, proud reminders of its beginnings. However, continual process improvements have kept the distillery at the leading edge of rye distilling. With so much rye grown locally that makes sense. In fact, Alberta Distillers is the only Canadian distillery to make both base and flavouring whiskies entirely from rye grain. Alberta Distillers remains the largest purchaser of rye grain in the west, contributing more than $6 million annually to the incomes of local rye farmers. Although most of the whisky distilled by Alberta Distillers is made from 100 percent unmalted rye, from time to time the distillery also mashes corn, wheat, unmalted barley, and triticale for certain blends. Except for some of the corn, all of this grain is grown in western Canada. Alberta is not corn country so the distillery must arrange to bring in what it can't buy locally from the American Midwest. This variety of grains contributes to a range of different whiskies, each with its distinct characteristics. Alberta Premium is always 100 percent rye, but Alberta Springs, which is the distiller's favourite, may differ among batches, as does Tangle Ridge.

Alberta Distillers is also the last remaining distillery in Canada to grow its own enzymes. According distillery manager Rob Tuer, a microbiologist by training, commercial enzymes are made for corn: "Sure they'll work on rye, but our own enzyme also attacks the cell wall components which deals with the viscosity problems. Our enzymes make sure the starch is available and doesn't gum up the works."

Alberta Distillers specifics

Distilling whisky is a generic process, yet each distillery approaches it a little bit differently, one reason each distillery's whisky is unique. So just how does Alberta Distillers convert "small prairie grains" into big Canadian rye whiskies? Twenty times each working day, grist is loaded into one of three batch cookers and mixed with water and natural enzymes to make a mash. Once cooked, the mash is held in a drop tank until a fermenter is available to receive it. Alberta Distillers uses a continuous batch process, meaning that each of its eighteen fermenters is in constant use, being filled, fermenting, being emptied, or being cleaned. Three or four cooker batches are needed to fill a fermenter, so each day twenty batches are cooked to keep all eighteen

Straddle carrier moving filled barrels to maturation house.

fermenters going continuously on a three-day fermentation cycle. Yeast is added as soon as there is enough mash in the fermenters to cover the agitator. Then, once the mash has fermented, it is pumped into a beer well – a reservoir – where it is held until it goes to the beer still. Maintaining a reserve of fermented beer allows the distillery to run its only beer still 24/7 without having to stop and restart between batches or if there's a glitch somewhere in the process.

Alberta Distillers uses three different distillation processes to make spirit for its flavouring whiskies. The high wines may be put directly into barrels as soon as they come out of the beer still, or they may be redistilled, or "doubled," in a stainless steel pot still called a batch kettle. This is called doubling because approximately half of the water is removed without losing any congeners or spirit. A third approach uses the batch kettle like a traditional pot still. Copper demisters in the beer still and in all the columns ensure sulphury off-notes are never found in the new spirit.

Flavouring spirit is filled into new wood and ex-bourbon barrels for ageing. These barrels are later reused to mature base whisky. This is because flavouring whiskies behave differently in the barrel than base whiskies do. While the subtle base spirit draws character out of the wood, the robust rye flavourings are already bursting with raw character just waiting to be finessed by the oak. Although they are often sold in bulk when still young, Alberta's rye flavourings really come into their own at about six years of age. Perhaps that's why for its younger whiskies Alberta Distillers often uses rye flavouring that is a bit older than the other whiskies in the blend.

The whisky matures in both pallet and rack warehouses, up to nine barrels high. Maturates from different warehouse locations are themselves noticeably different. At any one time more than 450,000 barrels of whisky are maturing in ten warehouses on site. Given Calgary's dry climate, the raw spirit that is diluted down to about 78 percent alc/vol before being put into barrels loses water as it ages, coming out of the barrel at about 81 percent alc/vol.

Tasting the nascent whisky

Alberta Distillers makes a base spirit – called Canadian Whisky Spirit, or CWS – that smells sweet and almost oily when it comes off the still. Kathy Pitchko, recently retired spirits quality assurance manager, calls this "a pretty neutral product, probably the most neutral in the west." She admits, though, that it retains a rye character and is generally smoother and rounder than neutral spirits or vodka. Sipping it from a glass reveals hints of dry grain along with promises of peppery rye spices. Maturation quickly brings changes and after three years in the barrel the so-called

The filling hall.

neutral base whisky has begun to pick up whisky-like woody notes, which enhance a range of native rye spices on the nose. The palate is soft and dried-grain flavours from the newly distilled spirit are more obvious. At this point it's whisky and ready to be shipped out in bulk to some commercial customers. However, those willing to wait just two more years are rewarded with a base that is very much rye whisky, loaded with sweet and peppery spices. And that's before the flavouring whisky is blended in. After ten years in the barrel the base whisky has picked up a range of crisp woody notes – not dry tannic wood but fresh and spicy oak with hints of vanilla and a touch of maple syrup. Though mild, the base now tastes like fully mature rye whisky. "This is the substrate or platform on which we add the rye flavouring whisky for Alberta Springs," says Pitchko.

"For a three- or four-year-old product the age of whisky used in blending is pretty consistent," she continues, "perhaps varying up to three months." Maturation is not an exact science, and as it gets older the whisky in some barrels ages more slowly than that in others. As a result, a bottle of 10 Year Old whisky may include some older whisky that the blender felt needed a couple more years to mature properly. However, the age stated on the label is always the age of the youngest component. After each batch has been blended and adjusted until the quality panel approves it, the final blend is put back into barrels to marry. This smoothes out any differences in colour and flavour.

Think local, sell global

Each year Alberta Distillers produces about 20 million litres of whisky, about 5.75 million litres of which are bottled at the plant in Calgary. It's quite an operation, with two bottling lines that combine state-of-the-art computer processing with low-tech but highly effective human quality control. Machines invert the empty bottles, wash them with compressed air, flip them back over, then fill them with whisky. Machines put on the caps and affix the distinctive labels. Then each one of these bottles is inspected and packed by hand into one of the 640,000 cases they will fill.

With over 200,000 cases sold each year, Alberta Premium is the best-selling all-rye whisky in the world, even though almost all of it is sold in Canada. Despite its success at home, the distillery's name remains largely unknown to consumers elsewhere. While it does export more than 14 million litres of whisky each year, most of this is sold in bulk and packaged by others who prefer to put their own name on it. Much of this bulk whisky ends up in the United States, but as many as fifty-five countries, including South Africa, Malaysia, Japan, Britain, Sweden, and France, also import whisky in bulk from Alberta Distillers for bottling. In recent years, independent bottlers in the United States and around the world have found that Alberta Distillers is also a reliable source of the very best American-style straight rye whisky.

Calgary is no longer the struggling city in one of Canada's struggling provinces that it was when Alberta Distillers was founded. Major discoveries of oil have changed the province forever. The Alberta government that supported the early growth of the distillery back in 1946 became the first legislature in Canada to end its monopoly on the sale of alcohol and the selection of whiskies available when, in 1993, it announced the privatization of the retail liquor business in Alberta. One hundred and twenty Albertans work at the distillery now and, although it may be in foreign hands, the distilling philosophy at Alberta Distillers remains, as Rob Tuer proudly points out: "Homegrown, grassroots, and local."

Lord Calvert Canadian – U.S. version
40% alc/vol

Caramel and sizzling pepper slowly unfold into mild rye, dill pickles, fresh fruit, and limes as autumn fruit stands and fresh spring flowers bathe in crème caramel. AD

Windsor Canadian
40% alc/vol

Classic Canadian rye, rich in smooth caramels and burnt sugar. Simple, yet very active as black pepper engages cloves and cinnamon in a fiery display while a slippery feel emphasizes its mouth-filling richness. AD

Chapter 18

Black Velvet

In 1973, International Distillers and Vintners (IDV) built a distillery in Lethbridge, a southern Alberta town that straddles the banks of the Oldman River, not far from a rattlesnake-infested desert called The Badlands. They named their new plant Palliser. Today that distillery produces about 18.5 million litres of beverage alcohol annually, most of it Canadian whisky. The majority of that whisky is the ever-popular Black Velvet, which explains why the name Palliser, very common in this region of Alberta, has been changed to the brand-specific Black Velvet Distillery. But the history of IDV's distillery began more than a century earlier, long before Alberta became a province of Canada.

In 1857, two brothers, Walter and Alfred Gilbey, then in their mid-twenties, had just returned to Hertfordshire, England, from their service in the Crimean War. Seeking a business opportunity, the brothers began importing wine to England from South Africa. By 1869 their business had grown enough to require new premises in Camden Town. There, in 1872, they built a distillery and began to make gin. Soon they were exporting their gin around the world, introducing it to Canada in 1906. Demand for Gilbey's gin grew to the point that their Canadian sales manager, C. P. Douglas, suggested the Gilbeys consider building a dedicated distillery in Canada. However, before he could

Danfield's Limited Edition
21 Year Old.

convince decision makers back in London, American Prohibition intervened.

Prohibition resulted in a small number of individuals famously amassing huge personal fortunes by selling Canadian whisky to American bootleggers. However, despite the amount of illicit trade, and with notable exceptions, Canada's distilleries struggled throughout this strange time in history. Since the days of the Civil War, the United States had been the largest customer for Canadian distilled spirits. Prohibition decimated that market. Still, Douglas persisted, and in 1931 he managed to convince the owners that they should build a gin distillery in Canada. On September 11, 1933, just months before Prohibition ended, the first drops of Canadian Gilbey spirit flowed from the stills at their Toronto plant.

By 1946, Gilbey distillers Crosbie Hucks and John S. (Jack) Napier were experimenting with making whisky in the Toronto distillery. Their largest impediment was a lack of warehouse space. Gin can be sold almost as soon as it is distilled; whisky must mature in oak. Once extra warehouse space had been secured, Hucks and Napier learned that their whisky tasted much better if they left it in wood longer than the law required. Over the next few years, they developed a number of Canadian whiskies, including one, introduced in 1951, that Napier dubbed "Black Velvet." Bulk sales to the U.S. soon made Black Velvet the leading brand for Gilbey's Canada.

In 1962, a change in ownership structure resulted in a change of name: Gilbey's became International Distillers

Black Velvet Reserve 8 Year Old
40% alc/vol

Hard rye, fresh-cut lumber, and bursts of sizzling pepper are drenched in creamy sweet butterscotch and blackstrap molasses. Black fruits blanket zesty undertones of grapefruit peel. A decadent delight. BV

Danfield's Private Reserve 10 Year Old
40% alc/vol

Hard rye crisps, creamy sweet corn, freshly chopped firewood, barley sugar, and pink grapefruit, with warming pepper and saltwater taffy. A peppery, pithy finish. BV

Danfield's Limited Edition 21 Year Old
40% alc/vol

Fragrant cedar and crispy oak, then peppery spice with masses of sweet and tart fruit. Lilacs, spices, and hard wet slate tinged with pickles become blistering white pepper, cinnamon, ginger, and cloves. BV and Vintners (IDV). A series of mergers, acquisitions, and divestitures followed, the first of which came in 1972 when Grand Metropolitan Hotels acquired IDV.

Moving west

The 1970s were heady days for the Canadian whisky industry. The lighter-style Canadian whiskies that were exported to the U.S. were strong mixing favourites for highballs and cocktails. Along with many other Canadian whisky brands, Black Velvet was riding high, all around the world – so high that the Toronto distillery could not keep up with demand. So, in 1973, IDV decided to build a second distillery, this one about 3,500 kilometres to the west, in Lethbridge, Alberta. Originally the Lethbridge plant was to supply Black Velvet Canadian whisky along with IDV's other hugely successful product, Smirnoff vodka, to the western U.S. market. However, a decline in sales across the global whisky industry in the 1980s led Grand Metropolitan to close its Toronto facility and move all production to Lethbridge. This was a time when many Canadian distilleries were forced to close, but Palliser managed to prosper, giving it the distinction of being the only branch plant to survive as a full-service distillery in the aftermath of the 1980s consolidation of the Canadian distilling industry.

Since 1999 the distillery has been owned by Constellation Brands. Although whisky was quite profitable, the company's primary business interest was wine and in 2009 Constellation sold off most of its value-priced spirits. However, it kept its high-volume, mid-premium brands, including Black Velvet. At the same time it moved

Black Velvet Distillery.

production of the Schenley brands, which it also owned, from the Valleyfield Distillery to Lethbridge. This is how two Schenley brands with strong ties to Quebec, Golden Wedding and OFC, came to be made in Alberta. The name Palliser was officially changed and the Lethbridge plant became known as the Black Velvet Distillery. Constellation designated the Black Velvet brand a division of Schenley's, and moved Schenley's head office from Valleyfield to Lethbridge. Black Velvet Distillery is now the last remaining spirits plant in the worldwide Constellation organization.

While all these corporate transactions were taking place, blenders at Black Velvet were creating new products and introduced two very limited premium whiskies, which they named Danfield's. To differentiate these whiskies, they also established a marketing department within the company, giving it the name Williams and Churchill. Danfield's Limited Edition 21 Year Old remains at the pinnacle of the Black Velvet whisky range.

Whisky forts

When IDV arrived in 1973, Lethbridge already had a long whisky history as the site of the notorious Fort Whoop-Up, a trading post brazenly established in 1869 by American traders from Montana, just 100 kilometres to the south. In finagling buffalo hides from the Blackfoot Indians, these traders' primary currency was called "whisky," though it was really raw alcohol shipped in five-gallon cans and mixed on site in various recipes to give it colour and flavour. It was this unconscionable trade that gave Fort Whoop-Up (its official name was Fort Hamilton) and other American trading posts the nickname "whisky forts." The devastating effect on the Aboriginal population, and the ensuing lawlessness, led to Canada's first declaration of prohibition and the formation, in 1873, of the North West Mounted Police (today's Royal Canadian Mounted Police). Those original Mounties established Fort MacLeod a short distance away but Fort Whoop-Up continued as a trading post until it was finally abandoned in 1893. A hundred years after the Mounties arrived to end the whisky trade, the Palliser distillery began producing Black Velvet, one of Canada's most successful whiskies, a libation with absolutely nothing in common with the damning firewater concocted at the original Fort Whoop-Up.

Black Velvet specifics

Black Velvet distillery is small by Canadian standards, but each week it receives eight to ten railcar loads of corn. Why corn when Lethbridge is on the edge of the prairies? Because that is what Gilbey's distilled back in Toronto when the recipes were developed. Toronto is right in the middle of southern Ontario corn-growing country. Not so, Alberta. As

MacNaughton
40% alc/vol

Creamy maple, fudge cookies, then hints of oak. Mild pepper gradually heats up with touches of ginger and nutmeg. Simple with nice weight and balance. BV

Schenley Golden Wedding
40% alc/vol

Sweet, light, syrupy body sustains slight earthiness amidst warming rye spices, medium pepper, citrus zest, and flowers. Vague floral notes and jammy fruit slathered on caramel crisps. Nicely balanced. BV

Schenley OFC
40% alc/vol

Classic hard peppery rye, softened by caramel, vanilla, and bourbon, then slathered in buttery corn. Lazy caramel tones awaken to whispers of sweet pickles and Portuguese piri piri. BV

a result, Black Velvet distillery buys and ships its corn from grain dealers, Canadian when possible, and also from the American Midwest. The approximately 1,500 metric tonnes of rye grain used annually for flavouring is grown locally in Alberta. But something new was added to the mix when production moved from Toronto to Lethbridge: Gilbey's did not use glacier-fed Rocky Mountain water to distill Black Velvet back east.

Grain arrives by Canada grain car.

Operations in Lethbridge are automated, with a distributed control system running the process from the time the grain arrives until the final spirit is produced. This has cut production staff from eight people per shift to two. The plant operates four shifts per 24-hour day, employing sixty people, along with a few part-time workers who help with the bottling lines. Fifteen of these Black Velvet employees have been trained as tasters and are responsible for daily quality review analyses of the plant's various products. The plant may be automated but the quality process requires the human touch. A minimum of twelve tasters sit on any one quality panel.

For base whisky, Black Velvet cooks a mash of straight corn in continuous jet cookers before sending it, in rotation, to one of eleven fermenters, where dry yeast is added. After twenty-four hours the mash reaches about 8 percent alcohol and by the end of fermentation it is at 13 to 14 percent.

Black Velvet distillery makes its base whisky in a modern, three-column continuous still composed of a beer column, an extractive distillation column, and a rectifying column. As it emerges from each of these columns the spirit passes through a copper condenser. Some of the high wines that come out of the beer still are diverted into holding tanks for barrelling to be matured into bourbon-style corn flavouring whisky.

Rye flavouring is mashed and distilled for a three-week period twice a year in May and September. For rye flavouring whisky, 10 percent barley malt is substituted for most of the microbial enzymes. No corn is included in the mash for rye flavouring. Flavouring whiskies are distilled solely in the beer column then matured for two to six years before being added to newly made base spirit, in a process dubbed "blending at birth." This blend of old and new is then put into once-used bourbon barrels from Buffalo Trace distillery at 77 percent alc/vol for at least three years before being bottled. Blenders at Black Velvet believe the flavours integrate better if they spend a long time together in the barrel.

As is common in many Canadian distilleries, barrels are stored on end on pallets for maturation. This means they are dumped and filled through the head rather than through a bung hole in the side. Because the summers are very hot in Lethbridge and winters bitingly cold (in spite of the occasional chinook), the warehouses are heated to keep them just above freezing. The shifts in the seasonal temperatures are beneficial for the whisky maturing within. On average, the angels' share amounts to about 3 percent, annually, with larger losses in new or dry barrels that soak up a lot of spirit. At any one time there are some 340,000 barrels, stacked six-high on pallets, resting in three separate warehouses.

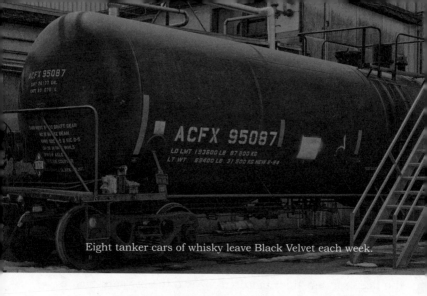
Eight tanker cars of whisky leave Black Velvet each week.

Each year one hundred rail-tanker cars full of Black Velvet are shipped to Carson, California, and Owensboro, Kentucky, for bottling. Transportation is such a large component of the cost of making whisky, and the United States is such a large consumer of Black Velvet, that it makes good economic sense to ship it there in bulk for bottling. Black Velvet destined for Canada and all other non-U.S. markets worldwide is bottled right in Lethbridge. Black Velvet remains a Canadian and an American favourite, just as it was back in 1951 when Crosbie Hucks and Jack Napier created it.

Chapter 19

Canadian Mist

When Harold Ferguson first arrived to work at Canadian Mist distillery in 1969 he remembers seeing wild turkeys scattering across the yard. "Those birds can fly!" the Montreal-born and Toronto-raised distiller exclaims, recalling his startled introduction to the fowl. Four decades later, advancing suburbia has ended these close encounters at the once-rural distillery where turkeys and deer felt safe to wander. It's a subtle reminder that whisky is, in fact, an agricultural product, bound tightly to nature and to the land. During his forty-odd years at Canadian Mist, buying grain from local farmers whom he knew by name, Ferguson maintained that link to nature, at least symbolically. Under his watch, which extended right up until his retirement in 2010, Ferguson rerouted a sewer line to save a tree, and one year, to mark Earth Day, he planted thirty-five more trees, one for each Canadian Mist employee.

Collingwood whisky.

David Dobbin and Don Jacques.

Huron Street crosses the downtown core of Collingwood and then turns onto the divided multilane Pretty River Parkway that leads to the suburban sprawl that has grown up around the distillery. David Dobbin, who now manages the distillery, arrived in a very different setting, but as he comes to know the plant and the town, it is clear to Dobbin that Ferguson has left a permanent fingerprint on Canadian Mist. Dobbin spent the early part of his career in the food manufacturing business, so a move to Canadian Mist seemed like a logical next step. Soon after he arrived at the distillery, Dobbin realized two things: making whisky quickly gets in your blood and learning to do it well is a long, slow process. That's why he relies on Canadian Mist's distiller, Don Jacques, to make many of the technical decisions.

Collingwood is a couple of hours north of Toronto. It's just down the road from Wasaga Beach, a famed summer playground on the clear waters of Lake Huron's Nottawasaga Bay, which is part of Georgian Bay. In the 1960s, Kentucky's Barton Brands had been working with the now-defunct Melchers Distillery in Berthierville, Quebec, to develop a Canadian whisky tailored to American tastes and the company was so successful that management at Barton decided to build a plant of its own to keep up with demand. With its pure Georgian Bay water and easy access to the nearby U.S. market, Collingwood was an easy choice. And it didn't hurt that the government was offering incentives to encourage businesses to locate there. Although it is not a highly labour-intensive industry, distilling whisky does generate a lot of tax revenues.

Once the site had been selected, in 1967, it took only five months to bring the distillery into production. Canadian Mist has consistently been one of the best-selling Canadian whiskies in the U.S. ever since, occasionally claiming the number one spot. The 1970s was an era in which the sales of Canadian whisky enjoyed unprecedented success, and all the major distilleries were expanding, making Canadian Mist a prime target for takeover. And that is exactly what took place before the decade was a year old. In 1971, venerable drinks company Brown-Forman Corporation, also of Kentucky, purchased Canadian Mist from Barton Brands.

Canadian Mist specifics

Established in the 1850s, Collingwood, with its deep harbour, had developed as a shipbuilding town serving the Great Lakes, and later as a port with massive waterfront grain elevators. In the early days of Canadian Mist, corn would arrive by laker from the American Midwest. That was before corn varieties more suitable to Ontario's short growing season had been developed. The shipbuilding is gone now, the lake terminal silent. Ontario-grown corn arrives at the distillery by truck. Though many things have changed, the whisky itself has not. The plant, processes, and ingredients have remained as they were in 1967. Canadian Mist is formulated for just one market, and made in this single distillery. If that sounds like a recipe for vulnerability, perhaps it also explains the weekly tests of the fire system. More recently the Canadian Mist line has been expanded to include several new expressions, Canadian Mist Black Diamond and the aptly named Collingwood.

Canadian Mist is blended right at the distillery from a single base whisky and one rich flavourful rye. The base whisky is creamy, sweet, and mouth coating when it first comes off the still. After a day in stainless steel tanks waiting to be put in the barrel, hints of cereal appear. It's high in alcohol, but only the deadest palate would call this a neutral spirit. After three full years in the barrel the base whisky has gained a white-wine colour, and the raw sweetness of Indian corn has evolved into a unique mix of vanillas, creamy corn syrup, more obvious cereal tones, and an unexpected dash of chocolate.

The base whisky for Canadian Mist begins with 100 percent Ontario dent corn, about 30 percent of it grown locally. The corn is ground and mixed with water, thin stillage, and a small amount of barley malt. This produces a slurry, which is then pressure-cooked in a stainless steel cooker to release the starch. Once it is cooked, the slurry is cooled in a flash cooler, a stainless steel conversion chamber, where unrefined natural enzymes are added to catalyze the conversion of starch to sugars. Using unrefined enzymes during mashing increases the complexity of the final whisky. The resulting mash is pumped into one of twenty 60,589-litre stainless steel fermenters, where commercial distiller's yeast is added. Three to five days later the resulting beer is triple distilled in stainless steel column stills.

As with most Canadian whiskies, the beer is not filtered before the first distillation and solid residues from the grain are drained off with the alcohol-depleted beer from the bottom of the beer still. The second of the three distillations is an extractive distillation in which the spirit from the beer still is diluted with water before being redistilled. Since fusel oil does not mix with water, this second distillation is used to remove it. The final distillation further refines the distillate, removing most of the water and undesirable congeners before the new distillate is pumped into stainless steel holding tanks ready to be put into barrels. With six column stills, that is, two sets of three stills, several batches can be processed in this way at the same time.

Stainless steel is rugged, long lasting, and easy to keep clean. But it lacks a key component of successful whisky stills: copper. When this subject is raised with Ferguson, he scratches his forehead and begins enigmatically, "When hiring, I'd always hire the farm guy; they're innovative problem solvers." And then he starts in about Bill and his duck plucker. "Copper is important," he says. "We use sacrificial copper like the bourbon guys do. Some use copper packing, copper pipe, Kurly Kate. We use copper rods, but first we put them through Bill's duck plucker." Bill, it turns out, is

Harold Ferguson and Tom Hartle coiling sacrificial copper.

an avid duck hunter who works in the distillery. And Bill, it also turns out, is such an avid duck hunter that he made a machine to pluck his ducks and, being also the innovative problem solver Ferguson values so highly, wondered what would happen if he stuck one of those copper rods in his duck plucker. A few minutes later he had turned a long copper rod into a short copper helix with infinitely more surface area. These copper helices are placed in the vapour section of the beer still, where they do their magic, removing sulphur notes and smoothing out the delicate spirit. "The spirit contacts the copper in the vapour phase," says Dobbin. "It's not as effective in the liquid as it is in the vapour." Canadian Mist also uses a copper doubler, copper in the condenser tubes, and copper piping – just to be sure.

Whether he learned the harmony of nature intuitively on his grandfather's Quebec dairy farm, or as a science student at Hamilton's McMaster University, Ferguson insists on treating the whisky-making process as an ecosystem. "It's always in a state of dynamic equilibrium," he says. "Our job as distillers is to make sure the yeast, our fermentation partners, are right out of nutrients at the right time." This state of equilibrium begins right from the start, because, as the retired distiller explains, "If you don't stress the yeast cells they'll do what you want them to." The temperature has to be right for the fermentation to proceed properly, but it also has to be right at every stage of the process, including when the grain is dried. If it's overdried, starches in the grain can be caramelized in the dryers and overdried grain is less fermentable. In the perfect system, all of the starch in the grain would be converted to sugar by the enzymes, and at the end of fermentation the yeast would have consumed all the sugar, leaving behind protein-rich spent grains containing no fermentables. These spent grains could then be dried and sold as feed for livestock.

For flavouring whisky Canadian Mist uses a mixture of unmalted rye, malted barley, and corn. It's all Canadian rye nowadays, much of it grown in Ontario, with a bit brought in from western Canada. When they can buy good rye locally, that is what they do, but in the past when Canadian rye crops were not suitable for whisky making, they brought in rye from as far afield as Scandinavia.

Sourcing barley malt is another story. Some distillers believe that the best malt comes from barley varieties grown in the Red River area in Manitoba, but making sure that Red River malt is received at the distillery is not as straightforward as it might seem. The difficulty has little to do with geography but a great deal to do with trade practices. Most of the malting barley grown in Canada is sold to American maltsters. The barley they use at Canadian Mist is grown for brewing and probably comes from Red River, but because malt is purchased from an American maltster, its origins are not always certain.

Barley is also grown in Ontario but it's not as good for making distillers malt as western barley. Years ago Canadian Mist tried growing some barley in Ontario and having it malted by a malt house in Toronto, but the experiment didn't work very well. The barley varieties used to make the best malt simply can't be grown in the Ontario climate.

Canadian Mist relies on commercially produced enzymes and yeast for its base whisky but not for its flavouring whisky. The Canadian Mist proprietary mash bill is fermented using the distillery's own strain of yeast, which it has specially grown and dried according to strict specifications. Canadian Mist provides the yeast culture to the grower and verifies the DNA fingerprint of each batch to ensure consistency. The distillery follows a five-day cycle, with Thursday's and Friday's mashes distilled on the following Monday and Tuesday. But mash for the flavouring whisky is left to ferment for up to five days to maximize the flavour. Generally speaking, flavouring whisky is fermented longer than base whisky at most Canadian distilleries for exactly this reason. Straight off the still, the new distillate for the flavouring whisky is already rich in malty, mashy notes with hints of butterscotch that will complement caramel and vanilla to be drawn later from the barrel.

The new distillate is reduced to barrel strength with water from Georgian Bay and put into charred white oak barrels to mature. The water in Georgian Bay is so clear that divers

Lake freighters brought grain to Collingwood terminal.

come from around the world to explore the many ship-wrecks. Canadian Mist has a steady supply of barrels from Brown-Forman Cooperage in Louisville, Kentucky. There's no mistaking Brown-Forman barrels: they use a custom rivet with a raised *B* on it to close the hoops. There is also no guessing about the heredity of the barrels used to mature Canadian Mist. Because the maturation process follows the laws of physics and of chemistry, knowing precisely what they are starting with helps the blenders know exactly what to expect. After three years of maturation, flavours of fruit and spices float on aromatic undertones of dried grain. As older barrels are slower to mature whisky, they are used only a limited number times before they are retired.

But if Canadian Mist makes just two distillates, how does it get the panorama of flavours into the final product? To start, between once-used and twice-used barrels there is a lot of difference in flavour. As a result, part of the company's blending secret is in the way it uses a mix of these different barrels. Warehousing too plays an important role. Collingwood winters are so cold that the warehouses need to be heated to keep them above freezing temperatures. But unlike the tall rack warehouses used by some distillers, at

Canadian Mist
40% alc/vol

Sweet mashy cereal with earthy tones, bright oranges, hot pepper, flowers, nuts, citrus pith, and cola. Dry grass and beery sour mash develop into cranberries, cream sherry, and allusions of chocolate milk. CM

Canadian Mist Black Diamond
43% alc/vol

A big, fruity whisky with sizzling pepper, chocolate-covered ginger, and sweet mash in effervescent cola. Concord grapes, rosewater, caramel and orange bitters. Nice weight. CM

Collingwood
40% alc/vol

A hugely expressive fusion of black cherries, rosewater, tingling chilies, and sweet pipe tobacco. Juicy, lip-smacking fruitiness grows steadily hotter and spicier with gently tugging peach-pit tannins. CM

Canadian Mist the warehouses are only six metres high, so there is not much of a temperature gradient and there are no real sweet spots in them. Rather than keep an entire batch in one spot, each season's whisky is distributed among warehouses, in part to guard against disaster, but also to average out any unseen differences. Each warehouse holds up to 38,000 barrels and at any one time there are over 100,000 barrels on hand. Blending whisky that has aged in different warehouses brings all the little variables together, which explains both the consistency and the range of flavours in Canadian Mist.

The biggest market for Canadian Mist continues to be in the United States, which explains the dash of American blending wine that is added to each batch. Once it is blended, the whisky is trucked in bulk to Kentucky in tankers for bottling. In Louisville the only thing added is water to reduce it to bottling strength, then, like all whisky, it's filtered. Filtering removes any little bits of wood, charcoal, or other unwanted particles. Some distilleries chill their whisky and filter it before it is bottled, but not Canadian Mist. Instead, the amber whisky is passed through more gentle carbon-filled pads to ensure that the integrity of the whisky is preserved.

More recently, Canadian Mist distillers collaborated with Brown-Forman blenders Chris Morris and Steve Hughes to create an all-new blend of Canadian Mist whiskies. Called Collingwood, this premium whisky contains a higher proportion of older rye whisky than is used for Canadian Mist. But there is another twist. Once the whisky has been matured and blended, it is held in the marrying vats for almost a year with toasted maplewood barrel

Tanker trucks take mature Canadian Mist to Kentucky for bottling.

staves floating on the surface of the tank. The toasted maple imbues the mature whisky with a rich fruitiness unique in Canadian whisky.

"Very few people can say they've worked for the same company for forty years," observed Ferguson shortly before he retired in the summer of 2010. It sounds like a pretty satisfying forty years though, for the big-city boy who turned his first job out of school as a lab technician into a life as the master distiller of one of Canada's best-known exports. David Dobbin has now firmly seized the reins of management at the Canadian Mist distillery, but he freely admits the trepidation he feels about following in the footsteps of such a master.

Chapter 20

Gimli Distillery

In 1875 when the first wave of Icelandic settlers arrived in what was to become Gimli, on the western shores of Lake Winnipeg, they slept in tents and used broken-up boards from flatboats for flooring. Today's Gimli, population approximately 6,000, gives no hint of their hardship, but gravestones in the small Icelandic pioneer cemetery speak softly but eloquently of epidemic and misfortune. It's still a long way from almost anywhere else: Montreal and Toronto are another time zone away and to the west there's 1,500 kilometres of prairie grain fields before you arrive in Calgary, near the foot of the Rocky Mountains. However, Gimli is a short ninety kilometres of straight (mostly) divided highway north of Winnipeg. The highway passes near Gimli's fishing harbour before reaching the northern edge of town, where row upon row of warehouses foretell arrival at the large block-like Gimli distillery,

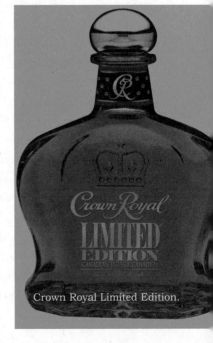

Crown Royal Limited Edition.

now officially known as Diageo Global Supply, Gimli Plant. Among these forty-six warehouses, 1.4 million barrels of whisky sit quietly maturing.

In the late 1960s demand for Crown Royal and V.O. had grown well beyond what Seagram's Waterloo distillery could comfortably supply. Seagram's also owned six other distilleries in Canada, each producing its own brands. However, business was booming and building another one seemed to be the most practical way to meet demand. By 1969 their Gimli plant had come on stream.

Seagram's original intention was that Waterloo would focus on making Crown Royal, while Gimli did the lion's share of distillation for V.O. This is what Seagram's wanted to happen, but consumers thought otherwise. Instead, plummeting sales and the increasing popularity of white spirits created a glut of whisky in the 1980s, leading to the closure of the Waterloo facility with all production moving to Gimli. By 1992, having absorbed production capacity from other Seagram's distilleries, the Gimli plant was itself operating at full capacity.

By the time it was sold to drinks giant Diageo in 2001, the Gimli distillery was responsible for Seagram's entire line of products, making it the last Seagram's plant to survive intact as a distillery. Although it still maintains a human touch, this is one big machine. Since Diageo has assumed ownership, production of V.O. has shifted to Diageo's other Canadian distillery in Valleyfield, Quebec. Although Gimli continues to make flavouring whiskies for V.O., Canadian 83, and Five Star, 90 percent of the spirit distilled there is now used for Crown Royal. None of the Gimli spirit is sold as bulk whisky.

Crown Royal Black
45% alc/vol

Sweet, peppery, and brawny with oak char, vanilla, licorice, and ginger slathered in crème brûlée. Slightly oaky bourbon tones meet rum-like molasses. Finishes with floral perfume and bourbon char. GI

Crown Royal De Luxe
40% alc/vol

Vanilla pods, caramel, nutmeg, and dusty rye with hints of pine needles afloat in mild bourbon. Sweet and peppery with hints of grain that open into garden herbs. GI

Gimli specifics

The giant distillery is not far from the shores of Lake Winnipeg, as large as a small sea and filled with clear, clean water. However, the Gimli distillery also sits above a huge aquifer and draws its water out of a deep well on its own property. This water is rich in magnesium, and with a touch of calcium chloride salt added it is ideal for making whisky.

Corn for base whisky comes from farms in Manitoba, while corn grown in the U.S. corn belt is preferred for the bourbon-style flavouring whisky. As much as possible, rye flavouring whisky is distilled from Manitoba-grown rye. The grain is milled in a hammer mill – spinning plates of metal that smash it into small pieces. Separate mills, each adjusted slightly differently, ensure that the grist is milled to the optimum size for each particular type of grain.

Unusual square fermenters for flavouring whiskies.

Since 1983, Gimli has used high-pressure continuous cooking for one of its two base whiskies. The mash is sent to a jet cooker, where it is heated almost instantly to 125° Celsius, then passed through cooking tubes. Continuous cooking is all about volume and speed, and the whisky makers at Gimli aim for a cooking rate of about 8.5 tonnes of corn per hour. The second base whisky, called batch base, is cooked in batches as the name implies, as are mashes intended for flavouring whisky.

Once the mash has been cooked and cooled, and all the starches converted to sugars in a dedicated conversion tank, it is pumped into one of twenty-eight fermenters. Sixteen of these fermenters, each of which holds the equivalent of three batches of cooked mash, are used for base whisky. As soon as there is enough mash in the fermenter to cover the base the operator opens a bag of dry commercial yeast and throws it in to begin its work. After about sixty hours the mash is fully fermented and the beer is emptied into a common hold-ing tank until it is needed for distillation.

At Gimli, mash for flavouring whisky spends seventy-two to seventy-six hours in one of twelve square stainless steel fermenters. These longer ferments develop fruitier flavours. Because the tanks are open there is always a small amount of "contamination" from bacteria. "It drives the guys in the lab crazy," says distiller Larry van Leeuwen, "but it's tradi-tional to use open containers; the bacteria add something special to the flavour." Two batches of cooked mash will fill a flavouring fermenter. This mash goes into the fermen-ters at 20° Celsius but because there is no agitation the action of the yeast heats it up to 32° Celsius.

In addition to dry yeast used for base whisky, special pure strains of live yeast for flavouring whisky are grown right at the distillery in a bank of nine yeast tubs. Each strain of yeast imparts its own special flavour to the whisky. The yeast is grown in a specially formulated grain mash in yeast tubs that look remarkably like small fermenters.

In all, five spirits are distilled at Gimli. These include continuous base corn whiskies; batch base corn whiskies; a typical, corn-based bourbon, officially known as CBW (corn-based whisky); rye flavouring; and a high-rye batch whisky unique to North America and likely to all the world. This second rye whisky is distilled in Canada's only operat-ing Coffey still, brought in from Seagram's now-defunct LaSalle plant in Quebec. From these five spirits, dozens and dozens of different whiskies are produced, based on how they are aged.

All of these spirits begin with distillation in a beer still to create high wines. These high wines may then be sent to a

Mini-fermenters for growing yeast.

continuous rectifier, a batch rectifier, a column and kettle still, the Coffey still, or straight into barrels. Gimli's continuous base whisky, the core spirit for Crown Royal, is distilled in a four-column still (the first column of which is the beer still). This ensures a relatively pure spirit with a subtle grain-like bouquet and very low levels of fusel oils, aldehydes, and esters. Base whisky goes straight from the rectifiers to holding tanks, from where it will be filled into used oak barrels.

For batch base whisky the high wines are redistilled in a copper kettle and column still. A column and kettle operates something like a Coffey still in that condensed spirit is collected in a receiver then reboiled in a 53,000-litre copper pot, or kettle, from where it enters the bottom of a column that sits directly above it. As in a traditional pot still, the heads (foreshots) and tails (feints) are collected separately and only the centre cut, the spirit distilled in the middle of the run, is used to make whisky. Heads and tails are sent to a continuous rectifier, where any remaining spirit is drawn off for vodka.

Bourbon-style spirit goes directly from the beer still into a holding tank without a second distillation. From there it is filled into brand new charred oak barrels for ageing. In fact, at Gimli all flavouring whisky is matured in new oak, which probably accounts for the distinctive high-vanilla bourbon-like flavour of Crown Royal. Rye-grain whisky is distilled in a two-column continuous still. Fermented rye mash that will be distilled in the Coffey still first passes through the beer still, then loads into the Coffey still from the bottom. Although copper plays a key role in making clean spirit, copper doublers at Gimli are conspicuously absent. Instead, Gimli employs copper demister pads in the top of each still.

At Gimli the new spirits are matured in charred new white oak barrels, first-fill bourbon barrels, and refill barrels, depending on expectations of future blending needs. At any one time about 19,000 barrels sit on site waiting to be filled with spirit. These barrels have made the long journey from Kentucky north to Gimli, where 1,000 of them are filled, six at a time, each working day. New barrels are filled directly, used ones are given a quick rinse with water to ensure all the previous spirit has been removed. Gimli also has a small but special group of barrels sourced from the Cognac region of France, which are used to make a special cognac-finished whisky called Crown Royal Cask 16. It's a blend of mature whiskies that spend a short time in these cognac casks before being shipped off to Amherstburg, Ontario, for bottling. At Gimli, whisky is aged in "bonds" of usually 540 barrels. Bonds are equivalent to batches in that all the spirit in a bond has been produced at the same time and given the same treatment from start to finish.

Once the whisky has matured it is "dumped" in batches, 400 barrels at a time. Whisky is aspirated out of the barrels through a hole in the barrel head, and shipped off in one of Diageo's seventy railcars to blending facilities in Valleyfield or Amherstburg, for blending and bottling. With five different spirits, three types of barrels, and an infinite range of ageing periods, there are many blending permutations indeed. Thus, individual brands of whisky may include upwards of fifty different Gimli-produced whiskies mingled together, each one contributing its own special something. To reduce shipping costs, once they have been blended, some of Diageo's non-Crown Royal brands may be sent on to Relay, Maryland, for bottling. However, all Crown Royal, regardless of the market is bottled in Canada.

Because the whisky is matured in 540-barrel bonds, a quality control team is able to take representative samples each year, beginning when the bond is three years old. Once the bonds have been evaluated, the formula for each whisky brand is adjusted slightly to maintain the same flavour profile. "It can't be close," says blender Joanna Scandella, "it has to be exactly the same." But to all appearances, a modern distillery like Gimli is a factory, so why wouldn't the whisky be the same from year to year? Well, to begin with, grain is like grapes. Each year is a different vintage. "Take 2009, for instance," says former plant manager Kevin Rogers. "2009 was a good year for rye. It's very, very spicy." Gimli may look

Crown Royal Limited Edition
40% alc/vol

Elegance, complexity, and balance begin austerely with cinnamon apple, nutmeg, vague vanilla, and oak. Restrained floral vanilla, crispy oak, and dry grain speak of corn while bitter orange, cloves, and ginger tell of rye. GI

Crown Royal Reserve
40% alc/vol

Expressive synthesis of sweet fruit, bourbon, floral vanilla, glowing pepper, and subtle woodiness. Slightly minty, accenting dates and cherries, while an alluring earthy perfume and bitter lemon underscore the wood. GI

industrial, and a lot of the whisky-making process is automated, but in the end it's not a computer but the blender's nose that calls the shots.

During those early years of hardship, the first settlers in Gimli set up their own form of local government (New Iceland), a school, and a newspaper. With the arrival of the railway in 1906, there would be no looking back. Today many of their descendants still celebrate their Icelandic heritage in an annual festival, the Islendingadagurinn. But they are Canadians, one and all, and 365 days a year they are the makers and the custodians of Canada's best-selling whisky, Crown Royal.

Chapter 21

Glenora Distillery

B y a Scottish burn in a Scottish glen, on a Scottish isle in the Scottish province of New Scotland, in a spot where locals converse in Gaelic and students study that ancient Celtic tongue, there sits a distillery. And though it was designed and built by Scottish distillery architect David Forsyth, and until 2007 distilled from nothing but Scottish barley, this seeming Caledonian treasure does not make Scotch, at least not legally. To look through the windows at its Speyside-made copper pot stills, to take in its highland surrounds, and to taste its Glen Breton single malt, you'd be hard pressed to say why not. No, this is not Scotland, but "New Scotland," otherwise known as Nova Scotia, and this is Glenora Distillery, the oldest single malt distillery in Canada. Much is made of Scotland's contribution to whisky making worldwide, and nowhere is this more explicit than in the tiny town of Glenville, Inverness County, home to the first Canadian distillery where this proves to be true. If Canada has a Little Scotland, Cape Breton is it. And Glenora it is that makes its dram.

Glenora Distillery is tiny. Although it is licensed to produce up to 250,000 litres annually, actual production is closer to 50,000. Still, Glenora is the largest malt whisky producer in Canada and is the only one with mature whisky on the market.

Glen Breton Battle of the Glen.

Bruce Jardine, a retired civil servant, built Glenora in 1989-90, under the tutelage of experts from Scotland's Bowmore Distillery. He was supported in this venture by government economic development funding that was intended to create jobs in an area of high unemployment, It was Bowmore that acquired all of the equipment for Jardine. Bowmore set up the distillery and worked with distillery staff for months, training them how to make malt whisky, just as their forefathers did in Scotland. Not surprisingly, its mature whisky, although unpeated, retains Bowmore's trademark floral notes.

There is plenty of vacant land in Cape Breton and the 265-hectare distillery site right on MacLellan's Brook was chosen carefully. The brook carries soft, crystal clear water from twenty springs that flow out of red Cape Breton Highlands granite and Mabou Highlands marble, right to the distillery. MacLellan's Brook was reputed in the past to feed numerous illegal stills making local hootch called Cape Breton Silver. Ideally situated in the rugged isolation of Cape Breton, the brook bounces rock to rock on its way to the Gulf of Saint Lawrence. A 3,785-kilolitre holding pond in front of the distillery ensures that, regardless of seasonal water levels in the brook, MacLellan water is always available for distillation and, in the event it is ever needed, to put out a fire.

In the past, bootleggers selling right off the still saw an immediate return on their investment. Today, licensed distillers need pretty deep pockets to survive the years waiting

Glenora Distillery.

Glen Breton 10 Year Old Single Barrel Ice Wine Cask #23
62.2% alc/vol

Lively sherry wood, pepper, pickles, and mellifluous dark fruits soar brightly over an earthen pedal bass. Cloves, blue clay, and astringent citrus notes give way to an interplay of bitter herbs and creamy, soothing milk chocolate. GB

Glen Breton 17 Year Old Ice
54.6% alc/vol

Fruity, and perfumed with brown sugar, wet earth, dry leaves, pepper, and roasted grain. Sweet, salty, and slightly soapy aspects weave through blazing pepper and bracing underripe kiwi. GB

for their first whisky to mature. Early cash flow problems forced Glenora to sell some of its newly distilled spirit as soon as it was produced. They called it Kenloch Silver. However, revenues were not enough to keep the doors open. In 1994, after several false starts and the death of Jardine, another local, Lauchie MacLean, purchased Glenora and its stocks of maturing single malt whisky. With no distilling experience himself, and sensing his staff still had much to learn, MacLean again brought in Scottish experts to ensure the processes were as they should be and the spirit was of the highest quality.

Glenora remains a craft operation. Indeed a significant proportion of its revenue comes from some 12,000 tourists who annually visit the distillery, many of them staying on site in the adjoining nine-room, six-chalet, post-and-beam inn with its fine dining room. It's a refined but affordable experience that draws return visitors from Europe and the United States. As one of the goals of Glenora was to support local employment, in the summer, during distilling's quiet season, the five distillery workers shift their focus and tend to the inn, and thus avoid having to "cash their unemployment stamps" (collect Employment Insurance). In all, fifty workers keep the inn and distillery operating, making a significant contribution to the local economy.

Today at Glenora Distillery, unpeated malted barley is trucked in from Alberta and stored in a forty-tonne grain silo. Each day, four days a week, a new batch of whisky begins with barley malt being transferred from the silo into a two-roller grinder using an auger. In the roller mill the malt is cracked into a rough meal consisting of about 7 percent flour and 12 percent husk, with the balance as grist – barley sugar in the making.

Glenora specifics

About two metric tonnes of cracked barley at a time are loaded into a round copper-topped stainless steel tub, or tank called a mash tun. When making malt whisky, the mash tun is the equivalent of a cooker. This is where the soluble sugars are extracted from the mash for fermentation. Because malted barley contains ample enzymes to convert all of the starch to sugar, the malt need not be cooked. Rather, it is simply mixed in a slurry with hot water, which activates the enzymes and dissolves the sugars. This water, now called wort, is pumped into the fermenters, or washbacks as they are called when making malt whisky. To make sure all the sugars are passed on to the washback, the mash tun is filled with water and drained three times for each batch of whisky.

The first water – 7,000 litres at 65° Celsius – dissolves most of the sugar out of the malted barley. A second mash, using 3,500 litres of water at 75°C, dissolves out the remaining sugar. A final 7,000-litre mash at 85°C picks up any residual sugar, before being directed to a brew tank (a heated storage tank), where it is held to be used later as the first water for the next mash. The combined sugar-laden first and second waters, or wort, are cooled to 20°C using a heat exchanger. Then over a period of about eight hours it is fed into one of three Scottish-made British Columbia fir washbacks. Unlike continuous distilling processes where leftover grain from the fermenting process is not separated out until it exits from the beer still, with malt whisky the unfermentable parts of the grain are filtered out in what is called a "lauter tun." The sieve-like bottom of a lauter mash tun allows the wort to be drained off while leaving the grist behind for additional mashing with the subsequent waters. This means that a clear wort is sent to the washbacks. The temperature of the cooled wort gradually creeps back up to 32°C as the yeast does its work converting this wort into beer, or wash as malt whisky distillers call it. Glenora's wort spends sixty hours fermenting in the washbacks to produce a wash with about 8 percent alcohol ready for distillation.

When the distillery was being built two 5,600-litre copper pot spirit stills from Forsyth and Sons, of Rothes, Scotland were installed, and this is where all the distillation occurs.

These stills were not commissioned for Glenora. Rather, Bowmore had purchased them secondhand after they had served ceremonial duty in a royal celebration. The price was right but it did create the need for certain methodological compromises later on. Normally malt whisky is distilled twice, first in a wash still to produce low wines with an alcohol content of about 22 percent, then in a smaller spirit still where the alcohol content is increased to about 72 percent. This was the plan for Glenora; however, when the distillery was under construction money was tight and instead of installing an authentic wash still, one of the spirit stills was designated to distill the wash. Thus, both stills are the same size, so charges of low wines from the wash still to the spirit still are smaller than they would be if a more typical larger wash still were used. There is talk now of installing an actual wash still as was originally planned. This would increase Glenora's production capacity to about 400,000 litres, though care would be needed to ensure the flavour profile of the whisky was not affected. Because the rest of the distillery was built before the decision was made to distill wort in a spirit still, installing a wash still now would also bring distillation capacity in line with fermentation outputs. Currently the washbacks produce enough wash daily to require two distillations in the undersized spirit-cum-wash still.

Mashing, fermenting, and distilling are done four days a week with a fifth reserved for filling barrels with spirit. Each day's distillation is directed to a holding tank to await barrelling day. Unlike in a continuous column still, the makeup of the spirit changes during distillation. Early spirit that contains undesirable esters and aldehydes is called foreshots

Distiller Daniel MacLean.

and is generally discarded or recycled back into the next spirit charge. Fusel oils and heavy alcohols that are distilled near the end of a distillation run are termed tails and are usually discarded or sold as industrial alcohol. The spirit distilled in the middle of the run, which is called the centre cut, is used for making whisky. The greatest skill a stillman needs is the ability to identify exactly the right time to make the cut. At Glenora, this is the job of Daniel MacLean. He mixes the spirit coming off the still with water, and when the mixture no longer turns cloudy the heads have passed and the centre cut is directed into a holding tank where it waits to be redistilled. MacLean verifies this tried and true approach with the time-honoured traditional method of nosing and tasting. Yes, he has equipment to guide him, but the final decision comes down to his experience and his well-tempered nose. The new spirit coming off the spirit still at 72 percent alc/vol passes through a copper shell and tube condenser, then is diluted to 63 percent to be filled into 170-litre American bourbon barrels used previously to mature Jack Daniels.

Maturation takes place in earth-floored wooden "dunnage-style" warehouses. It is a tradition that Scottish malt distilleries mature their whisky in these low, unheated warehouses built flat on the earth, and once again Glenora has followed Scottish tradition. At Glenora these warehouses have neither heat nor power, leading to very slow maturation during the long winter months. This explains why Glen Breton single malt doesn't really hit its stride until its midteens. Individual batches are vatted by hand, diluted down to bottling strength with MacLellan's Brook water, and then sent to a tiny bottling line where four operators fill four bottles at a time. It is here where the craft nature of Glenora is

Bottling Glen Breton single malt whisky.

most apparent, as the bottling line workers hand-fill each bottle after filtering the whisky through paper filters. Whisky that will be bottled in smaller 250-millilitre bottles, is filtered through paper coffee filters to remove any charcoal or other debris that might have come from the barrels. Each bottle is held up to a light and individually inspected before it is hand-packed into six-bottle cases. This labour-intensive process turns out 30,000 bottles a year, which is barely enough to keep up with demand.

In 2000, the first 1,000 cases of a no-age-statement eight-year-old called Glen Breton Rare were released in Canada, creating a feeding frenzy among expatriate Cape Bretoners across the country. Despite rave reviews from non-whisky writers (and, quaintly, one written by the local doctor), connoisseurs treated the whisky as something of a novelty. It had been made from aged spirit that was redistilled after taste tests showed that some of the initial batches were not quite up to snuff. Glenora's novice distillers, perhaps in an effort to squeeze every drop they could out of the mash, had waited too long to stop collecting the centre cut. Rather than being discouraged – and why should they be when their whisky sold like proverbial hotcakes? – distillery staff tuned their processes and continued to put away barrels of whisky, leaving them to age for ten, fifteen, and then twenty years. The distillery now produces about 50,000 litres of spirit each year and has settled on a respectable ten-year-old bottling called Glen Breton Rare as its core expression.

Although the distillery's unique signature is clearly evident in every bottle, there are noticeable differences as the batches advance from one to the next. "Our whisky is changing dramatically," says manager Donnie Campbell. In the past few years Campbell has begun to detect the aromas of local apple orchards and wild lupines that have found their way into the mature whisky. As the Bowmore flowers diminish, fruitier notes begin to take their place. A seventeen-year-old version that has been finished in Nova Scotia ice wine barrels, and a lovely fifteen year old called Battle of the Glen round out the line. Visitors to the inn and distillery have any number of special bottlings to choose from.

The reputation of Glen Breton Rare has now spread far and wide, with markets firmly established in Canada and the U.S., as well as in Japan, Vietnam, Spain, and Belgium. As its reputation grows, Glenora Distillery continues to expand its export trade.

Glen Breton Battle of the Glen
43% alc/vol

A complex interplay of fresh fruit, spring flowers, nutty grain, and hot pepper, with dry grass, fresh-cut alfalfa, minty herbs, inklings of rose petals, and a black licorice cigar. GB

Glen Breton Rare 10 Year Old
40% alc/vol

Strong, slowly fading floral perfume softens as vanilla, creamy caramel, and woody maple syrup flourish. Apples, black cherries, sweet tangerines, Turkish delight, and marshmallow nougat slowly emerge from an undefined fruitiness. GB

The Scotch Whisky Association has been a great though unwitting international promoter of Glen Breton, but in a way that had nothing to do with proud familial or clan links. In a suit that can only be described as bizarre, the association decided that Glen Breton Rare was too easily mistaken for Scotch single malt and demanded the word "Glen" be removed from the name. International media jumped on the story as an epic David and Goliath battle. Siding with David, their extensive coverage ensured that the distillery's name was constantly in the news. For Glenora this was a marketer's dream come true, even though it was a long and very expensive fight with no guarantee of success. In the end, however, the courts rejected the association's claim and sided with Glenora. Glen Breton continues to be produced as a Canadian single malt that proudly displays a large red Canadian maple leaf on its label, and a celebratory bottling aptly dubbed "Battle of the Glen" was added to the Glenora lineup.

That said, Glen Breton refuses to abandon its Scottish heritage. In an effort to learn more about the whisky business and how Scottish distillers engage their best customers, Campbell made a pilgrimage back to his Scottish roots. With a maple-leaf-sporting bottle of Glen Breton Rare 10 Year Old in his backpack, Campbell trekked from distillery to distillery, joining the consumer tour at each of them. Then, when the tour was over and the requisite drams tasted, he would pull out his own whisky for distillery staff to taste and comment on. Campbell listened carefully, and returned home inspired with ideas for new whisky expressions and for ways to add interest to the distillery tours at Glenora. Building on a steady stream of whisky tourists that visit the distillery, Campbell has plans to launch a

Manager Donnie Campbell.

whisky academy someday, nestled deep in the Cape Breton Highlands.

There was another upshot from the fight with Scotch whisky authorities in the motherland. The people who make Glen Breton are proud of their whisky and so confident of its quality that they place an extensive array of Scotch single malts right alongside it in the bar at their inn. Many single malts are represented, but the only one with a name beginning with "Glen" is Glen Breton.

"Would you like a Macallan?" the barkeep might ask. "Coming right up."

"A Balvenie? Here you go."

"Bowmore, Caol Ila, Talisker, or Highland Park? No problem."

Ask for a Glenfiddich though and you'll quickly be told: "Sorry, we don't pour that here."

With a sardonic wink, manager Donnie Campbell declares this is a precaution to avoid misleading anyone. Glenora Distillery in the town of Glenville, Inverness County, in the highlands of Cape Breton, Nova Scotia is just so Scottish, it wouldn't be difficult for visitors to forget they are actually in Canada.

Chapter 22

Highwood Distillers

igh River, Alberta, a town of 10,000 people, sits in that in-between place called the Foothills, where the flat prairie terrain begins its rolling climb toward the Rocky Mountains. Just thirty minutes south of Calgary, High River is most famous as the home of Joe Clark, Canada's former prime minister. But there's a hidden gem in High River: a small, barely known distillery that like its hometown is bigger than it looks. Well, in the flavour of its whiskies anyway.

Highwood whiskies.

In 1974, investors from Calgary hired a German eau-de-vie distiller to help them build a smallish plant, called Sunnyvale Distillery, walking distance from the heart of High River. The first raw spirit came off its unusual column still on April 1 that year, and other than its name – the distillery was renamed Highwood in 1985 – not much has changed since then. Highwood is still a small distillery, it is still independent, and it is still just a short jaunt from downtown High River. With just thirty staff, there's a friendly, even family feel to the place. "I guess everyone likes to think of their co-workers as a family," says distillery manager Michael Nychyk. "Highwood is a small place, like a cottage industry, and we try to keep our employees happy."

Working in the whisky business quickly becomes a calling, a vocation of sorts, and it has been no different for Nychyk. A job with one of Canada's major food chains turned into a career in whisky when former master distiller Glen Hopkins invited him to join the Highwood family in 2006 as the operations manager.

Highwood is unique among Canadian distilleries in that it mashes 100 percent wheat for its base whisky. Perhaps that is because wheat makes a fine, flavourful base whisky, and with a little different distillation process it can also be used to make light-flavoured spirit suitable for vodka. "We're not set up for corn," says Nychyk, "but we use a lot of it for some of our whiskies, so we buy corn spirit from other distillers – Alberta Distillers, Black Velvet, and Hiram Walker – and age it ourselves. We also have all the corn whisky that we got when we took over Potter's a few years ago."

Century Reserve 15/25
40% alc/vol

Plush, spicy cinnamon fruit slowly mellows through sweet marzipan, hazelnuts, and charred firewood into toasted oak. Starts in a pear orchard and ends in a lumberyard. HA

Highwood
40% alc/vol

Toffee, marshmallow, and fresh-cut wood with a biting, bitter, citrusy undercurrent. Peppery and quite warming with hints of tangerine peel. Creamy. HA

Highwood specifics

Making whisky is strictly a batch process at Highwood, and the process itself never varies. Each week seven batches of wheat go through the full cycle, from cooking through to distillation. Seven cooker batches of wheat become two batches of fermenting mash. These in turn become a single batch of beer ready for distillation. To start the cycle, about 2,500 kilograms of soft winter wheat are pressure cooked in 12,000 litres of water to create a 14,000-litre batch of mash. Although it is close to the Highwood River and connected to city water mains, the distillery has its own deep-water well to provide clean, potable water for cooking, mashing, and processing. The cooking process at Highwood is unique in Canada. The wheat is not milled but, harking back to the distillery's German heritage, enters the cooker whole. It quickly explodes in the heat of the cooker, releasing the starch. From the cooker the hot, cooked wheat is expelled under high pressure into a chiller. On the way, it slams against a hard surface called a bell, where any kernels that may not have burst in cooking explode on impact. An inspection of the spent mash reveals that wheat kernels almost never make it through the process without bursting open.

Conversion and fermentation begin as soon as the first batch is cooked. Over the next twenty-four hours, the six other batches are added to the fermenting mash as they become ready. The cooking/fermenting cycle takes about five days from start to finish, so cooking is done once every five days, followed by a seventy-two-hour ferment. It's an accurate and easy-to-repeat cycle that ensures that each batch is made exactly the same way and, importantly, results in a consistent beer with 12 percent alcohol by volume. Another day is then spent distilling the beer into new spirit.

High wines come off the stainless steel beer still at about 70 percent alc/vol. These are then reduced to about 40 percent and run through a custom-built kettle and column comprising a fifteen-metre stainless steel rectifying tower mounted directly on top of a stainless steel pot still. The tower, which has been painted red, is fed from the bottom by vapours coming from the pot still, creating a lot of purifying reflux and allowing very fine control of the components and concentration of the final spirit. The pot still is heated with a three-inch copper line that does double duty by also removing certain off-notes from the beer. The final product is a very clean spirit that is virtually free of fusel oil and, as a result, matures about one-third faster than corn spirit. A whisky that ages more quickly gives a faster return on

Beer still (a column still) in foreground, pot still in background at Highwood Distillers.

investment. Nychyk figures wheat whisky is at its optimum age at about ten years.

People unfamiliar with North American distilling practices sometimes look at stainless steel stills like those used at Highwood and jump to the conclusion that the spirit does not interact with copper during distillation. However, in addition to the copper coils in the pot still, the condensers and alcohol lines are all made of copper.

Wheat makes great base whisky, but it is rye that gives Highwood whiskies their particular kick. Every couple of years the plant switches over to mashing rye for a few months so it can distill its flavouring whiskies. Rye starch is very difficult to work with compared with wheat, as it becomes very sticky. This is why once they start distilling rye flavouring at Highwood, they try to make enough to use at various ages as it matures over the next ten years. At Highwood, the rye is cooked whole and fermented exactly as wheat is.

Although Highwood uses a single mash bill and distilling process for its rye flavouring whisky, as the spirit sits ageing in the barrels the flavour undergoes so many changes that every couple of years it seems like an entirely new whisky. Different ages of rye used as flavouring whisky contribute different flavours to the final product. With a new run completed every couple of years, Highwood always has a good variety of rye flavouring whiskies on hand.

Highwood buys only single-fill Jim Beam and Jack Daniels bourbon barrels, never using new barrels to age its distillates. But the demand for bourbon barrels is high, which is why, from time to time, they recooper and rechar them. Barrels are reused for up to fifteen years, or three fills. Once filled, the barrels are stored upright, on pallets, six ranks high, until the whisky is ready for blending. At any one time there are about 17,000 barrels of maturing whisky on site. The whisky is left to mature for up to twenty-five years in the extremes of the Alberta climate, with no temperature control in the warehouses except a little heat in winter. But winter can be bone-chilling in High River, which is why, come spring, residents watch the western sky for the telltale arc of dark clouds that signals a chinook – warm winds rushing down from the Rocky Mountains that can raise temperatures as much as thirty degrees Celsius in just a few hours and can signal an end to winter.

A powerful aroma of whisky greets you when you walk into the Highwood warehouse. Alberta has a dry climate and even though losses are significant, more water than alcohol is lost during ageing and the whisky that goes into the barrels as new spirit at 72 percent alc/vol has increased to 75 percent by the time it is drawn out for blending and bottling.

Blending is an art and for many people it is more: almost magic. As with every magician, it helps to know a few tricks, most of which can never be shared. One trick revolves around rye, the main component that controls the flavour of whisky. Control the rye and you control the flavour. Still, for blending, different ages of whisky are included, starting with eight to ten batches of matured

Potter's Special Old
40% alc/vol

Soft, voluptuous, creamy caramel on a bed of mild ginger and cinnamon. Classic crisp Canadian oak with hot white pepper all wrapped up in slightly pulling grapefruit rind. HA

White Owl Whisky
40% alc/vol

Sweet caramel, pepper, lemon custard, citrus pith, hints of oak, and dusty spicy rye grain. Cool citrus zing and peppery hot zip broaden into creamy toffee, sweet baking spices, and a touch of licorice root. HA

base whisky. Blending various batches ensures consistency and averages out any variation among batches. And this in its own way is another element of the distiller's magic. The biggest factor in selecting barrels for blending is flavour, but inventory is also a consideration. There is no dump trough at Highwood. Rather, the whisky is pumped out of the barrels and the blend is prepared using a recipe, then it is adjusted – a simpler form of magic – if necessary. Samples of all batches from the past several years are kept on hand to ensure consistency. The Highwood tasting panel compares the batch with the last two or three blends. All tasting is done at 20 percent to quickly reveal both the flavours and the flaws.

Specialty products

Highwood also produces several specialty whisky products. One of them, a sipping maple whisky, is a blend of Highwood wheat whisky with Quebec maple syrup. Another is a blend of three natural cherry juices with wheat whiskies. These are novelties to fill a niche in the local market, and that's about it. In a third experiment, however, Highwood has revived a long-lost Canadian whisky style called *whisky blanc* and this seems to have taken Canadian cocktail lovers by storm. The original *whisky blanc* was whisky that had been aged in copper barrels, ensuring that it had no woody flavours. Highwood's version is just the opposite: it is fully aged in wood. This is a clear whisky – as clear as water – but it is loaded with rye whisky flavours. The whisky, which is called White Owl and is priced to compete with high-end vodkas, is a blend of fully matured rye and wheat whiskies that have been filtered through powdered charcoal to remove any trace of colour. Of course, this process also removes some of the flavour, which is why the blend is quite rich in rye flavouring whisky. "My biggest problem with White Owl," admits Nychyk, "is keeping enough of the custom bottles and caps in stock."

Eight people work on the bottling line at Highwood, filling 150 bottles per minute. Highwood has adopted the more modern practice of washing the bottles with 40 percent vodka rather than air. Each filled bottle is inspected by hand to make sure labels, caps, fill lines, and so on are right before it is boxed by hand. It's labour intensive yes, but nothing like the miniature filling station where, in another display of the Highwood spirit, half a dozen employees hand-fill, cap, label, and pack miniatures, one by one, in what seems more like a relay than an assembly line.

Distilling tower.

In November 2005, seeking to expand their product line, Highwood Distillers bought Potter Distilleries of Kelowna, British Columbia, about a six-hour drive to the west. Potter's was not so much a distillery as a whisky broker with a bottling line but no stills. Highwood decided to move all of Potter's maturing stock to High River and has maintained the Potter's brands and formulas. Alas, they have not revived Potter's much-storied Bush Pilot's. Like Highwood's own Century Reserve whiskies, Potter's whiskies are all-corn whisky, so they are distilled elsewhere but aged at Highwood.

Tucked in behind a farm machinery dealer on the edge of a small prairie town, Highwood distillery really is a hidden gem, and all the more so because its whiskies are, for the most part, available only in Canada. Indeed, some are available only in Canada's western provinces. More's the pity, because some of these whiskies – the Century Reserve 15 Year Old with its liberal dose of much older whiskies, or the single-bond 21 Year Old, for example – really are worth seeking out.

Chapter 23

Hiram Walker & Sons

Established in 1858, Hiram Walker & Sons is the largest distillery operating in Canada today. Walker's is also the longest continuously operating beverage alcohol distillery in North America, but in truth most of the plant, as it exists today, was rebuilt in the 1950s. Only the Canadian Club Heritage Centre, a replica Florentine palace that Walker built in 1894, remains of the original distillery. In 1977–78 when the already huge demand for Canadian whisky was growing in leaps and bounds,

Hiram Walker distillery, operated by Corby's, is home to Canadian Club, Wiser's, and Gibson's Finest whiskies.

additional construction doubled the size of the distillery and a second still house was added. Updates since the turn of the twenty-first century have introduced computer-automated operations designed to give greater consistency of product.

During Prohibition, Walker's grandsons sold the distillery to the Hatch family, who in turn sold it on to a foreign conglomerate in the 1990s. In 2006 Pernod Ricard purchased the plant and since then it has been operated by Corby Distilleries on their behalf. When the Corby distillery closed in the 1990s, the Walkerville plant took over production of the Corby and Wiser brands. In 2008 production of most of the Gibson's Finest brands moved from Valleyfield to Hiram Walker's as well.

Canadian Club Black Label 8 Year Old
40% alc/vol

Prunes, figs, and lemon custard with spicy rye, fresh-cut cedar, then blazing pyres of pepper. Cloves and tingling ginger dissolve in bittersweet citrus pith. Canadian Club turned up a notch or two for Japan. HW

Gibson's Finest 12 Year Old
40% alc/vol

Earthy rye and ripe red cherries dissolve into crème brûlée, crisp oak, and spicy pepper. Clean oak and red cedar dissolve slowly into butterscotch. A humidor of rich, leathery tobacco. HW

A riverfront elevator with thirty-three silos holds a two-month supply of corn, almost all of which used to arrive by ship. However, grain freighters no longer dock at the distillery and today corn is delivered by truck. A little more than two-thirds comes from southwestern Ontario and the balance from the American Midwest. Rye grain, malted rye, barley, and malted barley are brought in by rail from the prairies. Walker's is unique in that it is the only Canadian distillery to mash malted rye. That is more of a challenge than might be expected, not because of any processing difficulties, but because rye is not normally grown for malting. This is why Walker's uses custom-grown and malted rye. Not surprisingly, this takes careful planning because, effectively, malted rye must be purchased a year in advance to give farmers and maltsters time to actually grow and malt it. And not just any rye will do. Walker's has identified a specific spring variety that is best for maintaining the flavour profile of one of its flavouring whiskies.

Hiram Walker specifics

When demand requires it, the Hiram Walker & Sons distillery is capable of running twenty-four hours a day, seven days a week, to produce 55 million litres of alcohol annually. Currently, 36 million litres of alcohol are produced each year over a five-day workweek, with the distillery operating around the clock. However, a five-day workweek certainly introduces some inefficiencies into the process. Continuous distillation requires that an equilibrium be maintained within the still. Each time the stills are shut down then restarted, precious distillation time is lost and energy is expended for the six hours it takes to get the columns back up to running temperature.

Grain arrives by truck at Hiram Walker elevators.

Corn for base whisky is cooked in a continuous cooker then filled into one of thirty-nine closed fermenters, where distiller's yeast is added. These fermenters are painted a creamy off-white colour to match the floors, which are tiled in a large turquoise and cream checkerboard pattern. This colour-coordinated fermenting room is an unusual sight in an industrial distillery and, somehow, a humanizing one.

Rye and rye malt are milled, then the rye is cooked in a traditional batch cooker while the malted rye is held back and added only after the mash has cooled down. Thus there is no need to add microbial enzymes. Walker's is the only distillery in Canada to use rye malt as an enzyme source. After fermentation using commercial yeast and a proprietary yeast strain that Hiram Walker himself isolated, the resulting beer contains about 6 to 7 percent alcohol. This could be increased to 12 percent with a few minor adjustments, but that would mean changing the 150-year-old recipe, a risk that neither the blenders nor the production staff believe is worth taking.

An all-copper beer still is used to make two types of rye flavouring whisky. After a single pass through the beer still, the spirit is quite aromatic with a fruity nose, smelling almost like peaches along with distinct overtones of grain, particularly when a bit of water is added. The second flavouring whisky begins much like the first. After being distilled in the beer still, it is redistilled in a 12,000-litre traditional copper pot. This second distillation focuses and enriches some of the flavours while lightening the spirit up a little bit. The clean, fruity nose already shows typical rye floral notes. Tasting it again after six years in new American oak barrels, the fruitiness remains, but new complex wood flavours are added and the floral notes have really moved to the fore. A touch of candy has broadened the palate. This is the whisky of the fabled Lot No. 40 and Wiser's Legacy.

Walker's base spirit is distilled to 94.5 percent then diluted to 78 percent for ageing. Although the stills are made primarily from stainless steel, certain sections are copper so there is no need to add sacrificial copper to them.

Copper is important in distilling, but because it plays an active role in the distillation, eventually it wears out. When this happened to the single pot still at Hiram Walker, Ian Ross, a chemical engineer who manages the distillery, was very concerned. Pot stills are made by hand and great care was needed to ensure the replacement still conformed exactly to the original. If it didn't, there would be a risk that flavours could change. Vendome Copper & Brass Works of Louisville, Kentucky was recruited to do the job. When all was in place and the new spirit started to come off the still, the distilling team at Hiram Walker breathed a collective sigh of relief. Nothing had changed.

The barrelling operation at Hiram Walker was tailor-built for the plant. Whisky arrives at the dumping-filling station from the warehouse on pallets of six barrels. The bungs, which are in the centre of the barrelhead, are automatically drilled out, two at a time. Mature whisky is aspirated out of the barrels, six at a time, by vacuum hoses, and within a few seconds the barrels are refilled with new spirit and new bungs inserted. Right away they are returned to the warehouses, where they are stacked six high. In an average eight-hour day, eight truckloads of barrels (about 1,400 barrels in all) are withdrawn from the warehouses some twenty minutes away in Pike Creek then driven over to the plant in Walkerville, where they are emptied, refilled, and returned to Pike Creek to restart the ageing process. In the Pike Creek warehouses the angels are particularly active during the first year of ageing, taking as much as 6 to 10 percent of the volume. After that, losses drop to about 3 percent annually.

The process for Canadian Club whiskies is slightly different from that for other whiskies distilled at Hiram Walker. For Canadian Club the component whiskies are blended before being filled into barrels. Because Wiser's, Corby's, and Gibson's whiskies are also made in the plant, the barrels for different products are kept separate to avoid any accidental transfer of flavours. After twenty to twenty-five years of use, the barrels are finally withdrawn from service.

Initially, the mature whisky that has been removed from the barrels will be sent to stainless steel holding tanks until it is needed for blending. One hundred and fourteen tanks in the tankroom can hold 9 million litres of various mature spirits, but according to Ross you can never have enough tanks for the blenders. Much of the whisky is blended and bottled on site, and every day two or three dedicated railcars loaded with bulk whisky leave the plant for bottling elsewhere.

As much as 40 percent of the whisky distilled at Hiram Walker is used for Canadian Club, its signature brand. As well, fully one-third of Walker's production is sold as bulk three-year-old whisky to U.S.-based producers. This is a versatile plant capable of producing a broad range of whiskies

Hiram Walker Special Old
40% alc/vol

Steely rye with hints of orange peel, zesty rye, a suggestion of chocolate milk, and rich, rum-soaked Christmas cake. HW

Lot No. 40
43% alc/vol

Dark, sour German rye bread, with dry grain, caraway seed, oak, and bitter dark molasses. A floral fruitiness matures into dark prunes, oranges, and aromatic vanilla, but really this is all about rye bread. HW

Wiser's 18 Year Old
40% alc/vol

Red cedar shavings in gingery, peppery butterscotch pudding, topped with wedge of lime. Slowly evolving complex aromas of cigar box and pencil shavings dissolve into dried fruit, grain, and leathery tobacco. HW and other spirits. And with a malted barley flavouring whisky still in production, theoretically Walker's could one day revive its Epicure single malt.

Just across the road from the distillery is the Hiram Walker bottling plant, where four modern bottling lines fill 300 to 400 bottles a minute. The bottles are rinsed clean with 40 percent vodka rather than air. Bottles are bulky, so the distillery has instituted a just-in-time handling system in which the bottles for the next day's run arrive at the loading dock at night, already packed in their twelve-bottle cartons. As a result, excess bottles are not stored at the plant. During the bottling process the bottles are removed from the cartons, filled, capped, and then put back ready to be shipped out.

The bottling lines are fully automated for efficiency, but the retooling that is necessary when there is a change from one bottle shape or size to another is very costly, so production runs are scheduled very carefully. Some wholesale customers demand plastic (polyethylene terephthalate, or PET) bottles for environmental reasons, to reduce weight, or to keep costs down, and the plant uses both glass and plastic bottles more or less equally. Plastic is seldom used for premium whiskies and is not allowed for whisky shipped to Europe. Whisky with a high content of rye must be chill filtered before it is bottled, as calcium oxalate crystals will form in the bottle after a few years on the shelves. This doesn't affect the flavour or quality of the whisky, but in the past consumers often returned bottles that had a haze in them. It's a nuisance that makes filtering the norm.

But whisky is not the only product of distillation. It's very typical for the spent grains left over from whisky making to

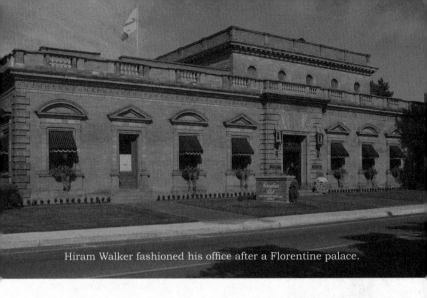

Hiram Walker fashioned his office after a Florentine palace.

be sold as animal feed. This is an added source of revenue at many distilleries and Hiram Walker is no exception. Walker's is a large distillery and the DDG (distillers dried grains) operation is also large, capable of holding up to 5,000 tonnes. Prices fluctuate, but at $100 a tonne, a by-product that might otherwise be regarded as waste is processed and quickly sold.

Were Hiram Walker to return today he might well recognize Walkerville, the town he built for his employees, although it is now fully contained within the city limits of Windsor. And though he might also recognize some of the whiskies being produced, he would almost certainly be surprised to see his distillery producing the whiskies that in his time were being distilled by his competitors J. P. Wiser in Prescott and Henry Corby in Corbyville. But Walker would be even more surprised to learn that his plant is now being run by Corby's successors and that their key brand is not Canadian Club, but Wiser's.

Chapter 24

Kittling Ridge Estates Wine and Spirits

Forty Creek
Confederation Oak.

As you wind down the steep road from Beamer Falls on Forty Mile Creek to the distillery below, Toronto's skyline, fifty-five kilometres away on the other side of Lake Ontario, glimmers in the hot summer haze through gaps in the mixed hardwood forest. Not so much a waterfall as a steep, bumpy ramp, Beamer scuds over the same Niagara limestone that the world's best-known waterfall plunges from, some sixty-five kilometres (forty miles) to the west. In the spring, thermals climbing the face of the escarpment vault migrating hawks into the sky, launching them homeward, north across the lake, an activity known as kittling. In just a few years Kittling Ridge Estates Wines and Spirits and its Forty Creek whiskies have become quiet ambassadors of this unique geography, until now known best by birders, hikers, and residents of nearby Grimsby, Ontario.

Kittling Ridge Distillery is just as distinctive as the geography around it. Owner and whisky maker John K. Hall is a chemist by education, a winemaker by trade, and a whisky maker by passion. Hall grew up in Windsor, not far from Hiram Walker's distillery, where he had set his sights on a career. But that was not to be. Instead, Hall did a stint tasting spices and botanicals at Campbell Soups before joining John Labatt's wine division, Ridout Wines, as an assistant winemaker. In 1989, when Labatt's decided to focus their business on making beer, Hall helped lead a management buyout of Ridout Wines, assuming the role of vice-president and general manager of Ontario sales and marketing for the newly created company, Cartier Wines. It was a successful business move that eventually propelled Cartier Wines to evolve into wine conglomerate Vincor, the fourth-largest wine producer in North America and eighth-largest in the world. As for Hall? By then he had chosen a different path: whisky.

If the aromas of Hiram Walker's fermenting mash educated his boyhood nose and his quality control responsibilities at Campbell's disciplined it, it was the process of making wine that nurtured his curiosity. Hall had not even visited a distillery when, in 1992, he struck out on his own, buying Rieder Distillery, the eau-de-vie operation that would eventually become Kittling Ridge. In 1971 Swiss distiller Otto Rieder founded the distillery with the intention of using local Niagara fruit to distill eau-de-vie. That was his passion, but by the time Hall bought the distillery, Rieder was supporting its eau-de-vie business buying and bottling bulk vodka and whisky and shipping it for sale in various markets, the most successful of which were in Asia. For a short while Rieder also bottled Canadian Mist under licence, for sale in Canada. "It was a good distillery," Hall says, "but no one in Canada was drinking eau-de-vie." Falling back on his winemaking skills, Hall obtained a provincial licence to make wine, and in 1993 he converted the distillery into a winery. However, he did not abandon distilling altogether, and was able to supplement his cash flow from wine with sales of vodka. At the same time, inspired by growing consumer interest in bourbon and Scotch, and his own natural curiosity, Hall also began distilling whisky.

Kittling Ridge specifics
Kittling Ridge distillery is unlike any you will ever encounter. To begin, the whisky distillery is very much integrated into the winery. Indeed, while Kittling Ridge mashes whisky for eight months of the year, during the other four months

the 40,000-litre, 25,000-litre, and ten 15,000-litre fermenters are used for making wine. Then, during whisky season, grain is fermented in the same stainless steel fermenters that during grape harvest were filled with wine. While some of these fermenters are uncovered to facilitate breaking the cap on fermenting red wine, the majority of the whisky is fermented in closed fermenters with pump circulation from the bottom to prevent sedimentation.

Barrels of wine sit ageing in the whisky warehouses – Hall calls them cellars – and both operations share the same bottling lines. In fact, the whole approach to making whisky bears an uncanny resemblance to the art of the winemaker. Just as he ferments and ages grape varietals separately, tailoring techniques to maximize the unique qualities of each, so he ferments and ages his corn, his barley, and his rye in separate batches. Careful attention is also paid to the yeasts, with brewer's and distiller's yeasts predominating, as they do in other distilleries. For corn mashes Hall adds wine yeast, as it produces fewer volatiles and thus fewer off-notes. The idea is that the fermented mash should capture the natural essences of the grains.

Grain is purchased already milled so there is no need for a mill on site. For the most part, barley malt is used to supply the conversion enzymes, but microbial enzymes are added if necessary to speed up conversion. Depending on the grain, the season, and the yeast, five to seven days of fermentation produce a fermented mash of about 8 or 9 percent alc/vol. While fermented corn mash is distilled in a copper column still, fermented rye mash and barley mash (Hall refuses to call them beer) are distilled in the two small, original, steam-heated copper eau-de-vie pot stills. The larger of these, at

5,000 litres, has a short rectifying column up above to encourage rising spirit to condense as "reflux" and fall back down into the short column. Hall believes this creates a richer spirit. The other column, a bare 500 litres, can only be described as mini. The fermented mash is usually run through one or the other of these stills just once, coming off between 62 and 70 percent alc/vol, so there is no need for dilution before barrelling. Hall believes that a single distillation minimizes the loss of flavour and, in vintner's lingo, "bruising" of the spirit. It also means that lots of congeners remain in the new spirit. The spirit that is produced by the 5,000-litre still is much softer than that coming from the 500-litre one, so they produce different results from the same mash. As in most small distilleries, heads and tails are routinely discarded.

The top-of-the-line whiskies distilled at Kittling Ridge are sold under the Forty Creek label. Forty Creek Barrel Select is the flagship whisky and each fall a small batch of a special new Forty Creek whisky is released. Kittling Ridge also produces two economy whisky brands, Canada Gold and Mountain Rock. The corn base spirit for these is distilled in a German-made copper column still and a stainless steel column. "It's important to have economy brands," says Hall. "The barrels still have a lot of life left in them after maturing spirit for Barrel Select. It's a huge cost if you have to discard them after one use. People generally consider new things to be better than used, but in the case of whisky barrels quite often used barrels are more valuable than new ones."

Barrel selection is paramount at Kittling Ridge Distillery, and because each barrel has its own personality the whiskies are tasted as they mature. The aggressive, heavy corn

Forty Creek Double Barrel Reserve
40% alc/vol

Caramel, butterscotch, and vanilla with lemon cream
biscuits, orange, and whispers of coconut, hot pepper,
mustard, and ginger. Sweet and sour rye, dry grain,
fresh sawdust, and zesty lime. KR

Forty Creek John's Private Cask No. 1
40% alc/vol

Bursting blasts of gingery spice, dark fruits, clean
wood, and crème caramel. Sultry fruits and dusky rye
spices with candied orange rind. Finishes in bitter rye
and glowing embers of spice. KR

spirit is tamed but not broken in heavily charred "alliga-
tor" barrels. White oak with a medium char shapes and
rounds the nuttiness of barley spirit, while lightly toasted
oak optimizes the spicy and fruity rye notes. Only when
each individual whisky has achieved the desired flavour
profile are they married together in common barrels. Hall
calls this his "Meritage whisky."

For the most part, Kittling Ridge uses American bourbon
barrels purchased in Kentucky and Missouri. But when he
found a grove of local oaks he realized would be ideal for
whisky making, Hall shipped the logs to a Missouri cooperage, where they were made into barrels, custom toasted,
and shipped back to Grimsby. Long, cold winters ensure
that Canadian oak is much more dense than its American
counterpart, and the harsh Canadian climate imbues it

Canadian oak.

richly with vanillins. Although the barrels had been seasoned carefully, after a year in Canadian oak the whisky was so loaded with extreme aromas that Hall feared he would end up having to redistill it. But patience was rewarded as time smoothed it out, creating an exciting Confederation Oak special release.

Forty Creek Barrel Select is a blend of whiskies aged in a mixture of light- and medium-toasted and heavily charred white oak barrels then reracked into barrels used first to age Kittling Ridge's Kingsgate sherry. The same approach is taken with Forty Creek Double Barrel Reserve, but rather than spending six months in sherry casks, Double Barrel Reserve is put to marry in high-quality, first-fill, ex-Kentucky bourbon barrels.

Forty Creek Three Grain, introduced at the same time as Barrel Select, included more barley whisky, but Hall withdrew it from the market to help build brand identity for Barrel Select. Whisky makers know that consistency is as important as name recognition, and that it is one of the keys to successful whisky brands. Hall agrees. But at Kittling Ridge, he says, blending is as much about creating style as consistency. Hall works hard to maintain the Forty Creek profile, and succeeds. It's still handmade whisky though, so each batch must be tweaked a little to accommodate the differences among the barrels.

Kittling Ridge is a growing enterprise with a staff of 130 and a 16,300-square-metre distillery, including a still house, barrel-ageing cellars, stainless steel storage and fermentation tanks, grain-handling equipment, finished goods warehousing, and five bottling lines. Yet despite this scale of operation – it's still tiny compared to some other Canadian distilleries – Kittling Ridge has not lost the handcrafted approach. Eleven staff on a bottling line hand-feed, inspect, and pack sixty bottles per minute. Two people and a machine could do it much faster, but automation is not part of the Canadian whisky heritage that Hall wants to rekindle.

The area called Kittling Ridge is typical of the Ontario farmland where many early Canadian settlers established tiny backyard distilleries using local grain from area gristmills. The land above the ridge is rich and flat, and Grimsby harbour provided ready access to market in nearby York. But if other Canadian distilleries promote their long heritage, tradition, and history, Kittling Ridge distillery makes much of its recent arrival on the scene. Is it a matter of confident, independent thinking or just a brash stirring of the pot that Hall, who is undeniably an innovator, claims to be trying to create what he calls a "New-World whisky style"? Has he not heard that the New World already has two distinct and internationally recognized styles: Canadian whisky and American bourbon? Let's hope nobody tells him, for in his reinvention of the Canadian whisky wheel not only is he breaking new ground – and a whole lot of rules – he's also coming up with one world-class whisky after another.

No matter whom you talk to in the Canadian whisky industry, everyone knows John Hall and his Forty Creek whiskies. "He's a breath of fresh air for the industry," says one competing distiller. "He's really done wonders for us." Forty Creek whiskies have developed a cult following in Canada, particularly in Ontario. However, their first success came not in Canada, but in Texas, where Forty Creek

John Hall, distiller.

Barrel Select was a big hit right from its introduction in 2003. Just as Canadian musicians and actors often go to the United States to launch their careers then come back home as stars, Forty Creek got its first real recognition south of the border. Aficionados have encouraged Hall to release his whiskies as single-grain corn, barley, and rye whiskies, at least in small quantities. "But then I wouldn't have enough to make my Forty Creek whiskies," he muses, clearly pleased that the best-tuned palates want them. We can only hope he might one day decide to give in.

Back in the 1960s when Hall was a kid looking for a job Walker's chose not to hire him. Isn't it ironic that today he's repeating founder Hiram Walker's feat of educating knowledgeable palates to demand Canadian whisky?

Chapter 25

Valleyfield

On an island in the Saint Lawrence River, in a typical old Québécois town, the *monseigneur* in the twin-spired Basilique-Cathédrale Sainte-Cécile ministers to the faithful. Some congregants work at the local distillery, as did their parents and their grandparents before them. Indeed, some have ancestors who now rest in the cemetery that lies directly beside the distillery on rue Salaberry. The town, Salaberry-de-Valleyfield, is about an hour's drive southwest from the site of the old Molson's distillery in the heart of Montreal. It's an industrial, column-stilled plant for sure, but set as it is on its long narrow lot – a throwback to the days of seigneurial land distribution – there is something decidedly human about Quebec's last operating whisky distillery. Somehow, the Valleyfield Distillery, now officially known as Diageo Global Supply–Valleyfield, looks like it belongs here.

The sign on the front is in French, as required by Quebec's language laws. Inside, the 230 staff converse freely in *la langue maternelle* but, like the townspeople, they'll quickly switch to English to greet an anglophone visitor. They are quick and proud to point out, however, that Valleyfield is the only distillery in North America that operates in the French language.

In the first few years of the past century, one Anatole S.

VO Now and Then.

Piedalue built a bakery on this site. He called his bakery Star Biscuits. Then, just a couple of years later in 1911, Piedalue sold his biscuitry to Édouard Hébert, better known as *le gros Hébert*, who converted it into the Golden Lion Brewery. The plant continued to brew beer all through the Depression years, until 1938. What did change several times, though, was its name. In 1923 it was the Salaberry Brewery, then six years later it became the Maple Leaf Brewery. Salaberry-de-Valleyfield is only 40 kilometres from the U.S. border and the brewery was particularly busy from 1920 to 1933, when Prohibition was in force.

In 1938 Quebec Distillers Company purchased the plant for a very different purpose. All through the Second World War they used it to ferment potatoes, grain, and molasses into alcohol for industrial and military applications. Then, in 1945, with the war finally over, the distillery was sold to Lewis Rosenstiel's Schenley Distillers Corporation and completely rebuilt as a whisky distillery. Rosenstiel and several partners had established Schenley in the United States during the early days of Prohibition, buying defunct distilleries and brands, and operating one of the few American firms allowed to produce and sell alcohol for medicinal purposes during Prohibition.

By 1946 the Valleyfield Distillery was exporting alcoholic beverages into the U.S. Two years later Valleyfield's first whisky, Golden Wedding, was ready for market. Rosenstiel had purchased the Golden Wedding name and a very extensive stock of American-made Golden Wedding whisky from Pittsburgh's Joseph F. Finch distillery during Prohibition. However, Golden Wedding was soon to become an enduring, high-volume, competitively priced Canadian whisky with impressive sales in the Canadian and U.S. markets, and around the world. During the 1950s Schenley reincarnated a number of other American whisky brands as Canadian whiskies, among them the Old Fine Copper brand, better known as OFC (and now called OFC–Old Fine Canadian), a very popular eight-year-old whisky at that time. Demand for Schenley's products blossomed and the distillery grew. By 1969 over 1 million barrels of spirit from Quebec-grown corn and other local grains had been distilled in the plant.

Today some people might cringe at the idea of whisky brands crossing international borders. Memory can be short and trade protectionism is now taken for granted, but geographic definitions for North American whiskies have not always been as rigid as they are now. Indeed, for at least a century and a half such restrictions were non-existent and at that time Canada had quite a thriving bourbon industry. Early Schenley bottlings of Ancient Age Bourbon, for example, were filled with whisky that was distilled in Canada. This was true also for Walker's Old Crow and many other well-known brands, despite their colourful and dearly held Old South legends.

In 1981 Schenley's Canadian operations were sold to a Vancouver family whose interest was piqued by the fact that Schenley had a branch plant distillery, called Park & Tilford, in Vancouver. The new owners quickly set out to modernize the Valleyfield Distillery. But the 1980s were a time of over-capacity in the whisky business worldwide, and Canadian Schenley needed a serious injection of funds that the new owners were not prepared to make. At some point, fearing their client was teetering into bankruptcy, the bank stepped in and found a new investor to take over the company. The distillery struggled through the mid- to late-1980s, and managed to remain in operation even as others were forced to close. In September 1990 United Distillers, a subsidiary of Guinness, the Irish beer company, bought the plant and its brands, and so began a roller coaster ride of mergers, acqui-sitions, investments, divestments, and reacquisitions. Since 2008 the distillery has been owned by Diageo, the world's largest drinks manufacturer. Diageo uses the plant to make distillate for V.O. and other Diageo whisky brands.

Among the many American whisky brands owned by Schenley was Gibson's. Gibson's is now a leading Canadian whisky brand, but its origins lay elsewhere. It was first dis-tilled in 1836 on the banks of the Monongahela River in west-ern Pennsylvania and was a well-known Pennsylvania rye whisky until Prohibition closed the distillery in 1920. In 1972, Schenley revived Gibson's as a Canadian whisky, using spirit distilled at Valleyfield. Although Gibson's had become one of Schenley's most prestigious brands in Canada, in 2001 it was sold to William Grant & Sons. Then in 2008 Gibson's found

Canadian 83
40% alc/vol

Initial spirit blossoms into butterscotch, muted rye spices, hot pepper, musty sandalwood, and citrus zing. Hints of steely rye gently tickle faint crispy oak. The favourite of Gimli, Manitoba. VA

Canadian Five Star
40% alc/vol

A classic Canadian mixer with caramel, hard rye, hot pepper and sweet fruit that diverges into dried herbs and vague maraschino cherry juice followed by a cleansing citrusy finish. VA

itself caught in the middle of the Diageo purchase and retooling, and moved new production to Hiram Walker's distillery. Nevertheless, Gibson's Finest Rare 18 Year Old is still blended and bottled at Valleyfield from old Schenley whisky that is continuing to mature in the warehouses there. Gibson's remains one of Canada's most sought after whiskies.

Valleyfield specifics

With such a long and convoluted history, it is no surprise that Valleyfield has its own production idiosyncrasies. For example, as distillery manager Martin Laberge explains, Valleyfield uses the same 100 percent corn mash to make two very different base whiskies. Both are distilled to the same alc/vol; however, one is distilled in continuous column stills, the other in batches, and the results couldn't be more different. With all other factors being identical, these differences must come from the stills. In whisky making the still makes an important contribution to the final flavour of the product.

Valleyfield's continuous base whisky is similar to that produced in some other distilleries. It's the batch base whisky that is really special. Rather than continuing through the rest of the columns, condensed high wines from the beer still are heated in a copper batch kettle and the vapours directed into an overhead column. This kettle and column process is akin to pot still distillation with the heads and tails recycled while the centre cut is used to make whisky.

The discarded heads, however, are rich in caramel, butterscotch, and chocolate, much like a rum and butter chocolate bar, and are a bit peppery on the palate. The tails smell sweet and fruity like bubblegum, but with unpleasant elements of cod liver oil. Tasted, though, they reveal distinct blackberry notes, generic fruitiness, more pepper, and bubblegum. Most interestingly, after tasting the tails, the heads seem to have transformed into a strong and rich hot chocolate fudge. These heads and tails, of course, are the extremes, but it is instructive to smell and taste them, as an ideal centre cut will include well-balanced elements of both. Valleyfield's centre cut is very rich and oily on the nose. with notes of camphor and mint, and it tastes quite spicy and peppery with mint (tails notes), caramel, and butterscotch (heads notes). It already has plenty of interesting flavours even before it is put into barrels.

While there are still some rye and bourbon flavouring whiskies from pre-Diageo days in the warehouses, today base whiskies from Valleyfield are blended with flavouring

Covered and uncovered fermenters.

whiskies shipped in from Diageo's other distillery in Gimli, Manitoba, to make such whiskies as V.O., V.O. Gold, Canadian 83, and Five Star. Since Diageo took over management of the plant, specialization has become the byword and no flavouring whisky at all is distilled in Valleyfield. Initially Diageo made great efforts to distill flavouring whiskies to match the Gimli profiles. However, flavourings are a distillery's signature and highly dependent on the stills, making it no surprise that Valleyfield's flavourings never quite tasted like those from Gimli. (Nevertheless, Schenley-style flavourings that were developed at Valleyfield have been perfected at the Black Velvet distillery.)

The cost of running a distillery is constantly increasing and can only be partially passed on directly to the consumer. Governments throughout history have garnered as much income as possible by taxing the production and sale of alcohol. A tiny increment at the production level translates into a large increase in bottle price. Therefore, economies are always being sought. One not so economical element of

Valleyfield's operation is the decision to close the distillery two days a week as inventories climb and warehouses fill up. A stop-and-start operation is expensive. Once the still is running and stable it can be relied on to produce quality spirit twenty-four hours a day. But come Monday morning when the stills are restarted, it takes some time for them to reach equilibrium again and much of the early spirit simply cannot be used to make whisky. It costs between twelve and thirteen cents a litre to redistill this below-standard spirit, says Laberge. Stop-and-start also increases wear and tear on some of the equipment.

Spirit from both the batch base runs and the continuous distillation is matured on site, mostly in reused barrels. Although the most rapid ageing is seen in the first couple of years, used barrels tend to deliver a slow and deliberate ageing process. This produces a smoother whisky in the long run, says Laberge, but it takes eight to twelve years to have a good balance between smoothness and the taste of whisky. In all, about 425,000 barrels of quietly ageing whisky sit in fifteen warehouses on site. To keep up with production, new warehouses have recently been added off site. Valleyfield uses pallet warehouses and five-storey rack warehouses but, uniquely among Canadian distilleries, in one of the warehouses the racks have been removed and the barrels are stacked in pyramids. "We got the cost of handling a barrel down from $2.40 to $0.40 using this approach," says former distillery manager Luc Madore, who came up with the idea.

But how do you take tasting samples from stacked barrels without moving them? Simple: a small hole is drilled in the side of the barrel, a small amount of ageing whisky is withdrawn, and the hole is filled with a tiny bung. Even so, bonds are spread among various warehouse types so that any initially unperceived differences will average themselves out.

Whisky is dumped in a traditional mechanical dump line at Valleyfield before being blended and bottled on site. Valleyfield has quite a large bottling plant with five bottling lines, plus an additional one for minis. About 290 bottles a minute are produced on each line. Prior to filling, each bottle is vacuum-washed to ensure any dust from the carton has been removed.

A lot of Canadian whisky history has happened in the only remaining whisky distillery in French-speaking Canada, from biscuits to wartime alcohol to the resurrection of a number of defunct American whisky brands. All

Seagram's V.O.
40% alc/vol

Opens slowly to cloves and ginger, earth, dark fruit, white cedar, freshwater plants, and hot pepper. Dusty and – with some imagination – floral. Sweet caramel dispersed by citrus pith and peel. VA

Seagram's V.O. Gold
40% alc/vol

Luscious caramel, hot pepper and clean fresh-cut lumber. Gingerbread fresh from the oven. Simple but delightful with its crisp, clean wood and succulent caramels. VA

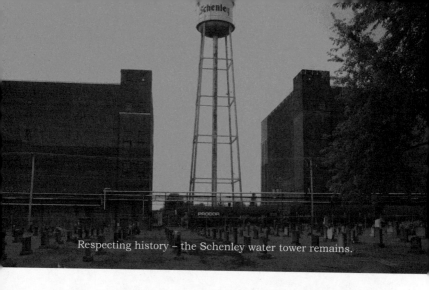

Respecting history – the Schenley water tower remains.

the while the distillery has maintained its solid reputation for quality, both within the industry and with whisky drinkers. It no longer produces its own whiskies from start to finish, instead distilling components for a number of popular Canadian blends, but the pride of the staff and determination of whisky men like Martin Laberge ensure that its reputation will remain intact.

Epilogue

he story of Canadian whisky is one of the creative use of available raw materials – grain and water – processed to meet the constantly shifting demands of the marketplace. Even Thomas Molson's move to distilling was a creative adjustment to his well-established beer-brewing business. As settlers moved west they brought with them the necessities of life and expertise in distilling. Always frugal, they made their whisky from local wheat using the leftovers from their milling operations. Turning waste into profit, and goodwill too, soon meant that almost every gristmill also had a still. When settlers from western Europe suggested adding a bit of rye, the rudiments of a new whisky style began to emerge.

Commercial and home-based distilling operations existed side by side. The few enterprises that survived were those that exported significant amounts of whisky to the United States. That cross-border tradition has deep roots. Since the 1860s Canadian whisky has been a favourite of American drinkers. When two decades later Hiram Walker decided to capitalize on this interest with a systematic approach to advertising, the result was a seemingly industry-wide switch to calling whisky Canadian regardless of where it was made.

The absence of competition from American distillers during Prohibition created the impression that Canada's production expanded to fill the gap. In reality, Prohibition was a mixed bag for Canadian distillers. The Bronfmans and Harry Hatch were businessmen who seized an opportunity, but not all Canadian distilleries flourished. However, Prohibition did cement the American predilection for Canadian whisky that had emerged some three generations earlier.

The cocktail fad of the Roaring Twenties became the cocktail fashion of the fifties and sixties, and Canadian whisky continued to be the mixer of choice. When people began to demand lighter whiskies in the sixties and seventies, Canadian distillers moved nimbly to meet the demand. The Canadian process of blending lighter and heavier whiskies together, along with good supplies of well-aged stocks, made that a relatively easy task. New lighter whiskies fuelled this trend.

Increasing interest in vodka in the eighties was not as easy to address and that period was one of corporate contraction and consolidation for Canadian whisky distilleries. Distilleries closed and brands were withdrawn. Even today Canadian whisky has not yet recovered from that decline and although it is still the best-selling whisky of any category in North America, sales of Canadian whisky continue to shrink marginally each year. If these trends continue, Canadian whisky will soon lose its ranking as the best-selling whisky in the U.S.

Distilling has changed remarkably since Thomas Molson fired up his father's dusty old pot still. Today, multinational corporations control the liquor business and own most of the distilleries worldwide. Distilling in Canada remains a billion-dollar business and a single product is keeping it alive: Canadian whisky. There is a huge market in Canada for vodka, gin, rum and other spirituous beverages. Most of these are also made in Canada, but only because many of those distilleries are already in operation making Canadian whisky. In many spirits categories the link between a recognized brand and its actual place of production has now been broken. Indeed some well-known vodkas originate in under-utilized (and government-subsidized) fuel ethanol plants. Canadian whisky remains the only spirit that must be produced in Canada.

However, in Canada profit margins for distillers are very low. From a simple economic viewpoint it makes little sense for a multinational firm to invest in its Canadian distilleries when, after all the taxes have been paid, the margin left for mark-up on production expenses is about 18 percent. The same level of investment in Scotland, in the United States, or in emerging nations can well bring double or triple that return. It is the extent of the international market for Canadian whisky, particularly in the U.S., that explains why with such limited margins these companies still support Canadian distilling. In effect, Canadian whisky has become a cash cow for multinationals to milk rather than an opportunity for investment and innovation. However, should it cease to be profitable to distill Canadian whisky, the rum, vodka, and gin distilleries will disappear as well, replaced by tanker trucks arriving from abroad.

Tax revenues may not change much, but Canada will have lost a big piece of its heritage. Should Canada's distilleries fail, not far behind will be prairie rye farms, Ontario corn farms, and a host of other industries. Economies of scale will simply relocate all distillation to the U.S. or abroad, where suppliers will fill the gap with just a few weeks' production. Current tax rates strongly favour Canadian beer and wine production. As a consequence, the distillation of spirits is pushed to the margins. The risk is real that with a couple of decisions in foreign corporate boardrooms a billion-dollar industry could disappear.

Then again, maybe distilling is simply coming full circle in Canada. Glenora Distillery in Cape Breton, against all odds, struggled valiantly through early problems with cash flow and initial distillation runs that, to be generous, relied on bad advice. Whisky experts and consultants chasing the dollar got in there early, took their fees, and left the distiller with spirit that, in the end, had to be recycled. Still they struggled on, and Glenora now has whisky that shares bar space proudly with the most popular single malt Scotches. Continued success seems assured as demand for their Glen Breton single malt whisky outstrips supply. Still, size matters: tiny Glenora produces in a year less than Hiram Walker can make in a day.

The consistent popularity of Canadian whisky is a matter of quality. In 1890 it became law that all Canadian whisky must be aged for at least two years. That was already the practice at a number of Canadian distilleries and American distilleries, but with an added government seal of approval that assured quality, sales of Canadian whisky surged. In 1974 that regulation was changed to require three years of ageing. Again, this speaks to quality, but it also creates difficulties regarding cash flow. When two years' ageing became law in 1890 virtually all of the small producers went out of business. Ageing is the most expensive part of making whisky. For new distillers today, the ageing requirements make it essential that they find other sources of income until their whisky can be sold. Of course, people want to age their whisky for the optimum period, and usually that means ageing longer than three years. However, in the U.S., where only nominal ageing is required, so-called "white whisky" has become the rage and a growing craft distilling movement has taken root to parallel the craft beer brewing movement of the 1980s. In Canada this craft distilling movement has been slow to catch on and there is a legal reason for that. Canadian distilleries are not permitted to sell white whisky, a further dent to their cash-flow prospects. Several distillers have found other innovative solutions.

In Ontario, Barry Stein and Barry Bernstein have gone through similar birthing throes with their Still Waters Distillery as Glenora did some twenty years earlier. Their goal is to produce Canadian single malt whisky, and until that whisky is ready to enter the marketplace they have found several ways to keep their cash flow positive. They began by importing barrels of Scottish single malt whisky and then blending it with tiny amounts of Canadian single malt. On the tongue there was no difference, but the Scotch Whisky Association and Canadian regulators required that it be bottled that way. Their bottlings were quite popular with single malt aficionados in Ontario and Alberta.

19th-century white whisky from Seagram's

Once their Carl-brand German pot still and rectifier were running, they began to make their own malt spirit, financing their malt whisky operations with sales of vodka where simpler rules apply. It is a vodka that is as close as you can get to whisky without actually being whisky. However, it is expensive to produce since it is made entirely from malted barley. Still Waters single malt vodka uses the same malted barley spirit that the partners are filling into bourbon barrels and custom-made new oak barrels. It's a luscious, creamy new spirit, one that whisky blogger Kris Shoemaker described as "candied red berry barley sugars, like Nibs red licorice." One year in refill bourbon barrels added coconut and pineapple, while that ageing in new oak had developed orchard fruits and tart wood tannins. Altogether, a very encouraging indication of another great Canadian single malt in the making. But it is still the vodka that pays the bills.

When Canadian extreme skier Tyler Schramm headed over to Scotland to do a master's degree in brewing and distilling, his plan was to return home to Pemberton, British Columbia, to make real potato vodka. Good plan; there are lots of potatoes in Pemberton. But distilling malt whisky was always in the back of his mind. Schramm successfully launched his vodka and followed it with a tempting gin. So much for taking care of the cash flow. Between batches of vodka and gin Schramm has been hard at work steadily distilling malt spirit from unpeated organic barley, putting away a few barrels at a time. In keeping with the trend to eat and drink locally, Schramm's Pemberton single malt whisky is distilled from British Columbia barley grown in Salmon Arm and up in the Peace River district, then malted in Armstrong, B.C. Adding some peated malt imported from

Nascent Still Waters single malt whisky.

Scotland means there are now two styles of malt whisky maturing in Schramm's warehouse. Schramm expects to wait well beyond the three-year requirement before his whisky is ready for bottling.

Farther west, on Vancouver Island, not far from Comox, a typical Scottish distillery called Shelter Point began distilling whisky in June 2011. It's an unpeated Scottish-style malt made by the much-celebrated Scottish distiller, Mike Nicholson. Shelter Point is a joint venture of Jay Oddleifson, a native of Gimli, along with his partners Patrick Evans and Andrew Currie, who built the Isle of Arran distillery in Scotland. The partners had two copper pot stills custom manufactured in Scotland then shipped to Vancouver Island by way of the Panama Canal. Normal start-up bumps were

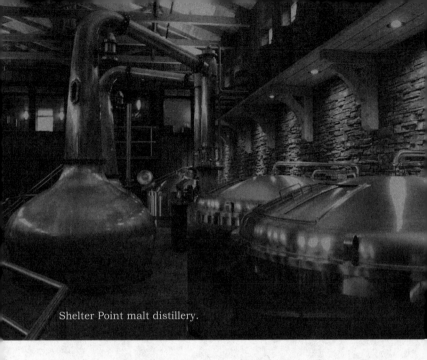
Shelter Point malt distillery.

compounded when customs officials decided to seize the stills as unlawful distilling equipment when the freighter carrying them from Scotland put in to port in Los Angeles to unload some cargo. With considerable toing and froing, the partners eventually succeeded in having their stills released to continue their journey to Canada. These extended delays ground everything at the distillery to a halt. The team at Shelter Point has taken another approach to generating income while they wait for their whisky to mature. They have developed a traditional Canadian rye whisky made from mature whisky purchased elsewhere. But again, regulators and regulations do not favour these small start-up distillers. Shelter Point rye is available for purchase only at the distillery or, amazingly enough, in South Korea!

Also on Vancouver Island, but farther south, near Victoria, Peter Hunt began distilling beer he had purchased from a local brewery. His intention was to add single malt whisky to an already successful line of gin produced in his tiny German pot still. And tiny is the problem, as it took many individual runs to fill a single barrel. While Hunt still has aspirations to make malt whisky, for now Victoria Spirits is most accurately – and perhaps hopefully – described as a promise of whisky yet to come.

In addition to the rye whisky that Shelter Point is selling, an Ontario company, Proof Brands, recently launched its own blend called "proof." It purchases whisky from distillers and custom blends it specifically for upscale urban cocktail drinkers. From the start it has been a success.

Highwood Distillers in Alberta has introduced a new concept: white whisky that really is whisky. A blend of rye and wheat whiskies up to ten years old, White Owl is filtered until it is as clear as vodka, and then it is filled into a very classy bottle and sold at a premium. Highwood can barely keep up with demand. Whisky snobs may turn up their noses, but cocktail drinkers are voting for it with their wallets.

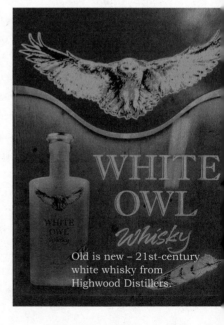

Old is new – 21st-century white whisky from Highwood Distillers.

In 2009 talk began of a "rye renaissance" in the United States. Rye whisky gets lots of coverage on the whisky web and in the American whisky press, but it really is quite a marginal product compared with bourbon. Nonetheless, when a few

U.S.-based independent bottlers decided to join this rye revival and began looking for rye whisky to bottle, they not only looked at home, they also sampled some Canadian rye whiskies. To say the least, they were impressed. When Dave Pickerell, renowned master bourbon distiller at Maker's Mark in Loretto, Kentucky, declared Canadian rye as the best rye whisky in the world, suddenly that whisky world took notice. The whisky web quickly was abuzz with plaudits for WhistlePig rye, a Canadian whisky Pickerell had sourced for a start-up distiller in Vermont. Others soon followed – Grand Grizzly in Mexico, Pendleton in Oregon, and from California, Masterson's Rye, all with premium bottlings of Canadian rye whisky. The reaction from connoisseurs has been practically gleeful. Perhaps this is where the future of Canadian whisky lies, in premium bottlings of powerfully flavoured whiskies. At least one major player thinks so.

If new things are happening with Canadian whisky, it makes sense that some of the lead should come from Canada's major market. And so it is that the Sazerac Company of New Orleans has hired the former master blender at Canadian Seagram's, Drew Mayfield, to launch a series of new richly flavoured Canadian whiskies. According to Kevin Richards, Canadian brand manager for Sazerac, their strategy is "to become the pre-eminent Canadian whisky supplier in the world with offerings for every consumer segment and taste profile including high-end products that will reshape consumers' expectations for how good Canadian whisky can be." That's a lofty goal indeed and does put Canadian producers on notice. Early releases, including Caribou Crossing Single Barrel, Royal Canadian Small Batch, and Rich and Rare Reserve, certainly delivered, raising the bar for flavour as well as for packaging. Sazerac has not revealed which distilleries they have contracted to produce these whiskies.

That same quality product and packaging bar is also being raised back home in Canada. Kittling Ridge Estate Wines & Spirits in Grimsby has established a stellar reputation since the turn of this century, based on a core whisky they call Barrel Select, and enhanced annually with a selection of low-volume special releases. It has now become a tradition for Canadian whisky enthusiasts to line up at Kittling Ridge each fall to pick up their preordered bottles, tour the distillery, and celebrate a little bit. These Forty Creek special releases carry premium prices to match their hand-crafted premium flavours, and they always sell out. Their three-grain whiskies finished in sherry wood, port wood, bourbon barrels, or in local oak wood, have become collector's items.

Kittling Ridge, Shelter Point, Pemberton, and Glenora have also introduced another novelty for Canadian distilleries: they invite visitors inside.

If all goes well, over the next decade or so five Canadian single malt whisky distilleries will have whisky on liquor store shelves: one in Nova Scotia, one in Ontario, one in

Still Waters Single Malt Vodka
40% alc/vol

Rich, velvety, and very malty with hints of toasted barleycorns, red licorice, and peppery caramel sweetness. Barley mash and nascent pepper hint at whisky flavours soon to come. SW

Saskatchewan, and two in British Columbia. Certainly Glenora has shown that Canadian distillers can go that route successfully. Who knows how many others will join them? But what about Canadian whisky? What about *real* Canadian whisky? What about Canadian rye? Single malt whisky certainly has the élan but for craft distillers living from one meagre sale to the next, it takes seemingly forever to mature. On the other hand, long before it is three years old, rye whisky is downright exciting to taste. Canadian whisky has built its reputation on its rye-flavoured whisky. Will any craft distillers take up the challenge? Still Waters has begun to.

To say the future looks bright for the Canadian whisky industry would imply hope that regulators will allow whisky making to become as profitable in Canada as it is in other countries. Relocating Canadian whisky making abroad is not an option, but closing their Canadian distilleries certainly is for those foreign owners who are enticed by greater margins elsewhere. For Canadian whisky itself, though, hope springs from those small distillers, the innovators and the individuals whose passion pushes them to take great risks. Some of these innovators continue to work away inside the big corporations. Think of staggeringly flavourful new whiskies such as Wiser's Legacy from Corby Distilleries Ltd., or long-time favourites such as Gibson's Finest. For yes, Canadian whisky is indeed rye whisky; so far it is the craft distillers who make malt whisky. However, single malt, regardless of where it is made, is scotch, if not Scotch. Perhaps hope lies in unique distilleries like Alberta Distillers, which is unquestionably the largest and best distiller of rye whisky in the world. Perhaps hope also lies with the tiny Highwood Distillers, where good reserves of aged whisky mean that the journey from initial concept to final bottle can take mere months, not years. Or with the passion of creative forces such as John Hall of Kittling Ridge and those odd contraptions he calls pot stills. Or perhaps hope finally lies in the efforts of the major distillers to convince regulators of the impact Canadian whisky has on so many sectors of the economy. At one time whisky was the single largest contributor to the Canadian treasury, the fabled goose that lays the golden eggs. Wouldn't it be ironic if instead of killing this particular Canadian goose, as happened in fable, Canadian regulators simply allowed her to fly elsewhere to lay her golden eggs?

A history distilled and a future bottled

The history of Canadian whisky is, in effect, a mirror of the history of Canada itself. The Canadian whisky we enjoy today has evolved over the more than two centuries it has taken to build our nation. From the recycled waste of English wheat millers and the rye-based *kornschnapps* of German farmers has emerged a uniquely Canadian whisky style, with the signature flavours of rye grain, but now based primarily on corn. Until recently, when hardy hybrids were developed, corn would not grow in the tough Canadian climate. Today, though, Canadian whisky is, as J.P. Wiser so aptly called it, "the mingled souls of corn and rye."

Of the hundreds of home distillers and many dozens of commercial hopefuls over the centuries, today a mere nine distilleries make the world's entire output of Canadian whisky. A careful search turns up no more than one hundred commonly available brands. Several craft operations are still in their formative stages and only time will tell if they will eventually make new contributions to this "species" we call Canadian whisky. Yes, Canadian whisky will continue to evolve. But there are obvious threats on the horizon. Taxation based on its classification as a spirit rather than its alcohol content is the greatest threat to its continued existence. Not far behind is the pressure from multinational corporations focused solely on the maximization of their global profitability, for which Canadian whisky is just one of several profit centres.

But the whisky world is waking up to Canadian whisky and declaring some of it as among the best whiskies in the world. Bolstered by new interest in rich and robust flavours, producers and bottlers, large and small, are taking chances on big flavour. Connoisseurs, confident in their own palates, are responding – enthusiastically.

Whatever the future may hold, whisky has played a major role in creating Canada. From its early service as a source of comfort on long winter nights (not to mention a primary tax source) to the employment it generates, to its role as a gentle ambassador of Canadian quality, whisky has played its role with distinction and with pride. And it is a role that it is determined to keep on playing in the future as it continues to unfold. Having read this book you now know more of what makes whisky Canadian, and what makes Canadian whisky unique. You sample it, you savour it, you enjoy it. As you sit by the fireplace on a cold winter's night, glass in hand, remember all those generations of Canadians who spent their lives creating it. And place yourself in that ever-growing group of those who, like you, also find simple comfort in its simple pleasures.

Glossary

Alc/vol. Alcohol by volume (also written abv or ABV), indicates the percentage of alcohol in a given volume of liquid.

Amylolytic enzymes. Enzymes that convert starch into sugar by breaking certain chemical bonds in the starch. Obtained from malted grain or fungi.

Aspergillus. One of several fungi that produce amylolytic enzymes.

Barrel. Round, convex, water-tight, wooden container made by wrapping heated, bent oak staves around flat oak end panels and binding them in a circle with metal hoops. Also called casks.

Beer. The alcoholic product of fermenting mash with yeast.

Bond. A single batch of whisky, all of which was produced at the same time using the same processes.

Bottling strength. Mature whisky is usually reduced with pure water to a consistent strength, often 40 percent alc/vol, for bottling.

Cask strength. The percent alc/vol of whisky in the barrel, usually greater than 60 percent.

Char. The process of heating the inside of a cask to burning point, creating a layer of charcoal, also called char, on the inside of the cask.

Chill filter. Whisky is cooled then filtered to remove components that would settle out over time, creating cloudiness in the bottled whisky.

Colourimeter. An instrument used to measure the colour of whisky for comparison to a standard.

Column still. A tall metal cylinder filled with horizontal perforated plates over which beer or high wines pass back and forth as they descend the column. Steam rising from the bottom of the column strips out alcohol and congeners as it rises until they pass from the top of the column to a condenser.

Common whisky. The most basic and least expensive whisky. Historically in Canada, whisky made without rye grain.

Condenser. A series of tubes that are cooled from the outside to condense vapours from a still into liquid state.

Congener. Any of a broad range of compounds that give whisky its flavours.

Corn. *Zea mays*, a tall native North American grass, the seeds of which are used to make whisky.

Dent. The variety of corn most commonly used to make whisky. When dry a dent forms in the crown of the seed.

Diastatic. *See* amylolytic.

Diastatic power. The ability of an enzyme to convert starch to sugar.

Distillation. Separation of individual components of a solution by collecting the vapours after heating the solution to a temperature where one component will vapourize but others will not.

Doubler. Much like a small pot still. Vapours from the main still are bubbled through condensate from the still, enriching the vapours that then flow to the condenser.

Endosperm. The portion of a seed that contains food, usually in the form of starch, for the new plant.

Enzyme. A naturally occurring protein that causes specific chemical reactions to occur. In whisky making, enzymes convert starch to sugar by breaking certain chemical bonds in the starch.

Ester. A sweet-smelling, often fruity congener in whisky.

Feints. The last vapours to come off a pot distillation or vapours collected at a feints port on a column still, containing aldehydes and other undesirable congeners.

Ferment. *As a verb:* to convert from sugar to alcohol and carbon dioxide though metabolic activity in yeast. *As a noun:* the process of fermenting or the time during the process when fermentation occurs.

Fermentables. Starch and other carbohydrates that may be fermented by yeast, usually after conversion to sugars by enzyme treatment.

Fermenter. The vessel in which fermentation occurs.

Flavourant. *See* congener.

Foreshots. The first distillate to come off a pot still or extracted from a column still, usually containing undesirable congeners.

Fusel oil. Undesirable heavy alcohols, primarily amyl alcohol, removed during distillation.

Gelatinize. To turn from a liquid to a gel. With starch this involves changes in molecular structure.

Grain neutral spirit (GNS). Flavourless alcohol produced by distilling and redistilling fermented sugars, until all detectable congeners are removed.

Grist. A coarse flour made by grinding grain.

Heads. *See* foreshots.

High wines. New distillate high in alcohol content and ready for rectification.

Hydrophobic. Congeners that are insoluble in water, but soluble in alcohol.

Ketone. A common component of foreshots, some ketones are sweet and caramel-like but most produce undesirable flavours if not removed during distillation.

Malt. Grain, usually barley or occasionally rye, that has been partially sprouted to activate the amylolytic enzymes, then dried.

Maltings. A facility where grain is malted.

Maltster. A business that produces malt.

Marrying. The practice of putting whisky that has been blended into barrels or vats for a period of time to let the mixture equilibrate and sometimes to draw additional flavours from the barrel.

Mash. *As a verb*: to mix ground grain with water in preparation for converting the starch to sugar. *As a noun:* a slurry of coarse-ground grain and water.

Mash bill. The mix of grains used to make whisky.

Mouthfeel. The way a whisky feels in the mouth. Usually characterized as creamy, mouth-coating, thin, or watery.

Nose. *As a verb*: to smell whisky for the purpose of identifying aromas. *As a noun*: the aromas found by methodically smelling a whisky.

Palate. The flavour and feel of whisky in the mouth. The ability to differentiate subtle differences in flavour and mouthfeel.

Pallet. The wooden base on which barrels of whisky are placed to facilitate storage and transportation by forklift.

Pot ale. The leftover residue in a pot still after the alcohol has been distilled off.

Pot still. A large vessel, usually made of copper, in which beer is heated to cause the alcohol and congeners to evaporate so they can be separated from water and undesirable congeners.

Potable. Safe to drink or consume.

Rack/rerack. Put whisky into barrels. More commonly used when partially matured whisky is transferred into different barrels.

Rack house. A tall warehouse, usually made of wood, in which whisky is matured. Some bourbon makers call it a rick house.

Rectify. A process of making raw whisky more drinkable by adding or removing certain flavours. Traditionally whisky was rectified by filtering through charcoal and or adding flavourings and colour. Today high wines are redistilled in a column still called a rectifier.

Rectifier. Traditionally someone who purchased raw alcohol and made palatable whisky by filtering it and adding flavouring compounds. Today the final column still used to produce or rectify new distillate.

Saccharifying enzyme. An enzyme that converts starch to sugar.

Sacrificial copper. Copper, often in the form of rods, tubes, or filings, placed in a still to react with certain undesirable chemicals in the beer or vapour, neutralizing or removing them.

Slurry. A liquid with a solid suspended in it. Ground grain suspended in water.

Small wood. Canadian law requires that whisky be aged in small wood, casks of less than 700 litres capacity. In practice distillers generally use casks with about 200 litres capacity.

Spent grains. The remains of the grain used to make whisky after the starch has been removed. Usually quite rich in yeast and protein and used to feed animals.

Still. A mechanical device used in whisky making to separate alcohol and congeners from water by heating them and taking advantage of differences in boiling temperature.

Stillage. *See* thin stillage.

Tails. *See* feints.

Tannin. An astringent chemical familiar in red wine, but also found in oak. In proper balance tannins can give a refreshing mouthfeel to a whisky.

Thin stillage. The alcohol-depleted liquid that is left over after distillation in a column still.

Toast. The preparation of a barrel by heating the inside of it until it turns brown, but does not burn. Components of the wood melt and change chemical structure, creating new flavours when whisky is matured in the barrel.

Vanillins. Various related chemicals found in oak that impart vanilla-like flavours to whisky.

Volatiles. Chemicals in foreshots, new spirit, and whisky that evaporate easily.

Wash. The fermented liquid or slurry that is fed into the still, also called beer.

Yeast. A single-celled organism that consumes sugar, turning it into ethanol and carbon dioxide. Yeasts also produce many of the desirable congeners in whisky.

Bibliography

Bramble, Linda. *Niagara's Wine Visionaries: Profiles of the Pioneering Winemakers.* Toronto: Lorimer, 2009.

Bronfman, Samuel. *From Little Acorns: The Story of Distillers Corporation-Seagrams Limited.* Montreal: Bronfman, 1970.

Broom, Dave. *Handbook of Whisky: A Complete Guide to the World's Best Malts, Blends and Brands.* London: Sterling Publishing, 2000.

Broom, Dave. *The World Atlas of Whisky.* London: Mitchell Beazley, 2010.

Brown, Lorraine. *The Story of Canadian Whisky: 200 Years of Tradition.* Markham: Fitzhenry & Whiteside, 1994.

Chartier, François. *Taste Buds and Molecules: The Art and Science of Food with Wine.* Toronto: McClelland & Stewart, 2010.

Chauvin, Francis X. *Hiram Walker and the Development of the Walker Institutions in Walkerville, Ontario.* Master's thesis, revised for Hiram Walker & Sons 1927. Unpublished.

Cope, Kenneth L. *American Cooperage Machinery and Tools.* Mendham, NJ: Astragal Press, 2003.

Cowdery, Charles K. *Bourbon, Straight: The Uncut and Unfiltered Story of American Whiskey.* Chicago: Made and Bottled in Kentucky, 2004.

Dempsey, Hugh A. *Firewater: The Impact of the Whisky Trade on the Blackfoot Nation.* Alliston: Fitzhenry & Whiteside, 2002.

Dendy, William, and William Kilbourn. *Toronto Observed: Its Architecture, Patrons, and History.* Toronto: Oxford University Press, 1986.

Denison, Merrill. *The Barley and the Stream: The Molson Story.* Toronto: McClelland & Stewart, 1955.

Faith, Nicholas. *The Bronfmans: The Rise and Fall of the House of Seagram.* New York: St. Martin's Press, 2006.

Gibson, Sally. *Toronto's Distillery District: History by the Lake.* Toronto: Cityscape Holdings Inc., 2008.

Goode, Jamie. *The Science of Wine: From Vine to Glass.* Berkeley: University of California, 2006.

Gray, James H. *Booze.* Toronto: Macmillan of Canada, 1972.

Heron, Craig. *Booze: A Distilled History.* Toronto: Between the Lines, 2003.

Dundurn, Hunt C.W. *Booze Boats and Billions: Smuggling Liquid Gold!* Toronto: McClelland & Stewart, 1988.

——— . *Whisky and Ice: The Saga of Ben Kerr, Canada's Most Daring Rumrunner.* Toronto: Dundurn, 1996.

Hunter, Douglas. *Molson: The Birth of a Business Empire.* Toronto: Penguin, 2001.

Jacques, K.A., T.P. Lyons, and D.R. Kelsall. *The Alcohol Textbook, 4th Edition.* Nottingham: Nottingham University Press, 2003.

Lea, Andrew G. H., John R. Piggott, eds. *Fermented Beverage Production, Second Edition.* New York: Kluwer Academic/Plenum Publishers, 2003.

Lefebvre Prince, Thérèse, with Mark Claxton, ed.
The Whiskey Man. Yorkton: City of Yorkton Municipal
Heritage Advisory Sub-Commission, 2003.

MacKinnon, Tanya Lynn. *The Historical Geography of the
Distilling Industry in Ontario: 1850-1900.* Master's thesis,
Wilfrid Laurier University, 2000.

MacLean, Charles. *Scotch Whisky: A Liquid History.*
London: Cassell, 2003.

Marrus, Michael R. *Samuel Bronfman: The Life and Times
of Seagram's Mr. Sam.* Lebanon, NH: University Press of
New England, 1991.

M'Harry, Samuel. *Practical Distiller.* Originally published in
Harrisburg, PA: John Wyeth, 1809.

Miles, Fraser. *Slow Boat on Rum Row.* Madeira Park, BC:
Harbour, 1992.

Molson, Karen. *The Molsons: Their Lives & Times,
1780-2000.* Willowdale, ON: Firefly Books, 2001.

Morris, John A. H. *Morrises' History of Prescott,
1800-2000.* Prescott, ON: St. Lawrence Printing
Company, 2001.

Newell, Dianne, and Ralph Greenhill. *Survivals: Aspects of
Industrial Archaeology in Ontario.* Erin, ON: Boston Mills
Press, 1989.

Newman, Peter C. *King of the Castle – The Making of a
Dynasty: Seagram's and the Bronfman Empire.* New
York: Atheneum, 1979.

Okrent, Daniel. *Last Call: The Rise and Fall of Prohibition.*
New York: Scribner, 2010.

Otto, Stephen A. *A Report on the Buildings at Gooderham
& Worts' Distillery and an Assessment of their Heritage
Significance.* 1988.

Piggott, J.R., R. Sharp, and R.E.B. Duncan, eds. *The Science and Technology of Whiskies*. Essex: Longman Group, 1989.

Poirier, Bernard. *Whisky with Dinner*. Burnstown, ON: General Store Publishing House, 1989.

Rannie, William F. *Canadian Whisky: The Product and the Industry*. Lincoln, ON: W.F. Rannie, 1976.

Roskrow, Dominic. *The World's Best Whiskies*. New York: Stewart, Tabori & Chang, 2010.

Rowe, David J., ed. *Chemistry and Technology of Flavors and Fragrances*. Oxford: Blackwell, 2005.

Russell, Inge, ed. *Whisky: Technology, Production and Marketing*. London: Academic Press, 2003.

Sargent, Charles S. *Manual of the Trees of North America, Volume One*. New York: Dover Publications, 1961.

Schneider, Stephen. *Iced: The Story of Organized Crime in Canada*. Mississauga: Wiley, 2009.

Shuttleworth, E. B. *The Windmill and Its Times*. Toronto: William Gooderham, 1924.

Slone, Philip, ed. *Beverage Media Blue Book 1958-59*. New York, 1958.

Teatero, William. *Notes of the History of Wiser's Distillery Limited*. Undergraduate thesis, Queen's University, 1977.

Travis, Gary L. "American Bourbon Whiskey Production." *Ferment Magazine*, n.d.

Turin, Luca. *The Secret of Scent*. London: Faber & Faber, 2006.

Wishart, David. *Whisky Classified: Choosing Single Malts by Flavour*. London: Pavilion, 2006.

Woods, Shirley E., Jr. *The Molson Saga 1763-1983.*
Toronto: Doubleday, 1983.

Wright, Steve. "Canadian Whisky – From Grain to Glass."
Ferment Magazine, n.d.

Acknowledgements

I n writing and publishing: Heartfelt thanks to my agent, Denise Bukowski, and her staff at The Bukowski Agency, John Greenwell, Elizabeth De Fancesca, and Erin Gallé; at McClelland & Stewart, my editor, Philip Rappaport, who encouraged my authenticity, Bhavna Chauhan, McClelland & Stewart president Doug Pepper, Josh Glover, Andrew Roberts, David Ward, and Anne Holloway; and to Dave Broom, author, friend, and mentor who encouraged me to publish. *Whisky Magazine* editor Rob Allanson and former editor Dominic Roskrow; *Scotch Whisky Review* former editor Marcin Miller; *Malt Whisky Yearbook* editor Ingvar Ronde; wordsmiths par excellence Kevin Burns, Charles MacLean, Chuck Cowdery, and Jim McKenzie, who taught by example; distiller Art Dawe, whose thoughtful criticism improved those parts of the manuscript he reviewed; and Janet de Kergommeaux who prepared the bibliography. All errors and omissions are my own.

Researchers and archivists: Marcia Stentz, Hudson's Bay Company Archives; Nora Hague, McCord Museum, McGill University; Sally Gibson, Gooderham and Worts Archives; Karen VandenBrink, City of Waterloo Museum; Susan Mavor, University of Waterloo Library; Gerry Boyce, Hastings County Historical Society; Bill Skinkle; Elena Kingsbury, Grenville County Historical Society; Mike Veach at bourbonenthusiast.com;

and authors of the website ellenjaye.com. Particular thanks to Art Jahns of the Canadian Club Archives for revealing discussions and access to his personal notes.

Distillers and whisky folk: Bob Denton, Mark Fox, Michael Farrell, Harold Ferguson, Tom Hartle, David Dobbin, Don Jacques, Steve Hughes, Tim Laird, Svend Jansen, John Hall, Beth Warner, Dan Tullio, Tish Harcus, Rebecca Fair, Howard Kirke, Rachel Kubacki, Carolyn McFarlane, Steve Wright, Trevor Walsh, John Swan, Mike Booth, Ian Ross, David Doyle, Kevin Rogers, Clint Sundseth, Dwayne Kozlowski, Larry van Leeuwen, Rob Tuer, Kathy Pitchko, Jeff Kozak, Rick Murphy, Rory Wright, Vicky Miller, Mike Miechkota, Chris Spearman, James Mmbando, Jan Westcott, Glen Hopkins, Michael Nychyck, Sheldon Hyra, Luc Madore, Martin Laberge, Denis Labelle, Donnie Campbell, Bob Scott, Daniel MacLean, Jay Oddleifson, James Marinus, Barry Stein, Barry Bernstein, Lorien Chilton, Tyler Schramm, Jim Knapp, Vincent D'Souza, Tia Bledsoe, Margaret Antkowski, Amy Preske, Drew Mayville, Jeff Norman.

Personal: Chris, Tori, Danielle, Matt, Seneca, Laurie, Al, Heather, Kristen, Drew, Sarah, Jordan, Olivia, Kim, Marco, Jonathan, Karyn, Carol, Donna, Dad, Mary Anne – my family. All the Malt Maniacs, All PLOWED, Charles Anderson, Johanna Ngoh, Lawrence Graham, Chris Bunting, Chris Raby, Nick Morgan, Kate Kavanaugh, Todd Holmes, Johannes van den Heuval, Serge Valentin, Tom Borschel, Olivier Humbrecht, David Winn, Dave Russo, Mark Gillespie, Alan Robinson, Craig Daniels, John Dube, Krishna Nukala, Peter Silver, Brian McHenry, Ralf Mitchell, Tim Bachelder, Martin "S'tan" Kari, Ulf Buxrud, Martin Brunet, Kris Shoemaker, Chip Dykstra, André Girard, Jason Debly, and so very many others.

Credits

Author's collection: 8, 23, 28, 37, 99, 118, 124, 133, 149, 176, 207, 210, 214, 218, 221, 224, 228, 230, 236, 241, 242, 246, 260, 265, 272, 282, 285, 293, 294

Black Velvet Distillers: 204

Brown-Forman Corporation: 213

Canadian Club Archives: 122, 157, 170, 174

Canadian Club, Corby Distillers and PMA Agency: 257

City of Waterloo Heritage Collection: xiv, 4, 5, 26, 105, 144

Diageo Canada: 225

Glenora Inn and Distillery: 235

Greg Cosgrove: 34, 46, 47, 73, 88

Hastings County Historical Society: 126

Jane Cameron: 7, 11, 15, 20, 21, 36, 40, 53, 62, 84, 194, 198, 200, 212, 248, 252, 256, 295

Kitting Ridge Estate Wine and Spirits: 266, 274

Prescott Museum: 182

University of Waterloo Library. The Seagram Museum Fonds: 66, 94, 137, 139, 291

University of Waterloo Library, The Seagram Museum Fonds and Diageo Canada: 277

Index - Tasting Notes

Index